The Key
to the Shenandoah Valley

ALSO BY EDWARD B. MCCAUL, JR.
AND FROM MCFARLAND

*The Mechanical Fuze and the Advance
of Artillery in the Civil War* (2010)

The Key to the Shenandoah Valley

Geography and the Civil War Struggle for Winchester

EDWARD B. MCCAUL, JR.

McFarland & Company, Inc., Publishers
Jefferson, North Carolina

This book has undergone peer review.

LIBRARY OF CONGRESS CATALOGUING-IN-PUBLICATION DATA

Names: McCaul, Edward B., Jr., 1951– author.
Title: The key to the Shenandoah Valley : geography and the Civil War struggle for Winchester / Edward B. McCaul, Jr..
Description: Jefferson, North Carolina : McFarland & Company, Inc., Publishers, 2023 | Includes bibliographical references and index.
Identifiers: LCCN 2023035539 | ISBN 9781476683980 (paperback : acid free paper) ∞
ISBN 9781476646244 (ebook)
Subjects: LCSH: Shenandoah River Valley (Va. and W. Va.)—History—Civil War, 1861-1865. | Winchester (Va.)—History—Civil War, 1861-1865. | Virginia—History—Civil War, 1861-1865—Campaigns. | United States—History—Civil War, 1861-1865—Campaigns. | BISAC: HISTORY / Military / United States | HISTORY / United States / Civil War Period (1850-1877)
Classification: LCC E470.3 .M33 2023 | DDC 973.7/37—dc23/eng/20230801
LC record available at https://lccn.loc.gov/2023035539

BRITISH LIBRARY CATALOGUING DATA ARE AVAILABLE

**ISBN (print) 978-1-4766-8398-0
ISBN (ebook) 978-1-4766-4624-4**

© 2023 Edward B. McCaul, Jr. All rights reserved

No part of this book may be reproduced or transmitted in any form or by any means, electronic or mechanical, including photocopying or recording, or by any information storage and retrieval system, without permission in writing from the publisher.

Front cover: Chromolithograph of Sheridan's charge at the Third Battle of Winchester (Library of Congress)

Printed in the United States of America

*McFarland & Company, Inc., Publishers
Box 611, Jefferson, North Carolina 28640
www.mcfarlandpub.com*

To those who encouraged my interest
in history early in my life:
my parents, Edward B. McCaul and Edith May;
Wall McCaul; Mr. Don Shirley;
Mr. William Pike; Mr. Austin Grim;
Miss Diana Burrus; and LTC David Mets

Acknowledgments

As with all books, there are numerous people to thank. Maps are crucial to any book about battles, and a number of people and organizations helped me obtain them. Jan Wagner, Ohio State University Library Map Room; Wilbur Johnston and Cissy Shull, Winchester-Frederick County Historical Society; Jim Campi, chief policy and communications officer, American Battlefield Trust; the research librarians in Handley Library; and Jeffrey Goldberg, cartographer, Department of History, United States Military Academy, all need to be thanked. Hal Jespersen needs to be especially mentioned as he drew many of the maps that are in the book. In addition, there are the wonderful maps in the *Atlas to Accompany the Official Records of the Union and Confederate Armies*. Unfortunately, these maps are too detailed and large to be included in the book. Still, anyone wishing to study the Civil War must be familiar with these maps.

Photographs and drawings were also important to this book. For these, I must thank David Lee Ingram, of Ingram-Hagen, who provided photographs of the Valley Turnpike, and Carole Downey of the Valley Turnpike Museum, Harrisonburg, Virginia, who put me in touch with him. In addition, there is the tremendous collection of photographs and drawings from the Library of Congress as well as the collection of James E. Taylor's drawings at the Western Reserve Historical Society.

I would also like to thank Mike Cannane and Charlie Hagan of the Kernstown Battlefield Association who were so kind as to give me a tour of the Kernstown Battlefields around Pritchard's Hill. They are very knowledgeable and were able to point out to me small geographic features that played a role in both battles.

A special thank-you needs to go to those individuals who proofed various versions of this book—John Montgomery, Allan Katzberg, Bill Dichtel, and the anonymous readers provided by McFarland. As always, my wife, Sherri, deserves very special thanks for proofing and for going along on numerous research trips. As usual, I take full responsibility for any mistakes in the book.

Table of Contents

Acknowledgments — vi
Introduction — 1

1. Winchester and the Shenandoah Valley — 11
2. Geography and the First Battle of Kernstown—22–23 March 1862 — 30
3. Geography and the First Battle of Winchester—25 May 1862 — 50
4. Geography and the Second Battle of Winchester—13–15 June 1863 — 63
5. Geography and the Second Battle of Kernstown—24 July 1864 — 79
6. Geography and the Third Battle of Winchester—19 September 1864 — 89
7. Geography and the Battle of Cedar Creek—19 October 1864 — 116
8. Control of Winchester — 129
9. Geography and History — 136
10. Geography and War — 144
11. Geography and Command Decisions During the American Civil War — 154
12. Geography, Technology, and the American Civil War — 169
13. Geography and the Future — 184

Appendix A. Macadamized Roads — 189
Appendix B. Major Battles for Winchester — 198
Appendix C. Confederate Invasions and Raids of the North — 202
Chapter Notes — 207
Bibliography — 217
Index — 225

Introduction

History has always been influenced by Geography.

This work is a philosophical history book. Thus, it will not be in the traditional mode of a history book written to tell the history of an event or events. The purpose of the book is to give the reader a better understanding of the overall impact geography has had on military actions and more specifically those around Winchester, Virginia. As such, not every aspect of each of the battles will be discussed, and some readers may find that their favorite incident in a battle has not been included. Still, I hope to inform the reader how important it was to each side to control Winchester, as the side that controlled Winchester held the initiative in the Virginia theater of war.

The word *Soldier* will be capitalized in this book when the word is being used as a proper noun to describe an individual who is in the army. Although some people may disagree with this capitalization, it is the method currently in use by the United States Army. The reason is that the word *soldier* has multiple definitions and the best way to differentiate an individual who is in the army from any other definition is to capitalize the word *Soldier*.

A large number of primary and secondary sources are shown in the bibliography. I have tried to quote only from primary sources rather than secondary sources. The secondary sources that are listed are works that I used to gain information, especially on the primary sources that their authors' used. Many of the secondary sources are excellent works that I would recommend especially for anyone wanting to learn more about the impact of geography and regarding battles for Winchester. However, anyone wanting to use the primary sources needs to be aware that many of them were written to promote a specific agenda, and some even change historical events to fit their agenda. Just because a source is a primary source does not always mean that it is reliable.

***

During the Civil War, the Shenandoah Valley was the scene of 326 engagements of various magnitude that are documented in the *War of the Rebellion Official Records of the Union and Confederate Armies*.[1] Many of these engagements occurred around Winchester, and it is estimated that the city was occupied and evacuated 72 times during the war.[2] Three major battles were fought in the immediate vicinity of Winchester, and three other major battles, First and Second Kernstown and Cedar Creek, occurred just south of the city. In addition, there were numerous smaller actions around the city. When I lived in Winchester as a teenager, I always wondered what made this small city so important that numerous battles were fought to control it. This question has intrigued me for years, and I have come to realize that geography played a pivotal role in determining Winchester's significance during the Civil War.

Although geography was a major factor in every Civil War battle, I decided to use Winchester and the six battles for Winchester as my main examples due to the fact that the city was so heavily contested throughout the war. The three battles that were fought in the immediate vicinity of Winchester occurred in different years although on different sides of the city. Two of the three battles that occurred just south of the city were fought at the same location, Kernstown, while the third took place just south of Kernstown. Controlling Winchester was key since whichever side held the city gained a distinct advantage in the Virginia theater of operations. Confederate occupation of Winchester or psychological dominance of the area allowed them to disrupt Federal operations. When Federal forces occupied the city, they controlled the tempo of operations in Virginia.

Unfortunately, it is no longer possible to view these six battlefields as they were at the time of the battle. The main reason is that Winchester has grown since the Civil War and currently covers the majority of five of the six battlefields. Still, there are excellent walking trails and interpretive signs for parts of the First Battle of Kernstown and the Third Battle of Winchester. The only battlefield that has remained relatively untouched is Cedar Creek, which is a National Battlefield Park. However, most of that battlefield is not in the park and is slowly being developed. Another change at all of the battlefields is the growth of trees, most of which would have been cut down during the Civil War. Consequently, the best time to appreciate the terrain around Winchester is late fall, winter, or early spring when there are no leaves on the trees. Even though the battlefields are not as they were during the Civil War, I would still recommend that anyone interested in any battle to visit that battlefield and walk the terrain. Even though walking a battlefield will not give you an understanding of the geographic impact of the operational, strategic, or grand strategy aspects of the battle, it will give you a better understanding of how geography influenced the tactical aspects of the battle. For those individuals who are unable to visit and walk the battlefields, I have included modern photographs of parts of each of the battlefields to help give the reader some idea of what the terrain looks like today.

***

The importance of the Shenandoah Valley and Winchester was recognized by leaders on both sides early in the war. General Stonewall Jackson stated, "They [the

Federals] want this Valley, and if the Valley's lost, Virginia is lost!"[3] Federal general Nathaniel Banks, Jackson's opponent at the First Battle of Winchester and Cedar Mountain, stated in his report on the First Battle of Winchester, "It was determined, therefore, to enter the lists with the enemy in a race or a battle, as he should choose, for the possession of Winchester, the key of the valley, and for us the position of safety."[4] Although Banks, who was a relatively unsuccessful politically appointed general, may not be considered a primary source for a military maxim, it must be remembered that Jackson stated just prior to the Battle of Cedar Mountain, "Banks is in our front, and he is generally willing to fight."[5] This, of course, is in contrast to some professional and political generals who were not willing to fight. In addition, President Abraham Lincoln, an astute judge of people, stated in August 1862, "I regard General Banks as one of the best men in the army. He makes me no trouble; but, with a large force or a small force, he always knows his duty and does it."[6] Both Jackson and Banks were correct. Having control of Winchester opened a northern avenue of advance for the Confederates and a southern one for the Federals. While controlling the entire Valley would be difficult for the Federals, destroying its economic value would effectively give the Federals "control" of the Valley as they could supply their units in the Valley while the Confederates would have difficulty doing so.

***

Geography is more than topography or the lay of the land. Although topography includes man-made modifications to the land such as roads, canals, railroads, and bridges, all of which are important considerations for any military operation, there is much more that needs to be taken into account. Too many people only consider topography when thinking about geography, but geography in its broadest definition includes natural resources, the environment (weather, climate, soil, vegetation), as well as topography. If geography is only defined as the lay of the land, too much information is missed that is probably more important than topography alone. In this book, the term *geography* will always refer to the broadest definition of the word.

Cities, the creation of humans, have impacted geography. First, they change the location's topography by creating their own topography. Roads can become canyons with some being dead ends. Rivers and streams can disappear beneath city streets, and hills and valleys can vanish. Natural vegetation disappears to be often replaced by non-native species in the controlled environment of a city park. Large modern cities have changed local geography by impacting the weather. These cities have become heat islands where the temperature is normally higher than that of the surrounding countryside. They can also act as "mountains" redirecting wind and storms. A city's constant need for large amounts of water for its population will impact nearby water sources. Then, there is the human waste and trash generated by the people in a city with the impact it has on the environment. No military commander can ignore cities, as they will influence any decision he may make.

It is important for the reader to understand that different levels of command have very diverse views of geography. There are four major levels of command in the military as shown in diagram I-1. These levels are grand strategy, strategic, operational, and tactical. Each level influences the adjacent levels and, in some cases, has influence on non-adjacent levels. Grand strategy, or policy, is conducted by the national leadership. During the Civil War, in the case of the Federals, this was Lincoln with his cabinet, and in the case of the Confederacy, it was Jefferson Davis with his cabinet. The strategic level is conducted by the military's high command. For the Federals, this duty eventually fell to Ulysses S. Grant after others had failed in this task. For the Confederacy, Davis controlled the strategic level, with the help of military advisors, until close to the end of the war when Robert E. Lee was made commander of all Confederate armies. The operational level is conducted by commanders in the field and, during the Civil War, could go as low as corps level. The tactical level during the Civil War was conducted by division level and lower leaders. All levels have a degree of flexibility to them as there is overlap between the different levels, and at times, individuals may plan or conduct operations at a higher or lower level. Geographically, the most important level is grand strategy, and the closer one gets to the tactical level, the more important topography (including man-made objects) becomes, although geography still cannot be disregarded.

The immense difference in the way an individual at the grand strategy level views geography compared to an individual at the tactical level can be best described by quotes from General Alfred von Schlieffen, chief of the German General Staff, and Sergeant (his rank at the time of the incident) Audie Murphy, who was at Anzio, Italy with the United States Third Infantry Division. After a staff ride in East Prussia, one of General Schlieffen's aides pointed out to him the beauty of the Pregel River. Schlieffen is reported to have commented, "An unimportant obstacle."[7] While the Pregel River may have been an unimportant obstacle at the grand strategy level, it would have been considered a major obstacle at the tactical level. In his autobiography *To Hell and Back*, Audie Murphy comments when he was walking across the Anzio beachhead to return to his unit, "As I plod along, I study the terrain instinctively. As a farm youngster, the land meant either hunger or bread to me. Now its shape is the difference between life and death. Every roll, depression, rock, or tree is significant."[8] The difference between how the two men viewed geography cannot be more striking.

Errors can and will inevitably occur at all levels. However, errors at the grand strategy level will most often have a greater impact than errors committed at lower levels. This is especially true if the war is a long one. For short wars, geography has a minimal impact, and topography becomes more important. But in a long war, geography reigns supreme, and topography becomes of secondary importance.

***

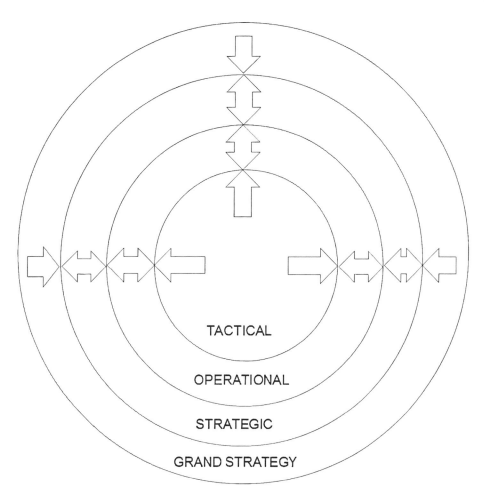

Diagram I-1: Levels of command.

Humans have been creating maps for centuries. The problem with maps is that there is a limit as to how much information can be included on one. Anyone viewing a map needs to be aware of what is important and relevant to the topographer and who their expected audience is. Most military maps will show the location of friendly and enemy forces and the topography of the area to include vegetation, roads, railroads, as well as the location of structures and built-up areas. In some specialized cases, trafficability, the ability for vehicles and people to travel across the terrain, will be included. Few will include information on the types of food raised in the area, the availability of minerals, the quality of the available water, manufacturing sites, or information on the local dialect. That information, at best, is left to the staff officer who is interested in that particular information. Consequently, the maps used by commanders seldom have all of the information they need or may want.

Humans have been able for centuries to change topography, but our impact on geography has been relatively limited. Still, our irrigation systems have allowed us to grow crops in locations where they would not normally be found. Deforestation and air pollution have impacted the climate in many locations around the world. Along with that, our ability to eliminate various species in the food chain has impacted the fauna and, thus, climate. One only has to consider the 1930s "dust bowl" created by improper farming methods in the great plain states of the United States, the steady depletion of fresh water in locations where irrigation is necessary for farming, and the impact of overfishing to appreciate how humans have changed geography. I will not be discussing in depth how humans have changed geography, but the reader needs to be aware that we have.

***

The first chapter in this book will give the reader a broad geographic overview of Winchester and the Shenandoah Valley. This chapter is important as it will allow the reader to understand why control of Winchester was vital to both sides during the Civil War. It will also give the reader an appreciation of how geography dictated the fighting in the Valley. Chapters 2–7 deal with the six major battles that occurred in the vicinity of Winchester and the impact geography had on each of them. Chapter 8 discusses how control of Winchester determined which side held the initiative in the Virginia theater of war. Although chapters 9–13 do not deal directly with the struggle for control of Winchester, I feel they are necessary so that the reader has a good understanding of the impact geography has had on history and warfare to include the American Civil War. In this case, I go from the specific to the general. Chapter 9 is a general summary of geography and history, while chapter 10 is an overview of geography and war. There are many other examples I could have included in both chapters, but I felt that I gave the reader a good overview. Chapters 11 and 12 deal with the Civil War. Chapter 11 explains how geography influenced command decisions during the war. To fully understand many of the decisions made during the conflict, it is important to have good knowledge of geography. Chapter 12 deals with how technology lessened the impact of geography in some situations but, at the same time, increased it in others. Chapter 13 deals with geography and the future. These chapters will provide the reader with a further and more general understanding of how geography influenced the struggle to control Winchester. Appendix A discusses macadamized roads, appendix B provides data on the six battles, while appendix C provides information on Confederate invasions and raids into the North.

I have used the battles for Winchester to analyze the influence of geography on these battles, the campaign leading up to each, and how the different levels of war view geography. This analysis is not meant to be a substitute for Carl von Clausewitz's trilogy of the people, the commander and his army, and the government.[9] Nor is it meant to supersede Clausewitz's statement that war is "a continuation of political intercourse, carried on with other means."[10] In addition, this book is not meant to be a full description of all aspects of the battles for Winchester, as there are many books that comprehensively discuss these engagements. Rather, the purpose of this book is to provide the reader with a better understanding of how geography influences war and how the different levels of warfare have competing views of geography.

All six battles for Winchester were unique with different geographic features impacting them. Each battle was decisive, although the victors were not able to attain all of their desired objectives. Each of the battles had markedly different situations and, except for two, a different set of opposing commanders. In four of the battles, the attacking force was successful and outnumbered the defenders. In the other two battles, the defenders outnumbered the attackers and successfully repelled their attack. Both of those battles were fought south of the city. The only things in common for all six battles were the desire of the attacking force to gain control of Winchester and that the larger force won.

***

Today, the United States Army trains its officers to evaluate future, current, and past campaigns and battles by nine principles of war: objective, offensive, surprise, mass, economy of force, security, unity of command, maneuver, and simplicity.[11] In addition, officers are taught to analyze terrain by determining its impact on observation, cover and concealment, obstacles, key terrain, and avenues of approach with each analysis being slightly different depending on the type and size of the unit. A geographic study supplements both of these methods but, more importantly, emphasizes a different view of a war, campaign, and battle. It is a view that has only become crucial since industrialization, although it has impacted wars, campaigns, and battles for centuries. An understanding of geography is important for today's political and military leaders, as it will influence their decisions and the consequences of those decisions.

History has always been influenced by geography. Although individual historical events can be studied without considering geography, any long-term or broad historical study must include its effects. The United States has been fortunate for most of its history because it has had access to a wide variety and plentiful amount of natural resources. In addition to abundant resources, it was protected from stronger nations by vast oceans until the advent of long-range aircraft. Great Britain is another example. Any history of Great Britain, which ignores the fact that it is an island with available high-quality coal and other mineral deposits, cannot be considered an adequate account of Britain's history. When the history of the world is studied, the impact of spices located in the Far East and the trade and exploration efforts generated by them cannot be ignored. The effects of geography on history are far reaching.

War and geography are inseparable even though many people only consider topography when studying military history. Weather, endemic diseases, and locations of natural resources have all had their influence on military actions. This is not to say the topographic features such as mountain passes, rivers, and swamps have not impacted military history, as they have. But it is important not to forget the influence geography, in the larger sense, has had. Just consider the consequences of the brutal Russian winter on Napoleon's army in 1812 or the impact the oil embargo had on Japan's decision to go to war in 1941. An excellent history of a war or military campaign will include the influence of geography beyond the effect of topography.

Anyone studying the effect of geography on history must also be aware that there are different levels of perception of geography—what is important to a city may not be important to a state or country. From a military point of view, a head of state will, and should, view geography much differently than a private in that nation's army. All of the other levels of authority between the head of state and the individual Soldier will have their own view of geography. The views held at each level will have their own bearing on how geography and history will interact.

***

Geography's impact on history is dependent on technology. Although technology cannot eliminate the influence of geography, it channels its effect. The invention and adoption of a major technology has the potential of changing the relative importance a society and its leadership place on different geographic features. The advent of the petroleum-burning internal combustion engine increased the importance of those regions producing oil while decreasing the importance of regions best suited for raising horses. The petroleum-based army was no longer dependent on farms to breed thousands of horses and mules as well as raising the vast amounts of fodder needed to feed these animals. Instead of fodder, millions of gallons of petroleum products were now required. Technology had replaced one geographically based need with another.

The Civil War was no exception when it came to the influence geography had on it. The South's lack of good, accessible sources of coal, iron, and other important minerals, when compared to the North, put it at a distinct disadvantage.[12] Then the advent of the steam engine negated the positive impact rivers would have previously had in the defense of the South. Although the climate in the Deep South held many endemic diseases for which Northern Soldiers were not prepared, the warm climate also allowed the North to conduct year-round campaigns in that part of the South. Geography is a double-edged sword that can be of use as well as a detriment to an army, navy, or air force.

Consequently, when considering Winchester's importance during the Civil War, much more than the surrounding topography must be considered. The climate in northern Virginia precluded long-term winter campaigns, but at the same time, Soldiers from the North did not have to fear endemic diseases. Food sources for the men and fodder for the horses were readily available during most of the year. When these were not, each side stayed relatively close to sources of supply. Both sides were dependent on the railroad and horse- or mule-drawn wagons since the nearby Shenandoah and Potomac Rivers were not navigable by military supply ships. None of these by themselves made the possession of Winchester crucial. What made Winchester important was the excellent road system that radiated out from it, the availability of food and fodder, and the fact that control of Winchester allowed Southern forces to easily move into the North while Federal control blocked this route. There were also large deposits of critical minerals (salt, lead, and iron ore) in the upper, or southern, part of the valley. These minerals became an objective of a number of Federal raids, but as long as the Confederates controlled Winchester, these sites were safe. Winchester was an attractor in the chaos of war. It was the key that unlocked the Shenandoah Valley or the lock that closed it.

It needs to be noted that the Shenandoah Valley was not the breadbasket of the Confederacy. This is a myth that has been perpetuated without a critical analysis. Although the Valley could easily feed a relatively large army that was within it, it was not possible, due to the lack of a southbound railroad, for food grown in the lower Valley to be shipped out of it to support distant Confederate armies. This topic will be more fully discussed later in the book.

The maps used in this book come from a variety of sources. First, there is the *Civil War Battles in Winchester and Frederick County, Virginia 1861–1865*, Winchester-Frederick County Civil War Centennial Commission. These maps overlay the battles onto a map of Winchester in 1960. Some of the maps used from the First Battle of Kernstown were created by Colonel Nathan Kimball, commander of the Federal forces, and used in his report in the *Official Records*. Other maps were drawn by Hal Jespersen, a cartographic expert. Although not used in this book due to the size and extensive detail on its maps, the *Atlas to Accompany the Official Records of the Union and Confederate Armies* show the terrain as it was (or close to what it was) at the time of each battle. I decided to use the same names for places and roads as shown on the period maps, even if the modern names are different, so the reader can find the locations I am discussing. However, I have tried to indicate the modern name of the locations when possible. When using data from a census report, I have used the same terms as are in the report, even if the terminology is no longer used today. The reader also needs to be aware that the Shenandoah River flows south to north. Thus, Winchester, at the northern end of the Valley, is in the lower part of the Valley. When I use the word "Valley" as a shortened version of Shenandoah Valley, I have capitalized it to indicate such.

The influence of geography must be recognized and appreciated by anyone desiring to understand the past and by anyone wishing to predict the future. There were other "Winchesters" in other wars, in other times. Each of these Winchesters was an attractor that drew more attention than one would imagine by a casual analysis. In the future, there will be new Winchesters, and an understanding of geography will help leaders predict where these Winchesters will be. My hope is that this book will allow readers to view geography in a different way than they have in the past.

1

Winchester and the Shenandoah Valley

The ebb and flow of Confederate fortunes in the Virginia Theater depended upon their ability to maintain control of Winchester.

Bruce Catton stated in *A Stillness at Appomattox*, "There may be lovelier country somewhere—in the Island Vale of Avalon, at a gamble—but when the sunlight lies upon it and the wind puts white clouds racing their shadows the Shenandoah Valley is as good as anything America can show."[1] Beauty alone does not make a location geographically important, and the question is, why was Winchester so heavily contested during the Civil War?

By tradition, the first houses in what was to become Winchester were built in 1732. Settlers continued to move into the area, and in 1738, the colonial assembly created Frederick County. Later a courthouse was built, and the settlement became known as Frederick Town. The town was renamed Winchester when James Wood, a prominent member of the community and the first court clerk, convinced the colonial government to change the town's name to Winchester, after his native town in England. Then, in 1752, Virginia's House of Burgesses granted a charter to Winchester, establishing it as a city. Throughout the French and Indian War, Winchester served as place of refuge for settlers fleeing from the Indians. Its population was large enough and its location good enough that George Washington had a fort built to defend the city in that war. During the American Revolution, a prison camp was established near Winchester holding British and Hessian (German) prisoners. By the time of the American Civil War, Winchester was a well-established commercial center for the northern or lower portion of the Valley due to its location and railroad connection. It was well connected to the surrounding communities with one major turnpike, eight additional roads or turnpikes, and one railroad radiating out from it.[2]

Winchester is 400 feet higher in elevation than Harpers Ferry and about 30 miles southwest of it. The city is approximately 15 miles west of the Shenandoah River, which hugs the base of the Blue Ridge Mountains as it flows toward the Potomac River. During the Civil War, the business quarter of Winchester was located in the basin of a little stream known as Town Run. In every direction, there is slightly rising ground with Fort Hill to the north, Church Hill to the east, Potato Hill to the south, and Academy Hill and Powell's Ridge to the west. Consequently, the city is located in a basin, and any effective defense of Winchester had to be conducted outside of the city. Opequon Creek is the closest stream of a significant size and, at its closest point, is about five miles east of the center of the city. Even though Winchester is not located near any navigable rivers, the site was chosen because of the pure water that came from the springs in the vicinity, the existence of an Indian village, and a major Indian trail that was broad enough for a wagon.[3]

In 1860, Frederick County, the county surrounding Winchester, had a total population of 16,546, which included 1,208 freed colored (the term used in the census) and 2,259 slaves, making it the 23rd largest county out of 148 counties in Virginia. Three of the other nine counties in the Valley had larger populations with Augusta, Rockbridge, and Rockingham Counties having more people and a greater number of slaves. Although Frederick County was not the most populated county in the Valley, Winchester was the largest city. Winchester had a population of 4,392, including 708 slaves and 680 free colored, making it the seventh largest city in Virginia out of 105 listed cities and towns. However, it needs to be noted that the 1860 census included what would soon become the state of West Virginia and that nine of the listed towns had a population of less than 100, while 62 of the listed towns had a population of less than 1,000.[4]

As previously stated, it is estimated that Winchester was occupied and evacuated 72 times during the war. Winchester was normally evacuated and then occupied by the opposing side because the defenders knew they could not successfully defend the city and had enough time to evacuate before being attacked. Evacuating the city was a wise decision since it was never successfully defended.

Map 1-1 shows how the high ground around Winchester made it very difficult to defend the city unless a large number of men were used, a force that neither side was willing or able to commit. Supporting map 1-1 is drawing 1-1, which is a view of Winchester from a fort on a hill northeast of the town. The drawing clearly shows the basin in which Winchester is located. An attacking force that was able to occupy any of the high ground adjacent to Winchester gained control of the city once they emplaced artillery. Winchester had to be defended outside of the city.

For the Federals to adequately secure half of the approaches to Winchester, a defending force would need to cover an arc of about ten miles in length. This distance could cover the western and southern approaches to Winchester and put the defender on the best defensible terrain around the city. However, their flanks would be open. For a comparison, at Cold Harbor the Confederate defenses were about five miles in length, and Lee with 60,000 men had no reserve. That Winchester was indefensible was well known to the Federal high command. In October 1864, General Henry Halleck wrote to General Grant, when he learned that a large number of troops were to be withdrawn from the Valley, about the need to adopt a line of defense against rebel raiders. In his correspondence, Halleck stated, "Winchester

1. Winchester and the Shenandoah Valley

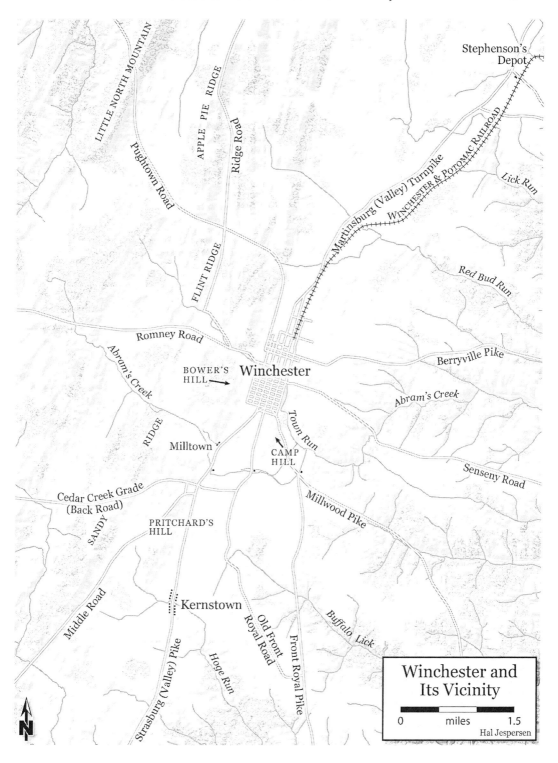

Map 1–1: Winchester and Its Vicinity.

Drawing 1-1: A view of Winchester from a fort (probably one of Milroy's forts, one of which was also known as Fort Jackson) on the hill northeast of the town (drawn by Edwin Forbes on 20 July 1862, Library of Congress).

and Strasburg are both reported as indefensible except by very extensive lines and large garrisons."[5] Halleck's information may have been based on a report from Brevet Major-General William Emory in August 1864 to General Philip Sheridan. Emory wrote, "This place [Winchester] is entirely indefensible; it is a basin surrounded by heights which are commanded by other heights."[6] Winchester's indefensibility was also obvious to some junior officers (who were not professional army officers) who were also aware that Winchester was indefensible. First Lieutenant James Hartley of the 122nd Ohio Infantry wrote his wife from Harpers Ferry after the Second Battle of Winchester,

> I used to wonder why it was that no force could hold that place [Winchester] and probably you may wonder the same. Therefore I will try to tell you the reason of it. Winchester is situated in the Shenandoah Valley in a very pretty place with elevations all around and presents no front to the enemy but can be approached from any or every direction. Our fort [probably Fort Milroy[7]] was situated on one of the elevations and when one of them is gained by the enemy they had an equal chance with those inside. And being liable to be approached so from every direction we could not tell from which the enemy was going to strike the hardest blow. At the time of our fight they kept us fighting them on one side all day Sunday until about five o'clock in the evening when they opened fire on us with their artillery from altogether a new direction where we did not know of them being at all. We then found or supposed that we were surrounded. Which afterward proved to be true. If I was going to fight the Rebels there again I would rather be on the out side [sic] and undertake to take the place from them than to be on the inside and try to defend it. It will take more men to defend the place then it will to take it. It can be surrounded as we were at any time and all communications cut off.[8]

The knowledge that Winchester was indefensible was not limited to officers as some nonprofessional noncommissioned officers realized this fact. Sergeant George Blotcher wrote after the Second Battle of Winchester, "I say at this point, the valley is nearly 20 miles wide and twenty thousand men, could not hold 5,000 me [sic] at base, in a valley like this because the small army could march on flank around the large army and let them set [sic]."[9] Although Blotcher may be exaggerating, his claim points out that the knowledge Winchester was indefensible was known by people of many ranks.

General Sheridan confirmed the indefensibility of Winchester when he was forced to retreat down the Valley in mid–August 1864 after General Early was reinforced with units from the Army of Northern Virginia. As Sheridan retreated north, he realized there was only one location "where a smaller number of troops could hold a greater number."[10] This location was Halltown, which is just outside of Harpers Ferry. Consequently, Sheridan did not try to make a stand at Winchester but retreated past it to Halltown.

For the Confederates, the problem was complicated by the fact that the high ground to the east of the city is much lower than the hills to the west. Still, Opequon Creek, east of the city, was a significant obstacle, and if a sufficient number of men were available, it made an excellent defensive barrier. However, the Confederates only directly defended Winchester once and were defeated in the attempt. Winchester was not defendable by either side with the number of men both sides were willing to allocate to the Valley.

Despite this, three major battles took place in Winchester along with three other major battles just south of the city. These battles were First Kernstown (22–23 March 1862), First Winchester (25 May 1862), Second Winchester (13–15 June 1863), Second Kernstown (24 July 1864), Third Winchester (19 September 1864), and Cedar Creek (19 October 1864). The defending forces were successful only twice, at First Kernstown and Cedar Creek. Both of these battles took place south of the city. At Kernstown, 3,800 Confederates attacked 9,000 Federals, while at Cedar Creek, approximately 15,000 Confederates attacked 32,000 Federals. In both cases, the defenders outnumbered the attackers by over two to one. For the battles in which the attacking force was successful, the attackers always outnumbered the defenders, and in two of the battles the attackers outnumbered the defenders by more than two to one. At First Winchester, 16,000 Confederates attacked 6,500 Federals; at Second Winchester, 12,500 Confederates attacked 7,000 Federals; at Second Kernstown, 13,000 Confederates attacked 10,000 Federals; and at Third Winchester 39,000 Federals attacked 15,200 Confederates.[11] In all cases, the victory went to the side with the largest force.

For the Federals, control of Winchester was necessary for the protection of the Baltimore and Ohio (B&O) Railroad as well as the Chesapeake and Ohio Canal, which were less than 50 miles from Winchester. If the Confederates controlled Winchester, Federal units had to be posted at numerous locations along the railroad and canal. This effort would tie down more men than the Confederates would have at Winchester. If the Federals controlled Winchester, they did not have to post as many guards along the railroad and canal as any Confederate units raiding either the railroad or canal would first have to get past Winchester, and if they did, they would be threatened with the possibility of being cut off. General Robert Milroy stated in his report after the First Battle of Winchester justifying his action to defend Winchester, "That railroad [B&O] never has been nor never can be kept from destruction while this place [Winchester] is occupied by the rebels."[12] Milroy's statement is supported by an assertion of General George McClellan who, although he was not a great battlefield commander, had an excellent grasp of geography. He stated in his book about his actions during the war, "I had often observed to the President and to members of the cabinet that the reconstruction of this railroad [B&O] could not be undertaken until we were in a condition to fight a battle to secure it. I regarded the possession of Winchester and Strasburg as necessary to cover the railroad in the rear, and it was not till the month of February that I felt prepared to accomplish this very desirable but not vital task."[13]

McClellan's statement, in addition to showing his lack of understanding of the political aspect of war, does show that some Federal commanders appreciated the positive impact control of Winchester would have for protecting vital Federal lines of commerce and transportation.

Beyond protecting the B&O Railroad, control of Winchester was important because it was the communication hub for the lower part of the Valley with one railroad and eight major roads intersecting there, as shown on Map 1-1. The Valley Turnpike (the current U.S. 11) was the best road since it was a macadamized road, meaning that it was an all-weather, smoothly packed gravel road. (See appendix A for detailed information about macadamized roads.) The Valley Turnpike went from the Potomac River at Williamsport, Maryland, south to Martinsburg (now in West Virginia), through Winchester, and on to Middletown, then down the western side of Massanutten to Strasburg, New Market, Harrisonburg, Staunton, Fairfield, and Lexington. The other major roads radiating out from Winchester, starting in the south and going counterclockwise, were Front Royal Pike (U.S. 522/340), Millwood Pike (U.S. 50/17), Millwood Road/Senseny Road, Berryville Pike (VA 7) a macadamized road, Martinsburg Pike (U.S. 11 and part of the Valley Turnpike) a macadamized road, Pughtown Road (U.S. 522), and Romney Road (U.S. 50).[14] The modern reader should not interpret the use of the word "turnpike" to mean an all-weather road, as some of the turnpikes were dirt or plank roads. No matter what material the road was made of, all turnpikes were maintained from the tolls paid by people using them. Since a toll was charged, construction of a turnpike required authorization by the Virginia State Legislature.

The importance of a macadamized road to troop movement needs to be understood as it directly influenced a number of military operations in the Valley. On an all-weather macadamized road, troops as well as wheeled vehicles could move substantially faster and thus farther than they could on a dirt road. This is especially true if the dirt road was muddy, particularly for Soldiers carrying 50–80 pounds of equipment and wearing wool clothing. It becomes even harder when it is hot and the road is rutted or muddy. The distance a large body of troops could travel on a macadamized road can be illustrated by the march of the Second Virginia Regiment on the 1st of June 1862. This regiment was the last unit to leave Winchester during Jackson's retreat up the Valley and were in danger of being cut off. When they retreated, they were able to march 36 miles on the Valley Turnpike in one day.[15] On the 1st of June, there is approximately 14¾ hours of daylight at Winchester. Assuming the regiment marched only during daylight, their rate of march would have been about 2½ miles per hour—assuming no stops. Although it is true that these men were highly motivated, as they did not want to be cut off and captured, their march would have been brutal, and they probably could not have achieved that distance on a rutted dirt road.

***

The Shenandoah Valley is considered to be that portion of the Valley that is drained by the Shenandoah River. The boundaries of the Shenandoah Valley are the Blue Ridge Mountains to the east, the Allegheny Mountains to the west, the Potomac River to the north, and the headwaters of the James River to the south. The boundaries of the Shenandoah Valley do not define the entire Valley as it continues into southwestern Virginia, although the terrain becomes more mountainous. The Valley also continues north into Maryland and Pennsylvania where it is called the Cumberland Valley.

Militarily, the Valley had areas where maneuverability was good and other areas where it was not. General Sheridan stated in his report on his 1864 campaign in the Shenandoah Valley, "The valley at Martinsburg is about 60 miles broad, at Winchester forty to forty-five, and at Strasburg twenty-five to thirty, where an isolated chain, called Massanutten Mountain, rises up, running parallel to the Blue Ridge, and terminates at Harrisonburg. Here the valley again opens out fifty or sixty miles broad."[16] Thus, parts of the Valley offered the opportunity for either side to maneuver, but there were choke points that were key defensive positions.

Photograph 1–1 is a photograph of the northern part of the Valley taken from Signal Knob, which is on the very northern end of Massanutten. This photograph shows how the Valley widens north of Massanutten and provides a very large maneuver area. Even with this considerable maneuver area, the major battles were centered on the Valley Turnpike. They congregated there because it was an all-weather road allowing units to move faster than they otherwise would. The turnpike was a high-speed avenue of approach that both sides wanted to control.

The southern portion of the Valley has a higher elevation than the northern portion. Consequently, the Shenandoah River flows south to north and empties into the Potomac River at Harpers Ferry. Thus, the southern portion of the Valley is known as the Upper Valley while the northern portion is called the Lower Valley. The Valley on the eastern side of Massanutten is named the Luray Valley, while the Valley on the western side is known as the Shenandoah Valley. The valleys on either side of Massanutten are substantially narrower than the lower portion of the Valley and are excellent defensive choke points.

Close to its headwaters, the Shenandoah River is divided by Massanutten Mountain, which runs parallel to the Blue Ridge and Allegheny Mountains for about 50 miles. The section of the Shenandoah River that runs on the western side of Massanutten is known as the North Fork, and the river on the eastern side is known as

Photograph 1-1: View of the northern part of the Shenandoah Valley from Signal Knob, the northern end of Massanutten. On the left/western side are the Allegheny Mountains and on the right/eastern side are the Blue Ridge Mountains.

the South Fork. The South Fork is considered to be the main stream of the Shenandoah River. The North Fork and the South Fork flow very closely to Massanutten Mountain. The two rivers join at Front Royal where the North Fork flows east, skirting the northern end of Massanutten. Just north of Massanutten, the Shenandoah River flows very close to the Blue Ridge. This leaves a large area between it and the Allegheny Mountains for maneuvering units. Neither the Shenandoah River nor the North Fork and South Fork Rivers were major obstacles to military operations and were not used for supply operations. The reason they were not major obstacles or used for supply boats was that unless they were in flood stage, which normally occurred only in the spring, they were relatively shallow and thus easy to ford.

The gaps, or passes, in the Blue Ridge Mountains can be seen on Map 1-2. The gaps are locations where the mountain range is not as high. Although the elevation is still significant, the elevation of each gap is substantially less than the adjoining mountains. Consequently, the majority of the roads were built where the passes cross the mountains. In the Blue Ridge, the major gaps are, from north to south, Vestal's Gap (near Harpers Ferry), Snicker's Gap, Ashby's Gap, Manassas Gap (where the Manassas Gap Railroad crossed the Blue Ridge), Chester's Gap (near Front Royal), Thornton's Gap, Fisher's Gap, Swift Run Gap, Brown's Gaps, and Rockfish Gap (where the Virginia Central Railroad crossed the Blue Ridge). Photograph 1-2 shows Ashby's Gap and the Manassas Gap. There are also minor gaps that were seldom used because they did not have good roads through them. In addition, there is a single gap through Massanutten Mountain, the New Market Gap.

1. Winchester and the Shenandoah Valley 19

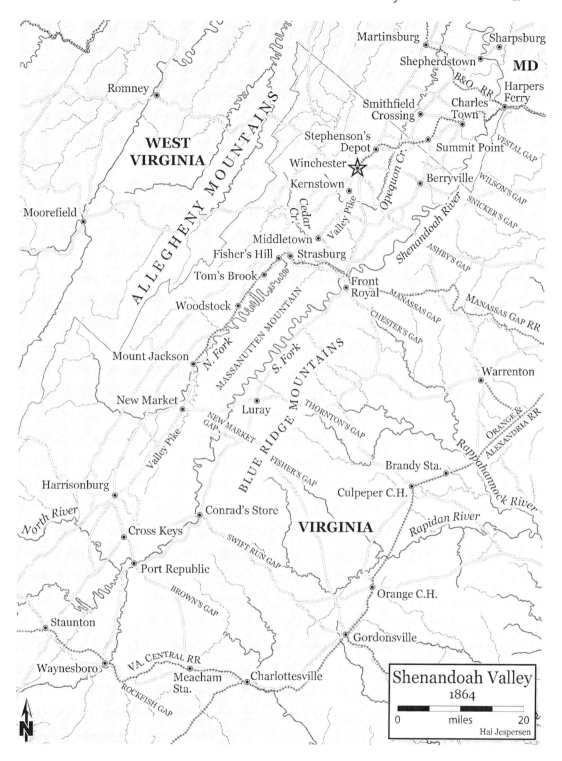

Map 1–2: The Gaps in the Blue Ridge and Allegheny Mountains.

Photograph 1-2: View of Ashby's Gap and the Manassas Gap taken from Signal Knob, the northern end of Massanutten. Ashby's Gap is to the left/north and Manassas Gap is to the right/south.

Any of these gaps, large or small, could be easily defended by a small number of troops. In most cases, once crossed in either direction, the terrain opens up, and units could deploy and maneuver. Three major exceptions to this are Vestal's Gap, Snicker's Gap, and Ashby's Gap. The western exits to all three of these gaps are close to the Shenandoah River, giving any unit defending the Valley a good defensive position. However, the gaps were only important when moving wheeled vehicles (artillery and wagons) or large bodies of troops, for as General Sheridan noted, "the Blue Ridge can be crossed almost anywhere by infantry and cavalry."[17]

Although there are also a number of gaps through the Allegheny Mountains on the western side of the Valley, they were rarely used during the Civil War. This was due to the fact that most of the rivers west of the Allegheny Mountains flow either north or south, blocking movement. In addition, the rough terrain and lack of forage to the west of these gaps made this area inhospitable to large military formations. Consequently, there were fewer major actions on the immediate western side of the Shenandoah Valley than on its eastern side. One major exception is the Battle at McDowell during Stonewall Jackson's 1862 campaign.

In 1864, General David Hunter and his army learned how few supplies were available west of the Valley during their retreat through West Virginia. Hunter and his army were forced to retreat after being defeated by Confederate forces. Hunter believed the only safe route was through the mountains of West Virginia. However, his men and animals suffered tremendously during their retreat. Alexander Neil, a surgeon in the newly designated Army of the Shenandoah, wrote to his family after the march, "We were on the verge of starvation coming over the mountains, the greater part of us getting not a bite to eat for four or five days."[18] General George Crook also wrote about the suffering the army went through in their march through West Virginia. Crook wrote in his autobiography, "From here [Scott's Cross Roads] we had about one hundred and fifty miles to traverse over a mountainous country, barren of everything in the shape of supplies."[19] Crook added, "We reached Kanawha Valley in a sad plight. Men were worn out from fatigue and hunger, all sadly in need of clothing. Many were barefoot."[20] Thus, because of the rough terrain, the lack of forage, along with the lack of farms where an army could get food, there were few major actions in the mountains west of the Shenandoah Valley. Nevertheless, both sides conducted numerous raids through the mountains.

Many people today have difficulty imagining the problems both sides experienced moving across the mountains of West Virginia. Our modern technology of easily transported, prepared food and cars or trucks traveling on all-weather roads obscures it. To appreciate these problems, one should drive U.S. Highway 250 between Staunton, Virginia, and Beverly, West Virginia, and pay attention to the steepness of the road and how it twists and turns. This highway traverses the same route as the old Parkersburg and Staunton Turnpike, which existed during the Civil War. A number of battles took place along this route including Droop Mountain and McDowell.[21] The small town of Beverly became an important supply depot and changed hands a number of times during the war.[22] Although there are some rich farming valleys between Beverly and Staunton, they are not very large or numerous. After one or two large military forces bivouacked in any of these valleys, the fields would have been stripped of their food and forage. Beyond the scarcity of forage, the steep inclines would have made it very difficult for horses, especially if they are weak from lack of nourishment, to haul heavy artillery guns and wagons up and down them. Consequently, the longer the war lasted, the harder it became to campaign in the mountains of West Virginia.

The Shenandoah Valley was much richer in farmland and had better transportation systems than the mountainous region to its west. In 1860, the Valley was serviced by three railroads and two canals. The northern-most railroad was the Winchester and Potomac (W&P), which went from Harpers Ferry to Winchester, a distance of 32 miles with stops along the way.[23] At Harpers Ferry, the W&P connected to the B&O Railroad, giving access to major eastern markets as well as the eastern ports. However, the W&P was designed for only light traffic. Still, it was more than capable of moving farm products and other light loads to and from the lower Valley. Having the railroad terminate at Winchester gave it a substantial commercial advantage over other cities and towns in the lower Valley.

Two railroads went east from the Valley. The Manassas Gap Railroad joined the lower Valley just north of Massanutten to markets in the east, as it went from

Strasburg to Front Royal and on to Manassas Junction. There, it joined the Orange and Alexandria Railroad. The upper Valley was serviced by the Virginia Central Railroad. It went from Richmond to the upper Valley (Staunton was one station) and on to Tennessee and other cities in the Confederacy. For the Confederacy, the Virginia Central Railroad was of much greater importance than either the W&P or Manassas Gap Railroads. Another railroad that deserves mention, although it was not in the Shenandoah Valley, was the Virginia and Tennessee Railroad. It connected Lynchburg to Bristol and continued on to Knoxville. This railroad was important because it connected Richmond with the resource-rich southwestern Virginia as well as the agricultural areas of eastern Tennessee.

During the Civil War, all products and merchandise were normally hauled to a train station by a horse-drawn wagon. All of the armies during the Civil War used wagons to carry their supplies once they were away from a railroad or navigable river. The problem for both civilians and the military was that horses can pull only so much weight and would eventually eat all they can carry or pull if the distance is too far. Consequently, there was a limit to the distance an army could haul its supplies by wagon if an adequate amount of forage could not be found for the horses. Trying to calculate this distance is difficult because there was not one standard supply wagon used during the Civil War. In addition, terrain had a tremendous impact on how heavy a load could be put in a wagon, and the quality as well as the health of the horses were other variables. Thus, it is challenging, at best, to determine the average weight of the wagons used during the Civil War and how much of a load they could carry.

The official weight of a Federal ambulance wagon during the Civil War was 2,115 pounds, and an approximate weight for a six mule wagon was 1,950 pounds.[24] Major Joseph Roberts stated in *The Hand-Book of Artillery* that a team of four horses could draw 2,400 pounds including the weight of the carriage or 600 pounds each.[25] Consequently, most of the weight is taken up by the wagon and not the cargo. Horses need to be well fed if they are to pull this weight every day. The 1865 U.S. Army's *Quartermaster's Guide* stated, "The daily ration of forage for horses and oxen is 14 pounds of hay and 12 pounds of corn, oats or barley."[26] Thus, a horse needs 26 pounds of feed every day. Assuming the weight of the cargo is 500 pounds for a four-horse team, the wagon can travel for only five days if no forage can be found other than what is being carried in the wagon. Therefore, a team and wagon can travel for only two to three days before it must start its return trip if no additional forage is obtained. On a good road, like the Valley Turnpike, this would ideally mean that a team of horses could pull a wagon for 60 miles before they would have to turn back. A more realistic estimate would be half of that, or 30 miles.

Beyond what was needed for the horses and oxen, a large amount of food and material were needed by the men. Lieutenant Colonel John W. Tyler, quartermaster for the Army of the Cumberland, informed Major General William S. Rosecrans in August 1863 that he estimated the following number of railroad cars would be needed to supply the army for one day.[27]

Supplies	No. of animals	No. of men	Pounds	Tons	No. of cars
Forage (grain only)	45,000		450,000	225	28
Rations		70,000	2,110,000**	105	13
Quartermaster's stores			160,000	80	10
Medical stores			32,000	16	2
Contingencies			112,000	56	7
Total per day			2,864,000	482	60

*Note—Although the table in the Official Records *shows 2,110,000 pounds of rations, that number must be incorrect as 105 tons would equal 211,000 pounds. In addition, 2,110,000 pounds of rations would be a little over 30 pounds per man while 211,000 would be 3 pounds per man, a much more reasonable figure.*

If a wagon could carry 500 pounds, the number of wagons needed for the Army of the Cumberland to transport one day's worth of supplies would have been 1,928. The total was probably larger since ammunition and ordnance supplies were not included in Lieutenant Colonel Tyler's calculations. These data show why the supply wagon trains for Civil War armies were so large.

Both of these examples help explain why Civil War armies, operating in areas where they could not live off the land, did not get very far from railroads or navigable rivers and why most campaigns occurred after the grass was high enough for the horses to eat. During the Civil War, Federal generals and supply officers knew that no army greater than 40,000 men could be sustained more than 100 miles from a railroad or navigable river.[28] It was because of this fact that when the Federal armies pursued the Army of Northern Virginia across southern Virginia, a pursuit that ultimately ended at Appomattox, Federal railroad units following the armies changed the gauge of the Southside Railroad from 5 feet to 4 feet 8½ inches, the gauge of the Federal military railroad.[29] This was done so that the Federal military trains could use the rails and keep the Federal armies supplied.

For a farmer, the issue was complicated by the need to make a profit. If he had to travel 60 miles to sell his grain or produce, he would not have much left after feeding his horse(s). Consequently, only the farmers living close to a railroad depot in the upper Valley could realistically sell food to the Confederate armies. Only Augusta, Rockingham, and part of Page County were close enough to Staunton for a farmer to make a profit taking his crops to the railroad there. In these three counties, the cash value of the farms in 1860 was $22,908,448. This was 6.2 percent of the cash value of all farms in Virginia. Further, the value of the livestock was $2,715,814 or 5.7 percent of the state's total, while bushels of wheat were 768,204 or 5.9 percent of the state's total. Even though the percentages were small, the value of the farms and livestock as well as the bushels of wheat produced was greater than the percentage of the population in these three counties, which was 59,266 or 3.7 percent of the total population of Virginia in 1860. Although the Shenandoah Valley was a rich farming area, the Valley was not the breadbasket of the Confederacy because of the lack of working railroads throughout the entire Valley.

Even if the Valley was not the breadbasket of the Confederacy, its agricultural production and location was vital to the Confederacy for a number of reasons. First, any army located in the Valley did not need to have the Confederate commissary supply food for the men or forage for the horses. General Joseph E. Johnston realized this in 1861 when he was in command of the Confederate forces in the lower Valley. In his memoirs, Johnston stated, "The rich country around us furnished abundant supplies of provision and forage, which the farmers and millers willingly sold on credit to the quartermasters and commissaries of the army. We neither received nor required assistance from the Commissary Department at Richmond, except for the articles of coffee and sugar, which were then parts of the Confederate soldier's ration."[30] Johnston went on to state that "under his [Major Kersley's] administration of the commissariat, 'the Valley' could have supplied abundantly an army four times as large as ours."[31] At this time, in 1861 before the Battle of the First Bull Run, Johnston's army was "not quite nine thousand men, of all arms."[32] Thus, Johnston felt the lower Valley could easily supply an army of 36,000 men without any support from the Confederate commissary. General Sheridan confirmed this, as he stated, "The valley itself was rich in grain, cattle, sheep, hogs, and fruit, and was in such a prosperous condition that the rebel army could march up and down it, billeting on the inhabitants."[33] This was one of the important aspects of the lower Valley: it could supply a large army without the army needing additional food from any other part of the Confederacy. This was significant since food and forage are bulky items requiring rail, ship, and/or wagon transportation, all of which were stretched beyond their capability in the Confederacy. The ability of the Valley to allow an army to be self-sufficient continued throughout the war until the Valley was devastated in 1864.

The loss of the supplies available in the lower Valley began when General Jubal Early was forced to retreat south, up the Valley, after threatening Washington in 1864. Lieutenant Colonel J. Stoddard Johnston, who served as General John Breckinridge's chief of staff during this campaign, stated after the war:

> This retreat necessitated the giving up of the richest part of the Valley, and surrendered all of our flouring mills which had been put in operation for the supply of the army. The portion of the Valley given up had been found rich in supplies of grain, none having been burned up to that time, and it not being uncommon to find two crops of wheat in the stack. But to utilize this for the army, on account of the scarcity of labor, details of soldiers had to be made to thresh out the grain, place the mills in order—most of them having fallen into disuse—and grind the flour.[34]

Even though General Early was able to regain control of the lower Valley, his defeat at the Third Battle of Winchester and his subsequent defeat at Fisher's Hill gave General Sheridan the opportunity to destroy the Valley's ability to supply a large force. Although Sheridan's destruction of food stock and forage was extensive, it occurred primarily along the main roads, especially the Valley Turnpike. However, it was along these roads that both sides foraged when moving through the Valley. Consequently, when Early moved back north, down the Valley, and attacked the Federal forces at Cedar Creek, his men were not able to easily find adequate amounts of food and fodder as they had in previous years. This hunger played a role in the desire for the Confederates to pillage the Federal camps they had overrun. This led to units becoming disorganized and more vulnerable to counterattack.

Lieutenant Colonel Johnston's statement further reinforces the fact that the lower Valley supplied little food to Confederate armies beyond one stationed in the lower Valley. The grain was available, but there were not enough men available to process it, much less transport it to the Virginia Central Railroad. The Shenandoah Valley was not the breadbasket of the Confederacy although the upper Valley did provide food to the Confederate armies.

As important as the Valley was for supplying any military unit located there, in reality, the Virginia and Tennessee Railroad and the associated supply depot at Lynchburg were logistically more important to the Confederacy. Captain Charles M. Blackford, a staff officer in General James Longstreet's corps, wrote,

> The strategic importance of the city of Lynchburg was very little understood by those directing the military movement of the Federal armies during the Civil war. It was the depot for the Army of Northern Virginia for all commissary and quartermaster stores gathered from the productive territory lying between it and Knoxville, Tennessee, and from all the country tributary to, and drained by, the Virginia & Tennessee Railroad. Here, also, were stored many of the scant medical supplies of the Confederacy, and here many hospitals gave accommodations to the sick and wounded from the martial lines north and east of it. Lynchburg was, in addition, the key to the inside line of communication which enabled the Confederate troops to be moved from our northern to our eastern lines of defense, without exciting the attention of the enemy.[35]

Beyond the supply depot at Lynchburg, the salt and lead mines along with the iron furnaces in southwestern Virginia were also very important to the survival of the Confederacy. Lieutenant Colonel J. Stoddard Johnston wrote,

> The armies at Richmond and elsewhere were dependent, as indeed were the people of a large part of the Confederacy, upon Saltville for their salt. The only lead mines in the Confederacy, from which the ammunition of the South was supplied, were in his [Breckenridge's] Department, and he was charged with seeing to the shipment of a stated supply. So also were the chief iron furnaces and forges, from which were furnished material for horse shoes for the whole army and for the military foundry at Richmond. Besides all this, he held the chief source of supply for both bread and meat needed for the army at Richmond.[36]

Thus, the supplies passing through Lynchburg gave people then, and now, the perception that all of the supplies had originated in the Shenandoah Valley.

The problem any Federal force had while operating in the upper Valley was that they were quite a distance from any friendly source of supply. Accordingly, they either had to have an extensive, vulnerable supply train or live off the land. Hunter chose the latter, so when he retreated through the mountains of West Virginia, his units suffered from the lack of supplies. In addition, any Federal unit in the upper Valley was under the danger of being cut off if Confederate units got between it and the lower Valley. The result was that very little damage was done to the upper Valley until late in the war. By then, the manpower and logistic differences between the Federals and Confederates began to show.

The Shenandoah Valley was the easiest route to the rich natural resources in southwestern Virginia especially when compared to the difficulties of moving across the mountains in western Virginia. Any Federal unit attempting to penetrate deeply into Confederate territory had to move quickly and lightly. Because of this, few efforts were made to destroy the lead mine, salt works, and other industrial sites in southwestern Virginia until late in the war. Having the only lead mine in the Confederacy, being able to supply enough salt to satisfy the needs of the entire Confederacy, and being a major source of iron and coal for the industries in Richmond made the upper Valley a resource that needed protecting.[37]

While the agricultural and mineral resources in the Shenandoah Valley were vital to the survival of the Confederacy, the Federals had difficulty attacking these resources. First, any Federal army moving south up the Valley would be moving away from Richmond, as well as moving into a more mountainous region. Still, such a Federal army would be a major threat to a critical source of supply and a major supply depot for the Confederacy. If an equivalent-size Confederate force followed the Federal Army, the Federal Army could either turn and fight, move into the mountains of western Virginia, or march across the Blue Ridge toward Richmond. There are obvious consequences with all of the options. To turn and fight would be risky since the Confederate Army would be between it and its supplies. Even if the battle was a victory, the Federal Army would still be in danger of being cut off. Retreating into the mountains of West Virginia would have been a logistic disaster as previously discussed. Marching on Richmond had possibilities, but if the passes were defended by Confederate units, it would be very difficult to force a passage through them. A pursuing Confederate force could also easily parallel the Federal Army's route and stay between it and its source of supplies with Richmond being many days march away.

Even though the Shenandoah Valley was not the breadbasket of the Confederacy, geography made it important to the Confederacy. First, as mentioned earlier, any Confederate unit stationed in the Valley could receive all of its food and forage from the Valley. This was important in lessening the strain on the overloaded Confederate logistic system. Second, as also previously discussed, control of the Shenandoah Valley gave the Confederacy access to the western states through the railroads that either went through the Valley proper or through the southernmost reaches of the Valley. Control of the Valley also gave the Confederacy a relatively safe location to place a major logistic center, such as the one established at Lynchburg. This was due to the fact that the upper Valley was easily defended because of the mountains to its west and the choke points on both sides of the northern end of Massanutten.

Third, and of equal importance, was that the Shenandoah Valley was a protected invasion route into Maryland and Pennsylvania as shown on Map 1–3 (Winchester is marked with a star). Any Confederate Army moving north would have the mountains to the east to screen its movements and only needed to leave a limited number of units behind to garrison the gaps through the mountains. Such a move would threaten the B&O Railroad, which was a major east and west supply route for the Federals, and the Chesapeake and Ohio Canal. Both of these were vital transportation arteries for the Federals, especially the B&O Railroad, and disruption of either caused difficulties for the Federals. The failure to adequately protect these resources was acutely demonstrated when General Early moved through the Valley in the summer of 1864 and disrupted movement on both of these arteries as well as threatening Washington. In addition, if a Confederate army stationed in Winchester moved north, it would be able to liberally forage from the fertile Federal farmlands.

The insert on Map 1–3, "Avenue of Invasion," graphically shows how the Valley provided a protective shield for any Confederate force moving north. However, both Confederates moving north and Federals moving south needed to ensure that the passes behind them were well guarded. Unfortunately, like any map, Map 1–3 cannot show all of the information a reader may want to know. Still, it shows why General Lee used the Valley for his movement into Pennsylvania. The map also shows why control of Winchester was vital to both sides. Unless Confederate forces controlled Winchester, they could not advance into Maryland or Pennsylvania. Conversely, Federal forces had to control Winchester to keep the Confederates south of the Potomac River while at the same time allowing them to move farther up the Valley. The Shenandoah Valley was an avenue of invasion for the Confederates.

It was through the Shenandoah Valley that most of the Confederate incursions into the north occurred; it was a dagger pointed northward. Excluding Kentucky, Confederate units invaded New Mexico, Colorado, Missouri, and western Virginia with the objective of controlling those regions. Confederate units also made raids into Federal-controlled Indian Territory and Kansas and made one raid into Ohio, one into Indiana and Ohio, and one raid/robbery into Vermont. All of these incursions failed for a number of reasons. More and larger military incursions of the north occurred through the Shenandoah Valley than anywhere else. These incursions include the General J.E.B. Stuart's Chambersburg raid in October 1862, the Gettysburg Campaign in June and July 1863, General Early's raid on Washington in July 1864, and Generals John McCausland and Bradley Johnson's Chambersburg raid in July and August 1864. Winchester was the cork that stopped or the outlet that allowed these incursions. Whenever the Federals controlled Winchester, there were no major raids into Maryland and Pennsylvania, but when the Confederates controlled Winchester, they were able to conduct raids into the north.

One of the exceptions to the Valley being an avenue of invasion was the Antietam campaign. During that campaign, Lee did not make extensive use of the Valley because the Army of Northern Virginia crossed the Potomac River at White's Ford, south/downriver from Harpers Ferry. Although Lee did not make use of the Valley to move into Maryland, the map makes it clear why Lee wanted control of Harpers Ferry. Controlling Harpers Ferry allowed him to use the Valley for resupply and safe communications with Richmond.

Control of Winchester, a relatively small city, dictated the pace and scope of

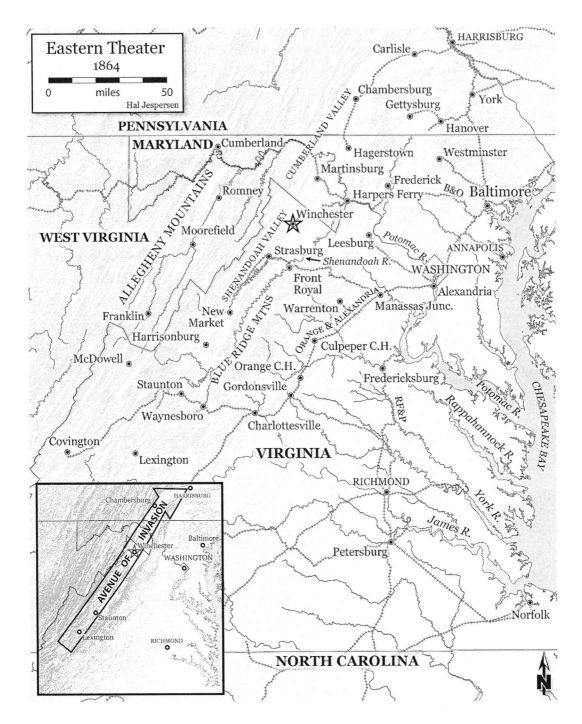

Map 1-3: Avenue of Invasion.

the war in Virginia. As long as the Confederates were strong enough to control the city, they could take offensive actions against the Federals. But when the Federals were strong enough to control Winchester, they were able to block major Confederate forces from moving north of the Potomac River. The ebb and flow of Confederate fortunes in Virginia depended on their ability to control Winchester. All of this was possible due to the orientation of the Valley, the location of Winchester as a major transportation hub, and the availability of food and fodder. Winchester was the center of an arc in which a Confederate force could tie down a greater number of Federal troops, because they would be needed to prevent the Confederate force from moving north or threatening Washington. When the Confederates controlled Winchester, they dictated the tempo of the war in the Virginia theater, but when the Federals controlled Winchester, they dominated events in Virginia.

2

Geography and the First Battle of Kernstown

22–23 March 1862

A small battle, due to geography, can have wide consequences.

Kernstown was a small village on the Valley Turnpike a little over three miles south of Winchester as shown on Maps 1–1 and 2–3.[1] What made Kernstown important was its location on the outer ring of high ground south of Winchester. Once an attacking force from the south seized control of the high ground in the vicinity of Kernstown, its options increased as it could now maneuver to the open ground to the east and outflank any defending units posted to the west of Winchester. Any Federal force wishing to control Winchester had to retain control of Kernstown and the surrounding high ground.

The First Battle of Kernstown was fought on the 22nd and 23rd of March 1862. It was a short fight with the main battle starting on the 23rd around 3:00 p.m. and ending at dusk, about 6:30 p.m. Officially, the battle was only on the 23rd, but on the 22nd, there was a preliminary fight/skirmish between the Confederate cavalry under the command of Colonel Turner Ashby and the Federal outposts just outside of Winchester involving fewer than 2,000 men. The fight on the 23rd was the smallest of the battles fought for control of Winchester with fewer than a total of 14,000 men involved that day. Still, it had a far greater impact on events than other much larger Civil War battles. Although it was a Federal tactical victory, it became a Confederate strategic victory. This battle was the first major battle in the Valley and is considered the opening battle for General Stonewall Jackson's famous Valley campaign. It is also the only battle Jackson lost.

Of the six maps included in this chapter, four of the maps were drawn for Colonel Nathan Kimball, commander of the Federal forces. His maps show the chronological sequence of the battle from the Federal view and were included in his report of the battle; thus, they are period maps. The fifth map is a more modern map showing the disposition of both sides in relationship to modern Kernstown. The sixth map shows the flow of the battle up to the Confederate retreat. As always, all of the maps need to be viewed for the reader to get a full understanding of the battle and how geography influenced it. There is a Confederate map of the battle, but unfortunately, it is very difficult to read. Consequently, I decided not to include it.

∗∗∗

In March 1862, at the grand strategy level, control of Winchester was not a major issue for Lincoln as the war was going well for the Federal government. Nashville, Tennessee, had been captured and the Federal government was now in control of large parts of Tennessee and Kentucky as well as western Virginia. Then the Confederate defeat at Pea Ridge consolidated Federal control of Missouri. In addition, the Confederate hope of breaking the Federal blockade of the James River had ended when USS *Monitor*'s appearance negated the advantage held the previous day by CSS *Virginia*. Still, Lincoln was very concerned about the safety of the capital, especially as General George McClellan had taken the vast majority of the trained units to the Fort Monroe area for his planned attack on Richmond. McClellan felt that he needed every available unit he could get if he was to be successful. As a result, he wanted to leave as few units as possible around Washington. This concerned Lincoln because he wanted the capital adequately guarded. The First Battle of Kernstown brought the safety of Washington into question as it revealed the possibility that the Confederates could, if they had won the battle, have strong, active forces north of Washington.

For Jefferson Davis, his geographic view of the war had not changed except that the Confederates had lost control of some very important areas. Aggressive action was needed, but he was not getting that from his commander of the largest Confederate army in Virginia, General Joseph Johnston. Then McClellan's movement to the peninsula southeast of Richmond created a significant threat to the Confederate capital forcing Davis to concentrate his efforts on that threat. Thus, in early March, neither Lincoln nor Davis were concerned about Winchester.

At the strategic and operational levels, McClellan and Confederate general Joseph Johnston had mutually opposite desires. McClellan wanted reinforcements, while Johnston did not want any additional units sent to McClellan. McClellan considered the Confederate forces in the Valley so weak that he instructed General Nathaniel P. Banks, commander of the Fifth Corps, on the 16th of March 1862, concerning the disposition of his corps, "Something like two regiments of cavalry should be left in that vicinity [where the Manassas Railroad crosses the Shenandoah River] to occupy Winchester and thoroughly scour the country south of the railroad and up the Shenandoah Valley, as well as through Chester Gap, which might perhaps be advantageously occupied by a detachment of infantry, well intrenched."[2] McClellan certainly believed in giving tasks to subordinate units that were, obviously, too much for them to handle. Still, his message shows how little he appreciated the Confederate threat in the Valley and how much he wanted troops for his campaign.

For the Confederates, the problem was that their forces in the Valley were too weak to challenge the Federal units advancing up the Valley. In addition, Johnston's retreat from Manassas exposed Jackson's eastern flank to attack through one of the passes going through the Blue Ridge Mountains. These two reasons forced Jackson to retreat from Winchester on the 11th of March. With the Federals now in control of Winchester, they had gained the initiative in Virginia. They had more than enough forces to defeat Jackson's small force in the Valley, secure Washington, and attack Richmond. The Confederates were on the defensive in Virginia and it appeared that the rebellion would soon be crushed. However, having the initiative means little if commanders are unwilling or unable to take advantage of it.

Jackson's retreat from Winchester up the Valley was deliberate, as Federal forces did not aggressively pursue him. Using the macadamized Valley Turnpike, Jackson slowly marched his units south and stopped just beyond Mount Jackson on the 17th. In reality, Mount Jackson was a hard day's march on the macadamized Valley Turnpike from Winchester, but Jackson was not under strong pressure and wanted to make sure that his forces remained close to the pursuing Federals. On the 19th, Jackson received a message from Johnston stating "that it was most desirable the enemy's force in the Valley should be detained there, and prevented from reinforcing General McClellan."[3] Based on Johnston's request to keep Federal forces in the Valley, Jackson continually looked for an opportunity to attack them.

Geography could have worked against Jackson as he was bivouacked on the western side of Massanutten Mountain. If a strong Federal force moved up the Luray Valley, on the eastern side of Massanutten, it would cut him off from communications with General Johnston. Such a force could also stop any reinforcements from Richmond getting to Jackson as well as preventing Jackson from reinforcing Johnston. However, any Federal force moving up the Luray Valley could be attacked on its flank by Jackson unless they placed a strong force on the road going through the New Market Gap, the only road going across Massanutten. Jackson's problem was that he needed to stay in contact with a superior number of Federal forces, yet not allow his force to be isolated. Luckily for Jackson, the Federal forces were only interested in containing Jackson since Banks' corps was responsible for the Valley as well as protecting the capital.

After assuring themselves that Jackson was not a threat, the Federals pulled their forces at Strasburg back to Winchester on Friday the 21st of March. Colonel Turner Ashby, commander of Jackson's cavalry, informed Jackson of this. Based on this information Jackson, "apprehensive that the Federals would leave this military district," decided to follow them.[4] The next day, Jackson marched his units about 21 miles to Strasburg using the macadamized Valley Turnpike. Jackson's advance was preceded by Ashby and his cavalry, and on the 22nd, there was a sharp engagement between the Confederate cavalry and Federal outposts just south of Winchester. The Federal outposts were quickly reinforced, and Ashby was forced to retreat. There were two main results from the skirmish. First, General James Shields, commander of the Federal forces, was wounded and incapacitated. This caused the command to fall to Colonel Nathan Kimball. Second, Ashby gained intelligence on the Federal forces in Winchester and found out that only four regiments remained there and that the other units had left the city.

Unfortunately for the Confederates, the intelligence Ashby gained was very misleading because there were actually three brigades of infantry consisting of 13 regiments, plus artillery and cavalry in the vicinity of Winchester. Ashby's information caused Jackson to continue his advance with the idea of attacking the Federals on Monday the 24th. By 2:00 p.m. on the 23rd, after a march of about 14 miles, his units were about a mile or two south of Kernstown and ordered to bivouac.[5] Regrettably for the Confederates, even though they used the all-weather Valley Turnpike, the men were not accustomed to hard marches. This, combined with the poor weather, caused many men to drop out and consequently were not available for the battle. The stage was set for the First Battle of Kernstown.

The Battlefield

The Kernstown battlefield is relatively small, but there were some geographic features that impacted the battle. First was the weather and the season. The ground was saturated due to rain and snow and this limited the cross-country mobility of both sides especially in the bottoms.[6] The wet weather also resulted in the men becoming wet and cold. In addition, some of the fields had been plowed and were saturated with water. Due to this, horses would sink to their fetlocks, the part of a horse's leg just above the hoof.[7] Obviously, this slowed down maneuvering by the artillery, cavalry, and infantry. This made control of the all-weather Valley Turnpike even more important. Since the battle took place in late March before the trees had fully leafed, they were not drawing large amounts of water out of the soil, which contributed to the bogginess in the bottoms. The lack of foliage also made it hard for units to move undetected, although if they were far enough into the woods and behind some terrain, they were very difficult to spot. Forage for the animals was also in short supply as the grass had not yet begun to grow. Whereas the Federal government could provide forage for their army, the Confederates were more dependent on local sources.

Second was Pritchard's Hill. The importance of Pritchard's Hill, which is located just to the west of the Valley Turnpike (Valley Road on Maps 2–3, 2–4, 2–5, and 2–6; Route 11 on Map 2–1; Valley Turnpike on Map 2–2; and Strasburg Turnpike on Map 1–1), was that it controlled the all-weather Valley Turnpike. Controlling the turnpike was essential due to the soggy ground making the dirt roads barely passable and off-road movement very difficult. In addition, from Pritchard's Hill, Kimball was able to observe the movement of many of the Confederate units. Then, due to the strong force of Federal artillery and infantry posted on Pritchard's Hill made the success of any direct assault on it costly and likely to fail, Jackson decided to maneuver to the west. Pritchard's Hill is shown on Map 2–3 as "A" and as "Pritchard's Hill" on Map 2–6.

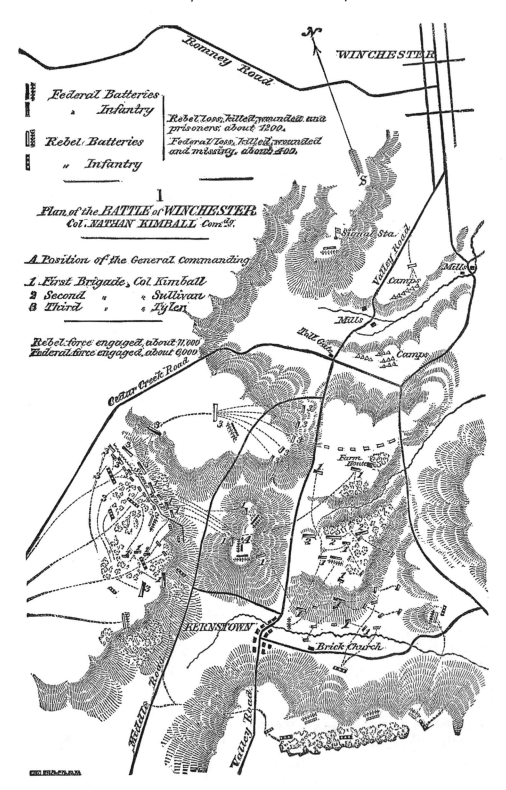

Map 2-1: The First Battle of Kernstown Overview (*ORA*, Series I, Volume XII, Part I, 362).

2. Geography and the First Battle of Kernstown

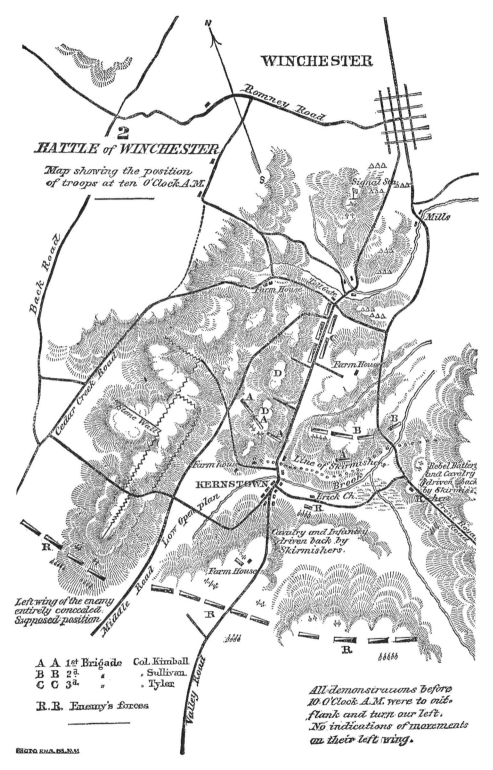

Map 2-2: The First Battle of Kernstown Overview, 10:00 a.m. (*ORA*, Series I, Volume XII, Part I, 363).

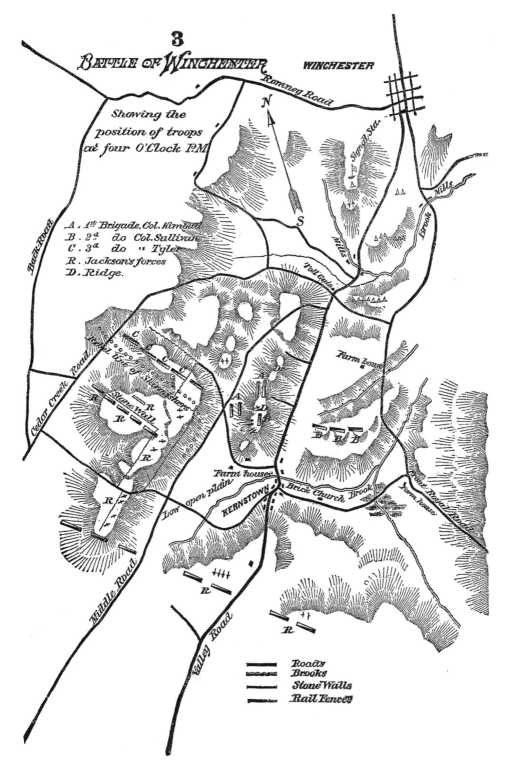

Map 2-3: The First Battle of Kernstown Overview, 4:00 p.m. (*ORA*, Series I, Volume XII, Part I, 364).

2. Geography and the First Battle of Kernstown   37

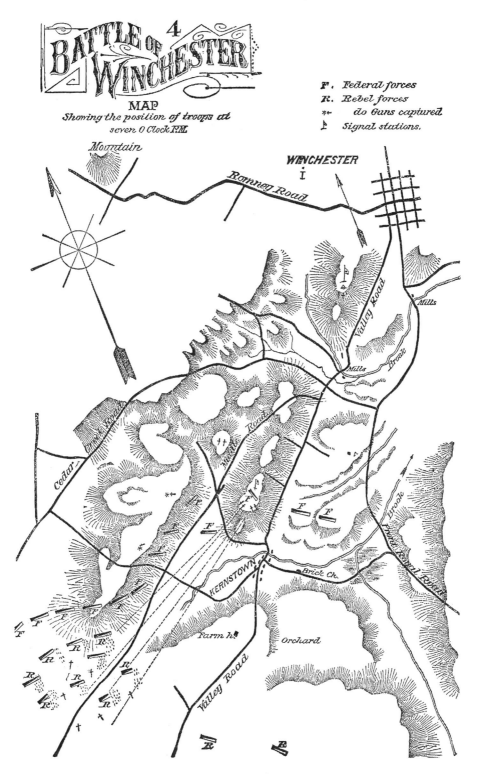

Map 2-4: The First Battle of Kernstown Overview, 7:00 p.m. (*ORA*, Series I, Volume XII, Part I, 365).

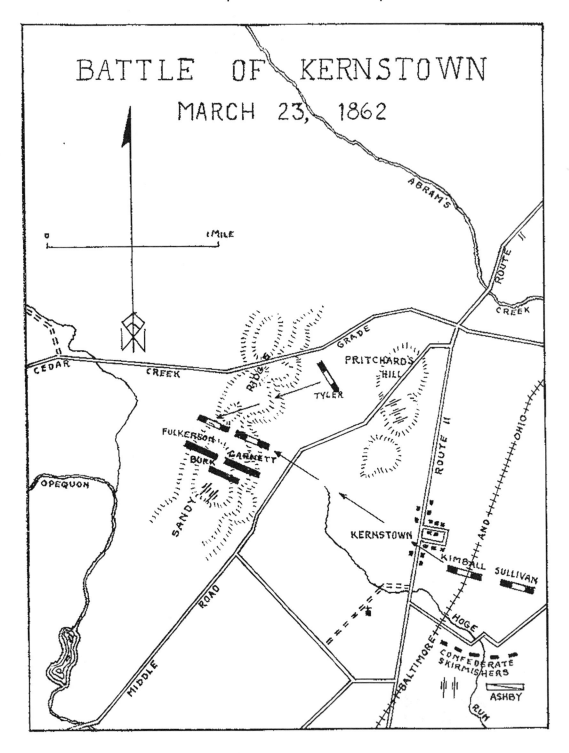

Map 2-5: First Battle of Kernstown showing the location of units in respect to Kernstown in 1960 (*Civil War Battles in Winchester and Frederick County, Virginia 1861–1865*, Winchester-Frederick County Civil War Centennial Commission).

2. Geography and the First Battle of Kernstown

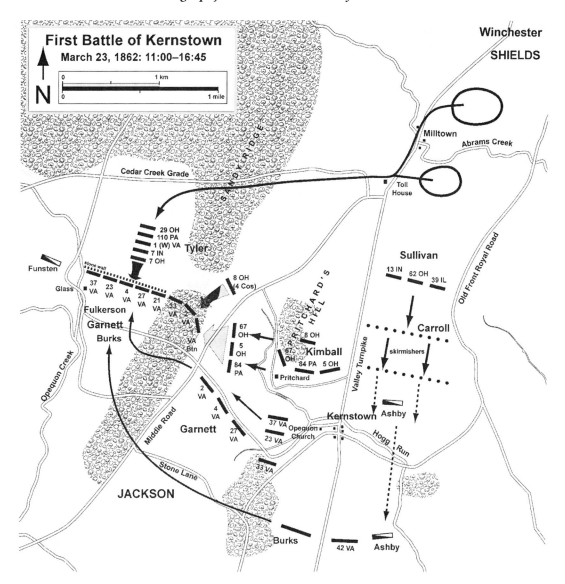

Map 2-6: The First Battle of Kernstown Overview (Hal Jespersen, www.cwmaps.com).

Pritchard's Hill is located just north of Kernstown and west of the Valley Turnpike. Any force on it can dominate both Kernstown and the Valley Turnpike. Photograph 2-1 is a view of U.S. 11, the former Valley Turnpike, taken from Pritchard's Hill. The photograph shows how any military force on the hill would easily dominate the turnpike. It also shows how Winchester has increased in size since the war and how the city now covers a large part of the Kernstown battlefields. Photograph 2-2 shows the view Kimball had from Pritchard's Hill toward the south. As the photograph shows, the terrain flattens out and anyone on Pritchard's Hill has an extensive view toward the south. Photograph 2-3 is a view of Sandy Ridge from Pritchard's Hill. Sandy Ridge is higher than Pritchard's Hill and blocks the view of what may be

Photograph 2-1: Photograph taken from Pritchard's Hill of U.S. 11, the former Valley Turnpike. Route 11 is located near where the first houses can be seen.

Photograph 2-2: View from Pritchard's Hill looking south.

happening on the western side of Sandy Ridge from an observer on Pritchard's Hill. Photograph 2-4 is a photograph of Pritchard's Hill taken from the vicinity of the Pritchard House. The hill dominates the surrounding area, and control of it gains the defending force a distinctive advantage.

Third was Sandy Ridge, which is located about one mile west of Pritchard's Hill and separated from it by a small valley and Middle Road, a dirt road that was not very passable due to the wet conditions. Sandy Hill is not one continuous hill, as it

Photograph 2-3: View of Sandy Ridge from Pritchard's Hill.

Photograph 2-4: View of Pritchard's Hill from the south.

is cut by a number of ravines. In addition, parts of it were heavily wooded and it was crisscrossed by numerous stone walls. The reason Jackson maneuvered to the west to Sandy Ridge was because it was higher than Pritchard's Hill, and he believed that any Confederate artillery placed on Sandy Ridge would be able to dominate the Federal artillery on Pritchard's Hill. Kimball, although he could have seen that Sandy

Ridge was higher than Pritchard's Hill, probably did not occupy Sandy Ridge at the beginning of the battle because he believed he was outnumbered and that the wet conditions would force the Confederates to stay close to the Valley Turnpike. Sandy Ridge is shown as "R" on Map 2-5 and as "Sandy Ridge" on Map 2-6.

Fourth, this part of the Valley has an abundance of rocks on top of or very close to the surface. Consequently, stone walls were very common in the area and were a significant factor in the battle. The fences channeled movement, provided protection, and forced the Confederates to open passageways through them for their artillery. Map 2-4 shows the stone walls on Sandy Ridge and highlights the one the Confederate main line was posted behind. By using this stone wall, the Confederates were able defend Sandy Ridge against a superior force until some of the men ran out of ammunition and retreated. Photograph 2-5 is a picture of a reconstructed stone wall at the same location as the Civil War-era stone wall used by the Confederates to defend their left/western flank on Sandy Ridge. The photograph shows the view the defending Confederates would have had of the Federal units attacking them. It also shows the folds in the ground that would have provided cover and protection for the attacking Federal infantry. Photograph 2-6 was taken from the perspective of the attacking Federal infantry of the stone wall the Confederates were behind. Although the Federals were attacking uphill, there were numerous folds in the ground, which would have provided protection when the men were lying down.

Fifth, the lack of local forage impacted the Confederate cavalry. At this time of

Photograph 2-5: Reconstructed stone fence at the location of the Civil War stone fence used by the Confederates to defend their left (western) flank on Sandy Ridge.

2. Geography and the First Battle of Kernstown

the year, the grass in the northern part of the Valley had not grown very much. Consequently, forage for the animals needed to be brought in or be purchased from local farmers. When a cavalry force is actively campaigning, as Turner Ashby's was, there are only limited opportunities to rest the horses and properly feed them. As a result, many of his men were not available for the battle, limiting his force to 150 men on the Confederate right flank and 140 on the left flank.[8] The lack of cavalry impacted Ashby's diversionary attack on the Federal left (eastern) flank as well as the ability of the Confederate cavalry on the left (western) flank to protect their retreating infantry.

During the First Battle of Kernstown, both Jackson and Kimball were acting at the operational and tactical levels. Each realized the importance of Pritchard's Hill. Jackson knew that he had to seize control of the hill to advance on Winchester while Kimball realized that it was an excellent defensive position. Consequently, both men directed a large number of units to either defend or seize the hill. At the tactical level, both men used the topography to place their units in the best positions possible. Still, due to the time/distance factor, neither man could directly control all of their units, resulting in many of the tactical decisions being made by lower level commanders. However, Kimball did have an advantage over Jackson in regard to receiving information and giving orders, as Lieutenant William Rowley was able to establish signal stations at various places on the battlefield and between the battlefield and Winchester for him.[9] Consequently, Kimball was able, for the most part,

Photograph 2–6: The view the attacking Federal infantry would have had as they advanced on the Confederate-held stone wall on the western side of Sandy Ridge.

to be aware of what was happening throughout the battlefield and was able to keep General Shields in Winchester informed.

A related issued to the limited control the two commanders had was that both forces mainly consisted of inexperienced officers and men. Although the men and officers on both sides fought gallantly, mistakes were made that would not have been made if the officers were more experienced and the men were veterans. First Kernstown was the only battle of the struggle for control of Winchester in which the majority of the officers and men were not experienced veterans. Consequently, in later battles for Winchester, both officers and men would be more aware of the tactical advantages and disadvantages the terrain held.

The movements of the units, especially the Federal ones, can be seen on Maps 2-3 to 2-6. These are a series of maps that were drawn for Colonel Kimball by Captain Eddy D. Mason of the 67th Ohio and thus are from the Federal point of view.[10] Map 2-3 shows the overall flow of the battle. Map 2-4 depicts the situation at 10:00 a.m. Map 2-5 presents the situation at 4:00 p.m. when the main battle began. Map 2-6 shows the situation at 7:00 p.m. at which time, the Confederates had retreated and the battle had ended. Map 2-2 gives a summary of maneuvers up to just before the Confederate retreat. These maps clearly illustrate the important role that the high ground and stone walls played in the battle, though they do not show what parts of the battlefield limited mobility or where the woods were located. As with any map, not everything can be shown and the person creating it needs to decide what is most important to them.

The Battle

While Jackson was moving toward Kernstown on Sunday the 23rd, Ashby, who was a very aggressive commander and had been reinforced with four companies of infantry, had started a battle. However, he was outnumbered and pushed back. The result of his attack was that it alerted the Federals and allowed them to occupy Pritchard's Hill with a strong force of artillery and infantry. From this hill, Federal commanders could see the advancing Confederate infantry as they went into bivouac.

Although Jackson considered waiting until Monday to attack, once he realized that the Federals could observe his army's movement and he knew "that the Federals had a position from which our forces could be seen, I concluded that it would be dangerous to postpone it [the battle] until the next day, as re-enforcements might be brought up during the night."[11] Pritchard's Hill was the key to dominating the Valley Turnpike and thus access to Winchester. General Shields, who wrote an extensive but biased report, stated, "On the west side of this road [Valley Turnpike], about a half a mile north of Kernstown, is a ridge of high ground [Pritchard's Hill], which commands the approach by the turnpike and a part of the surrounding country. This ridge was the key-point of our position."[12]

Jackson also realized the importance of Pritchard's Hill, as he ordered an attack on it by Colonel Samuel V. Fulkerson's brigade and the available part of General Richard B. Garnett's much larger brigade with Fulkerson's brigade in front. The plan was to attack Pritchard's Hill on its western side, as Jackson realized that the Federals had a strong position, "which prevented a direct advance."[13] However, some of the Federal artillery was relocated and was able to fire at the attacking Confederates. In addition, the men had to deal with low, marshy ground and fences. Fulkerson tried to protect his men from the artillery fire by getting a small grove of trees between them and the Federal artillery. Still, the relocated Federal batteries placed such effective fire on Fulkerson's unit that he moved his men to some nearby woods. Eventually, he moved his brigade to a hollow where Garnett's brigade was already sheltered.[14] Fulkerson and Garnett were then ordered to Sandy Ridge with the idea of outflanking the Federals on Pritchard's Hill.

Sandy Ridge is slightly higher than Pritchard's Hill. Thus, when the Confederates placed artillery on it, they were able to place very effective fire on the Federal units attacking them as well as the Federal infantry and artillery units on Pritchard's Hill. Once the Confederates occupied Sandy Ridge, Kimball ordered an attack on it. The initial attack failed due to the Confederate infantry being behind stone walls, the supporting Confederate artillery fire, and the attack being uncoordinated. As the battle progressed, the Federals reinforced their attacking units, and the Confederates reinforced their defending units. However, both Jackson and Kimball, as well as many of their subordinate commanders on Sandy Ridge, lost control of the fight, and it became a struggle between small groups of men trying to survive.

The topography of Sandy Ridge dictated the ebb and flow of the tactical battle. At one point in the fight, there was a race between Confederate and Federal Soldiers for a stone wall on Sandy Ridge. The Confederates won the race and inflicted a number of casualties on the Federals before they fell back. Later, as more Federal units arrived and the Confederates began to run out of ammunition, they were able to drive the Confederates from the stone walls and Sandy Ridge. A fairly accurate illustration of the successful attack by the Federals can be seen in Drawing 2–1. Photograph 2–6 shows the view the attacking Federal infantry would have had as they advanced on the Confederate-held stone wall on the western side of Sandy Ridge. Although it is not a steep slope, it would have been an exposed advance uphill against an enemy who was behind a stone wall.

Another topographic feature was that the main Confederate battle line was separated by a slight ridge that was high enough so that commanders on one side could not see what was happening on the other side. Consequently, when one side retreated, the men on the other side did not know that their flank was now open. When this happened and the Confederates received fire from their flank, a hasty and disorganized retreat began. Again, a small topographic feature can have a major impact on a battle.

As to be expected, the reports of the subordinate commanders, letters from

Drawing 2-1: The Federal charge on the stone wall (drawn by Edwin Forbes on 23 March 1862, Library of Congress).

individuals, and diaries emphasize the fury of the fighting and the topography of the battlefield. The men who were defending and attacking at the tactical level were much more interested in the lay of the ground than a bigger view of the overall geography of the battle. Fulkerson, along with the other Confederate commanders, mention a number of topographic features in their report. Major Frank Jones wrote in his diary, "He [Jackson] ordered me to lead the Rockbridge Artillery and three Regiments of the Brigade across the open fields and take positions on the right and long ridge overlooking the back road [Middle Road]. The enemy batteries had full play upon us but they did little damage and we soon reached the cover of the woods!"[15] As expected, the topography and how it either exposed or protected the men was more important to Jones than the overall geographic importance of the battle.

The same is true of the Federal reports. Lieutenant Colonel William Harrow, 14th Indiana Infantry, commented on an open meadow, a slight skirt of timber, and crossing a depression.[16] Lieutenant Colonel Franklin Sawyer, Eighth Ohio Infantry, commented on an open wood near a stone church, a force of the enemy concealed behind a ridge of ground, and a rail fence.[17] Even in letters home, Soldiers would write about important topographic features rather than the overall geography. Dr. Christian Schwartz with the 67th Ohio Volunteers, when writing to his family, mentioned woods and a stone fence.[18] In 1889, William S. Young, who was a private in the Seventh Indiana, wrote in an article in the *National Tribune*, "By the indomitable pluck, coupled with the ignorance of the danger of our situation, and by utilizing every stone, stump and tree as a shield from the enemy's fire, it became, as it were, a free-for-all."[19] This is a statement that is very similar to one that Audie Murphy made in his autobiography as shown in the introduction. To the men doing the fighting, little changes in the topography can mean the difference between life and death.

All of this is in contrast to Jackson's and Kimball's reports, as they were more interested in non-topographic subjects. Jackson's report mentions that his forces could be seen by the enemy and that is why he decided to attack on Sunday; the stone wall that was used by his men; commanders; orders; running out of ammunition; gallantry; General Garnett's order to retreat; the beginning of night ending the battle; numbers of men involved; and losses on both sides. Kimball's report is similar in that he mentions heights on the right of the road; actions of subordinate commanders and their units; the hill the Confederates were on; gallantry; and night ending the battle. Even well after the war, Kimball's article in *Battles and Leaders of the Civil War* contains only limited topographic information. Neither Jackson nor Kimball were very interested in the exact topography of the battlefield, for at their level, their concerns were about maneuvering units and how well leaders performed. Their view of geography was very different than those of their subordinates. One geographic feature both men mentioned is that the battle ended at dusk, which begins around 6:30 p.m. in that part of Virginia during that time of the year. Fortunately for the Confederates, it was a short battle. If it had started early, the Federal units would have had more time to pursue the retreating Confederates. This would have probably resulted in more Confederate losses in casualties and men being captured.

Shields' report is very different than either Jackson's or Kimball's. His report is self-serving and mainly discusses how great he is, how he tricked Jackson into attacking by feigning a retreat, and how he divined Jackson's intentions. Part of the absence of any real tactical value in his report could be because he was not on the battlefield due to the injury he suffered the previous day. Nevertheless, he wrote the longest report, five pages in length. However, his messages about the battle are worth analyzing to determine the impression Jackson's attack had on him and his corps commander, General Nathaniel Banks. On the 25th of March, Shields gives Jackson's strength as 15,000. On the 25th, he writes that Jackson is receiving 30,000 reinforcements and that Jackson had 11,000 men. On the 29th, he writes that Jackson was to receive 5,000 reinforcements from Front Royal and 10,000 from Sperryville but that high water stopped them from joining Jackson. Shields also writes, "Though the battle had been won, still I could not believe that Jackson would have hazarded a decisive engagement at such a distance from the main body without expecting reinforcements."[20]

Banks took command shortly after the battle and reinforced his forces in the Valley with Alpheus S. Williams's division.[21] Banks became very cautious, probably due to the heavily inflated size of Jackson's force. Consequently, his pursuit was slow. The pursuit was so slow that Kimball wrote in his *Battles and Leaders of the Civil War* article that on the 24th, "Major-General Banks, arriving as this movement [pursuit of Jackson] was being commenced, assumed command. He deemed it prudent to await reënforcements [*sic*], and our army remained in camp at Middletown and Cedar Creek that night, while the enemy escaped to Fisher's Hill."[22] Kimball's article was written after the war and had the advantage of hindsight, something Banks did not have. But for whatever reason, Banks' pursuit was ineffective.

The First Battle of Kernstown was a battle for control of a ridge and a hill. Whichever side controlled those two locations would win the battle. It took place near a very small town that few people could have found on a map, much less have known about. Still, its location near Winchester made it a significant battle. Geography made a battle so small that by 1864, it would probably have not received any significant notice by either the Confederate or Federal high commands. Although a close study of period maps and a full understanding of the available technology can allow a person to understand events at the grand strategy, strategic, and operational levels, a visit to the battlefield is necessary to understand the tactical events. Despite the many changes have taken place to the Kernstown battlefield, enough is left to give the visitor a good understanding of the tactical events. The First Kernstown battlefield is relatively small, the battle was short, and relatively few men were involved, but it was an event that influenced other "more important" events. It was a tactical event that due to geography, changed Federal plans at both the operational and strategic levels.

The Impact of the First Battle of Kernstown

The impact of this battle on the grand strategy level was tremendous. For the Federals, the common belief was that Jackson would have never chanced a battle without being assured of reinforcements. Jackson would probably not have risked a battle if he had known the true odds, but the Federal commanders were assuming Jackson thought as they did—very cautiously. This was an assumption Jackson would totally destroy during his Valley campaign. Even then, Federal commanders increased the size of Jackson's force to a size they thought was appropriate.

Jackson's thoughts about the battle, as stated in his report, were,

> Though Winchester was not recovered, yet the more important object for the present, that of calling back troops that were leaving the valley, and thus preventing a junction of Banks' command with other forces, was accomplished, in addition to his heavy loss in killed and wounded. Under these circumstances I feel justified in saying that, though the field is in possession of the enemy, yet the most essential fruits of the battle are ours.[23]

As far as Jackson was concerned, even though he lost the battle, he had gained a victory. The Federal commanders displayed more of a defeated attitude than Jackson did. Their fears were such that they heavily reinforced their forces in the Valley and added forces to those already defending Washington.

The problem for the Federals was that by reinforcing the Valley, they did not leave enough trained troops to defend Washington. As a result, General Irwin McDowell's corps, which McClellan expected to reinforce him, was reassigned to the defense of Washington. President Abraham Lincoln informed McClellan on the 9th of April,

> After you left, I ascertained that less than twenty thousand unorganized men, without a single field battery, were all you designed to be left for the defence of Washington, and Manassas Junction; and part of this even, was to go to Gen. Hooker's old position. Gen. Banks' corps, once designed for Manassas Junction, was diverted, and tied up on the line of Winchester and Strausburg, and could not leave it without again exposing the upper Potomac, and the Baltimore and Ohio Railroad. This presented, (or would present, when McDowell and Sumner should be gone) a great temptation to the enemy to turn back from the Rappahanock, and sack Washington. My explicit order that Washington should, by the judgment of all the

commanders of Army corps, be left entirely secure, had been neglected. It was precisely this that drove me to detain McDowell.

I do not forget that I was satisfied with your arrangement to leave Banks at Mannassas Junction; but when that arrangement was broken up, and nothing was substituted for it, of course I was not satisfied. I was constrained to substitute something for it myself. And now allow me to ask "Do you really think I should permit the line from Richmond, via Mannassas Junction, to this city to be entirely open, except what resistance could be presented by less than twenty thousand unorganized troops?" This is a question which the country will not allow me to evade.[24]

McClellan was upset by this and informed the president, "In my deliberate judgement the success of our cause will be imperiled…. I am now of the opinion that I shall have to fight all of the available force of the Rebels not far from here. Do not force me to do so with diminished numbers."[25] Although McClellan probably did not need another reason for his lack of action and future failure, the loss of McDowell's corps gave him an additional one.

The First Battle of Kernstown was a battle of wills, one that the Confederates won. The Federal commanders vastly overestimated Jackson's strength and appeared to be afraid of fighting him. Although he lost the battle, Jackson saw it as an overall victory since it kept Federal forces in the Valley and kept others from joining McClellan. A small battle in an unknown town, which, due to its geography, had an impact far greater than other much larger battles. Although the Federals still controlled Winchester and thus held the initiative in Virginia (in that they could have forced the Confederates to react to their movements), they failed to take advantage of it. The problem was that Jackson's attack gave the Confederates psychological dominance over the Federal's physical control of Winchester. The results of the First Battle of Kernstown were best summed up by Jackson in a letter to his wife on the 11th of April: "The great object to be acquired by the battle demanded time to make known its accomplishments. Time has shown that while the field is in possession of the enemy, the most essential fruits of the battle are ours."[26]

3

Geography and the First Battle of Winchester

25 May 1862

Confederate control of Winchester exposed Maryland and Pennsylvania to Confederate raids.

The First Battle of Winchester took place on the 25th of May 1862 and lasted about three to four hours. It was a very one-sided victory as Federal losses were over 2,000 while Confederate losses were around 400. The battle was part of General Stonewall Jackson's Valley campaign. Geographically, Jackson's Valley campaign was a success at all levels for the Confederates. The First Battle of Kernstown had occurred almost two months before this battle, and Abraham Lincoln and the Federal commanders had assumed that the threat from Jackson had disappeared. However, Jackson's capture of Winchester revealed how Confederate control of Winchester exposed Maryland and Pennsylvania to invasion. Consequently, when Jackson gained control of Winchester, the effect of the battle on the operational and strategic levels was significant, as Lincoln, in an effort to trap Jackson's forces, reassigned units to the Valley that had been designated as reinforcements for General George McClellan.

Maps 3-1 and 3-2 show most of the topographic features that were important during the battle. The battle took place just outside of the city limits of Winchester in 1862, and that is reflected on Map 3-1. Map 3-2 shows where the battle occurred in relation to Winchester in 1960. Even combined, the maps do not (and no map can) show all of the details of the battle. Still, they are valuable references when studying the battle.

***

The war was not going well for the Confederacy by the middle of May 1862. Although Jackson had achieved a small victory at McDowell and the U.S. Navy had been repulsed at Drewry's Bluff, many more disasters had occurred than victories: the Confederate Army invading New Mexico had been defeated at Glorieta Pass, forcing a retreat to Texas; the Confederates had been defeated at the Battle of Shiloh

3. Geography and the First Battle of Winchester

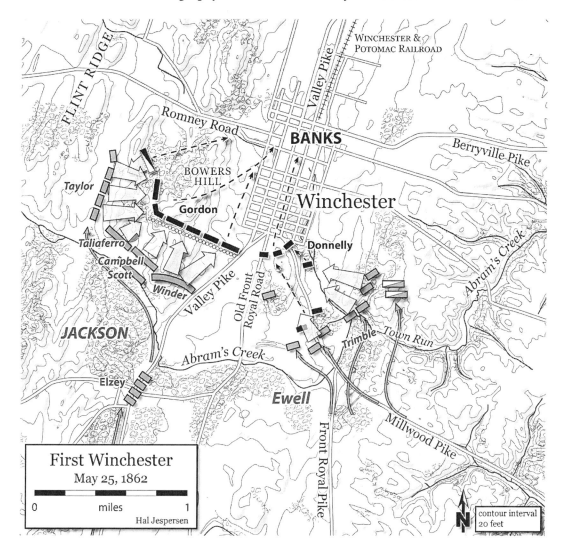

Map 3-1: The First Battle of Winchester.

and their commander, General Albert Sidney Johnston, had died from a wound; Island No. 10 had been captured, causing the Confederates to lose control of more of the Mississippi River; Fort Pulaski, outside of Savannah, Georgia, had surrendered; New Orleans, Louisiana, had been captured; Fort Macon near Beaufort, North Carolina, had surrendered; Yorktown, Virginia, had been evacuated by General Joseph Johnston's army allowing the Federal Army, under General McClellan, to continue its advance on Richmond; Norfolk, Virginia, had been evacuated, and the CSS *Virginia* had been destroyed; and General Johnston continued his retreat up the peninsula stopping just outside of Richmond. It appeared that the Confederacy was on the verge of collapse.

At the grand strategy level, for Lincoln, the war was going well, and it appeared that the nation would soon be reunited. He was confident enough about the safety

52 The Key to the Shenandoah Valley

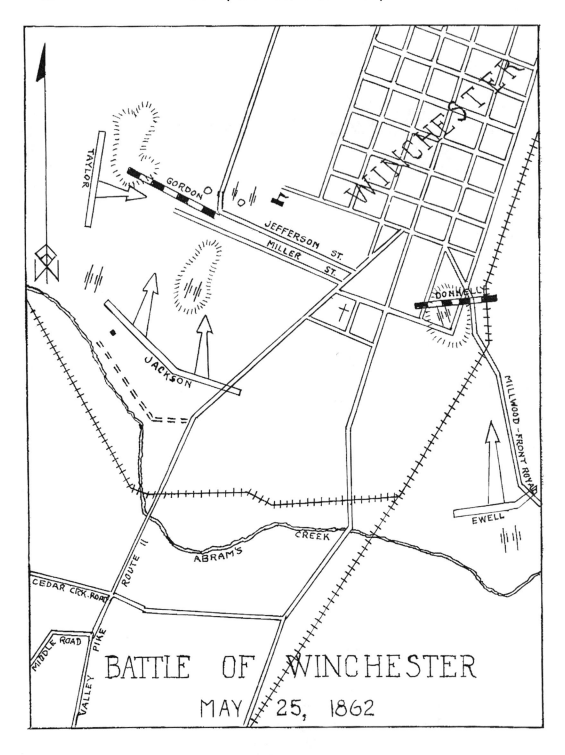

Map 3-2: First Battle of Winchester showing the location of units in respect to Winchester in 1960 (*Civil War Battles in Winchester and Frederick County, Virginia 1861–1865*, Winchester-Frederick County Civil War Centennial Commission).

of Washington that he released General Irvin McDowell's corps to march overland to support General McClellan's army. However, he was worried that the Confederate Army defending Richmond might slip away from McClellan and attack Washington before McClellan could come to the defense of the city. Consequently, McDowell was instructed to always keep his corps "in position to save the capital from all possible attack."[1] In this case, Lincoln was working at the strategic and operational levels.

Jefferson Davis was in the opposite situation of Lincoln. While they were both disappointed by the commanders of their largest army in Virginia, Davis was dismayed by the victories the Federals had achieved, especially McClellan's threat to Richmond. The threat was taken so seriously that Davis and some of his cabinet members had their families leave Richmond.[2] The Confederacy needed to retain or recapture needed resources, and for that, it needed victories.

At the strategic and operational levels, McClellan had been very successful. He was an excellent engineer, and his knowledge of geography was second to none. His plan allowed the Army of the Potomac to successfully bypass the river obstacles in northern Virginia. He was an outstanding trainer and had created a well-trained army that had confidence in him and was slowly advancing on Richmond with minimal casualties. But his success worried him, and he continually demanded more troops. He wrote to Lincoln and Secretary of War Edwin Stanton on the 14th of May 1862, "I cannot bring into actual battle against the enemy more than 80,000 men at the utmost, and with them I must attack in position, probably entrenched, a much larger force, perhaps double my numbers."[3] Although the army had confidence in him, McClellan did not have it in himself.

Even though Robert E. Lee had not yet lived up to expectations people had of him during his campaign in western Virginia and his engineering work on the Atlantic coast, President Jefferson Davis had complete confidence in him. Consequently, he had Lee assigned to duty in Richmond on the 13th of March 1862: "General Robert E. Lee is assigned to duty at the seat of government; and, under the direction of the President, is charged with the conduct of military operations in the armies of the Confederacy."[4] Davis now had an aggressive and confident advisor whose knowledge of geography was equal to McClellan's.

Lee was daring, and when other people saw problems, he perceived opportunity. At the strategic level, Jackson's success in the Valley would be one of Lee's greatest triumphs. Lee realized that success in the Valley would adversely impact ongoing Federal operations around Richmond as it would pull Federal units away from threatening Richmond. Consequently, he ensured that Jackson received and retained the units he needed for success. Lee's advice to Jackson included, "Whatever movement you make against Banks do it speedily, and if successful drive him back toward the Potomac, and create the impression, as far as practicable, that you design threatening that line."[5] General Joseph Johnston was also hopeful of what Jackson could achieve. After Jackson's victory at Winchester he wrote, "If you can threaten Baltimore and Washington, do so. It may produce an important diversion."[6] However,

Johnston tempered his message as he closed with, "Your movements depend, of course, upon the enemy's strength remaining in your neighborhood. Upon that depends the practicability of your advancing to the Potomac and even crossing it."[7] While geographic locations were referred to by both Lee and Johnston, neither man was interested in tactical-level geography but rather operational- and strategic-level geography.

During the Valley campaign, Jackson operated at the operational and tactical levels of command. At the operational level, Jackson outmaneuvered Federal general Nathaniel Banks by using the geography of the Valley to his advantage. (The reader may want to refer to Maps 1–2 and 1–3 while reading this section.) The main part of Banks' army was located at Strasburg, which is located on the western side of Massanutten at its northern end and on the Valley Turnpike. There was also a small Federal garrison at Front Royal, which is located on the opposite side of Massanutten from Strasburg. Unknown to Banks, he was now at a numerical disadvantage as most of his units had been ordered to Washington, and his strength went from around 35,000 to 9,000. In contrast, Jackson had been reinforced so that now his strength was about 16,000 compared to his previous strength of 3,500.

Jackson successfully moved his forces on the west side of Massanutten to the east side without Banks' knowledge. Once there, he attacked and overran the Federal garrison at Front Royal on the 23rd of May. Jackson's dilemma was not knowing what Banks would do. Jackson realized that if he advanced with his entire force to Winchester, Banks may move to Front Royal and then east toward Washington. If he advanced on Strasburg, Banks would be able to escape by using the Valley Turnpike and retreat through Winchester. Jackson decided to cover all options by having some of his cavalry make a reconnaissance to determine if Banks was using the Valley Turnpike to retreat to Winchester, while the rest of the army marched toward Winchester on the road from Front Royal. Jackson also ordered his cavalry to screen his left flank with the object of letting him know if Banks was trying to slip past him to the south. In all three cases, geography and the road network determined Jackson's and Banks' options.

Banks, once he realized that Jackson was threatening to cut him off, quickly retreated to Winchester using the Valley Turnpike on the morning of the 24th. For the race to Winchester, Banks had the advantage because his units were using the all-weather Valley Turnpike, while Jackson's forces were moving on dirt roads that had become muddy due to the rain and hail that had occurred the morning of the 24th.[8] Once Jackson learned that Banks was using the Valley Turnpike to retreat to Winchester he ordered most of his infantry to march west and intercept the Federal column with the rest of the army continuing on to Winchester with Richard Ewell. Although the Confederates were moving on dirt roads, they were able to attack Banks' retreating column near Middletown with about one-third of his command being cut off.

After the fighting around Middletown had ended, there was continual skirmishing between the advancing Confederates and the retreating Federals on the Valley Turnpike. The Federals were able to slowly retreat and delay the Confederate advance by using the terrain and the numerous stone fences to their advantage. The fighting continued until early morning when both forces were just outside of Winchester and physically exhausted, with some of the men falling asleep as soon as they stopped moving. Consequently, most of the men in both armies had only a few hours of sleep that night.

One reason Jackson pushed his men hard was because he knew that in order to capture Winchester, he had to control the high ground around it. He wanted to gain control of the high ground on the south side of the city before the Federals could occupy and fortify it. Jackson stated in his report, "So important did I deem it to occupy before dawn the heights overlooking Winchester, that the advance continued to move forward until morning, notwithstanding the darkness and other obstacles to its progress."[9] Photograph 3–1 was taken from Bowers Hill looking to the northeast toward Winchester. It shows how that high ground dominates the city, and once the Confederates controlled it, the Federals had no choice but to retreat from Winchester. Photograph 3–2 was also taken from Bowers Hill looking to the southeast. It shows how Bowers Hill dominated the southern approaches to Winchester. At its eastern-most end, Bowers Hill was less than a quarter mile from the Valley Turnpike. Jackson was right in wanting to quickly control these heights, for once he did, he in effect controlled Winchester.

Ewell's advance along the Front Royal Road stopped and started based on different orders from Jackson. Eventually, Ewell made a decision in the early evening, just prior to receiving an order from Jackson to resume his advance, to continue his advance on Winchester. Just outside the city, he ran into Federal units from Winchester and some fighting occurred. Due to the darkness, combined with confusion of night fighting, Ewell's command halted for the night.

The Federal units that were cut off by the Confederate attack at Middletown had a different set of geographic problems than the units that were able to continue using the Valley Turnpike. First, they had to decide which way to retreat. Initially, many of them retreated up the Valley with a few retreating westward. A few units tried to move to Winchester by moving west, then north, but most were unable to do so due to Confederate forces being in the way. Eventually, all of the units that were not able to get to Winchester, before it was occupied by the Confederates, moved westward into the mountains, staying away from Winchester and the Confederates. Unfortunately, this forced them to use poor-quality roads over rough terrain. The experience of the column led by Brigadier General John Hatch, commander of the cavalry, typifies what these units underwent to escape. Only the front part of his column was able to reach Winchester before the battle, as "the column was very long, and in moving over a bad road became divided."[10] The portion that became separated was finally able to cross the Potomac River with "32 baggage wagons, 1 battery wagon, and 1 forge."[11] In the end, although somewhat disorganized, the units that were unable to rejoin Banks before the battle were able to link back up after the battle north of the Potomac River.

The Battlefield

The First Battle of Winchester took place south and southwest of the city as shown on Maps 3–1 and 3–2. As a battlefield, the First Battle of Winchester covered only a small area, but as with any battle, it had important geographic features. There were actually two distinctive engagements within this battle. One was on the southside of the city on Camp Hill, which was located to the east of the Valley Turnpike and along the road to Front Royal. The second action was centered on Bowers Hill from which the Federals could cover the Valley Turnpike. For both of the engagements, there were the obstacles of Abrams Creek, which the Confederates had to cross to attack the Federals, along with the ubiquitous stone fences that seem to be everywhere in the Valley.

Although Abrams Creek is not deep and is not a major obstacle to infantry and cavalry, it was a significant obstacle to artillery and wagons. Consequently, Confederate artillery and wagons were forced to use the roads and bridges for any movement across the creek. The creek was the cause of another problem—mist/fog—that limited visibility. Many of the reports about the battle comment on the morning fog that "became so dense as to obscure for half an hour both the town and valley."[12] The fog was a meteorological phenomenon, but its presence was accentuated by the topography of the surrounding area. Even a small geographic circumstance can impact a battle with some effects being very significant.

The stone fences, which seemed to surround every farmer's field in the valley, provided excellent protection from small-arms fire for the defenders, allowing them to fire at attackers with relative immunity. However, if fired at by artillery, the stone fences became very dangerous to the defenders as the shards of rock created by artillery projectiles that would hit the wall became perilous and deadly missiles. Still, the stone fences were a quick defensive shield used by both sides.

As the battle took place in the immediate vicinity of Winchester, the city itself became part of the battlefield. When the Federal forces retreated, they had to retreat through Winchester with its confining streets and alleys along with the twists and turns they made. The Confederates had a similar problem as the Federals when pursuing them through the city but with the additional problem of looting as well as being slowed by friendly, thankful civilians wishing to congratulate them.

The Battle

The stage was now set for the battle, and topography became crucial to both sides as they prepared for the engagement. The two Federal infantry brigades were placed on high ground just outside of Winchester as shown on Maps 3–1 and 3–2.

3. Geography and the First Battle of Winchester

One brigade was placed to cover the Valley Turnpike on Bowers Hill and the other to cover the road from Front Royal on Camp Hill. Any artillery emplaced on Bowers Hill allowed that side to effectively control Winchester and the Valley Turnpike coming from the south. The view of Winchester and the Valley Turnpike from Bowers Hill can be seen in Photographs 3–1 and 3–2. Any force approaching Winchester from the south had to gain control of Bowers Hill if they wished to capture Winchester.

The two problems for the Federals were first that the attacking Confederates were also on high ground, and second, they were outnumbered. The problems for the Confederates were that they needed to cross a small valley and Abrams Creek to reach the Federal-held high ground and that the Federals were positioned behind stone fences. Although it is considered to be one battle, in reality the battle consisted of two different independent actions. Still, if one of the Federal brigades retreated, the other would also be forced to retreat.

Although Ewell's attacking force was smaller than Jackson's, it was an important fight in its own right with geography having a tremendous influence on it. One major geographic factor was the fog created by Abrams Creek that kept both sides from being able to see their opponent. This led the 21st North Carolina to suffer heavy casualties as they advanced when they were fired on by two Federal regiments whose location they were not aware of, eventually causing the Confederates to retreat. Then "a heavy fog having settled over the ground the firing ceased on both sides for almost half an hour."[13] This fog was accentuated by the gun smoke that had been created by the rifle and artillery fire. Once the fog had lifted, Ewell decided not

Photograph 3–1: View of Winchester from Bowers Hill.

Photograph 3-2: View to the southeast from Bowers Hill.

to continue directly attacking the Federals, as they were too well protected, but to maneuver to the right with the objective of outflanking them. However, before the Confederate maneuver was completed, the Federals had retreated due to their right flank on Bowers Hill being turned.

The fighting on the other side of the battlefield centered on Bowers Hill, which was actually a series of small hills and ridges. It was much more sustained than the fighting for Camp Hill due to the fact that the fog was not as much of a factor. Initially, the Confederates had to clear Federal skirmishes from some hills across the creek and in front of Bowers Hill. After General Charles Winder's brigade (the Stonewall brigade) crossed Abrams Creek and attacked, the Federal skirmishers retreated and the Confederates occupied a series of hills that were lower than Bowers Hill, giving the Federals a slight advantage. Once the lower hills were secured, Confederate artillery was deployed in front of the Confederate infantry, and a sustained artillery fight took place. Unfortunately for the Confederate artillery, they were exposed to both Federal artillery and rifle fire. However, the Confederate infantry assigned to protect the batteries were placed on the reverse slope and thus not exposed to the Federal artillery and rifle fire. McHenry Howard, an officer on General Winder's staff, wrote after the war,

> I do not well recall the details of the movement, but we were soon in occupation of this high ground [the high ground on the north side of Abrams Creek] on the north of this side road, and my first precise recollection is the Poague's (Rockbridge) and Carpenter's Batteries of the brigade were in position on it and firing on the enemy who held some also elevated ground

[Bowers Hill], almost on the south edge of Winchester. Our infantry regiments were supporting in rear, sheltered by the rising ground and somewhat apart. Our two batteries were exposed to a very sharp fire, both of artillery and musketry, and lost severely, particularly in horses. They were much annoyed at first by a line of skirmishers behind a stone wall, not far in front, until the General [Winder] ordered solid shot to be fired at the wall, which soon made them scamper back.[14]

Dips and folds in the ground can become very important terrain features to Soldiers while protective terrain, like stone fences, can become a detriment when engaged by different weapons.

Stonewall Jackson, realizing that heavy losses would occur if the Federals were directly attacked, ordered General Richard Taylor to move his brigade to the left and outflank the Federal line on Bowers Hill. Taking advantage of the terrain, Taylor was able to gain the right flank of the Federal's, and although they finally realized what Taylor was doing, they did not have sufficient men to stop him. Consequently, once Taylor's brigade advanced, they were able to outflank the main Federal line.

After the Federals were outflanked, the Confederate numerical advantage began to have a significant effect, and the Federals were forced to retreat. The difficulty for the Federals during their retreat was that they had to withdrawal through Winchester. Cities have their own geography, and the narrow streets and alleys created congestion and caused some units to lose their unity and become disarrayed. In addition, the Federals suffered the fury of some of the local residents. Colonel George H. Gordon, commander of the Third Brigade, wrote after the battle, "My retreating column suffered serious loss in the streets of Winchester. Males and females vied with each other in increasing the number of their victims, by firing from the houses, throwing hand grenades, hot water, and missiles of every description."[15]

Between the men being tired, being chased by the Confederates, confusing dust being raised by their marching in the streets, streets blocked by wagons, and civilians trying to harm them, their retreat through Winchester would have been confusing. However, the Confederates faced similar problems, as they were equally exhausted. But their difficulties were amplified by thankful civilians, needing to put out fires, and the looting of Federal supplies. General Winder wrote after the battle, "Just beyond [Winchester] I reformed the regiments as far as practicable, they having been much scattered in passing through the streets."[16] Jackson was unable to complete his victory and pursue the defeated Federals due to his cavalry being scattered and the infantry being exhausted.[17]

Banks' and Jackson's reports on the battle were mainly concerned with the movement of their units and that of their enemies, as well as their decisions and the battle with its aftermath. As with most other reports, they both emphasized the gallantry of their men and how much they accomplished. Both men did mention a number of topographic features such as hills, woods, and a stone wall. These same topographic features are mentioned in the reports of subordinate commanders, with some of them additionally commenting on fog the morning of the battle. As to be expected, the closer an individual is to the fighting, the more likely they are to mention topographic features.

The First Battle of Winchester was a geographic success for the Confederates at all levels of command. At the grand strategy level, territory that had been under Federal control was regained. Most of the citizens of Winchester welcomed the Confederate troops as liberators and were disappointed and upset when Jackson was later forced to retreat up the Valley. At the strategic level, Federal units that were to reinforce General George McClellan, were held back due to the implicit geographic threat the Confederate control of Winchester posed. McClellan used their retention to defend Washington as another excuse for his lack of success, but it is doubtful whether those units would have changed McClellan's fears of being outnumbered.

At the operational level, there were two successes. First, Jackson was able to use the geography of the Valley to outmaneuver Banks. Second, Jackson was able to immobilize more Federal strength than what was in his army. Again, this was due to the geography of the Valley and the location of Winchester. At the tactical level, the two Federal brigades were posted as well as they could have been. Farther out from Winchester was better terrain, but there were too few Federals to adequately defend the terrain. Offensively, Jackson's forces approached from two different directions and were on ground almost as high as the ground the Federals were on. Once the Federal units were forced to retreat, they quickly lost their organization and suffered more casualties.

After the Battle

The impact of the Confederate victory was immediate. Beyond sending additional troops to the Valley, Federal generals and Secretary of War Edwin Stanton feared that Jackson may be considering attacking Washington. Consequently, on the 25th of May, immediately after the First Battle of Winchester, General William McDowell included in his instructions to General James Shields, "As the national capital is an object of extreme solicitude, you will so arrange your movements as not to uncover it."[18] On the 29th of May, four days after the battle and based on intelligence from General Banks, Secretary Stanton wrote General McDowell:

> Considering the condition of the force in Washington, I submit it to your judgement whether at least part of King's force [General Rufus King, commander of the First Division, III Corps] should not be brought here. Is it not possible that the Potomac may be crossed below Harper's Ferry? If this be done in any force, Washington City will be in danger with only its present garrison. General Meigs suggests this latter contingency, and thinks the safety of the city requires an increase of the garrison. The transportation has been ordered to Aquia Creek, and the movement can be made as soon as the troops can reach the wharf.[19]

However, General McDowell recommended that the Washington garrison "might be increased from the North, but it would be a most damaging confession of weakness for us to throw into it our forces from the field."[20] It would seem that the fear of an attack on Washington would recede after Jackson left the Valley, but it did not. On the 22nd of June, General John Wool wrote Secretary Stanton, "If Jackson has the number of troops reported, [40,000 to 60,000 by General Franz Sigel's estimate[21]] I think we ought to be looking after Washington."[22] Thus, a victory at the tactical level influenced events two levels above it.

After the battle, Jackson moved his units toward Harpers Ferry, and although he threatened the Federal units there, he did not make any serious attacks. While he was doing that, stronger Federal forces were moving from the east and west to cut him off to the south and were closer to Strasburg than his units were. Jackson was forced to retreat and move south to avoid the oncoming Federal units. The advantage Jackson had was his units were marching on the all-weather Valley Turnpike, while the Federal forces were marching on dirt roads that had become very muddy due to rain. A macadamized road saved Jackson's army from being cut off and having to fight a superior Federal force.

When studying Jackson's Valley campaign and the First Battle of Winchester, the effect of geography at all levels of command cannot be ignored since its influence impacted all levels. Douglas Southall Freeman in his classic work *Lee's Lieutenants* commented, "Once Jackson learned the geography of an area, his interpretation of it was strategical; and when he came to a field of battle, his sense of position was sure, unhesitating and quickly displayed."[23] Jackson knew that knowledge of the Valley was essential. Consequently, he ordered Jed Hotchkiss "to make me a map of the Valley, from Harper's [sic] Ferry to Lexington, showing all of the points of offence and defense in those places."[24] Jackson, at his level of command—operational and tactical, realized that an excellent understanding of topography was crucial to success. Although he indirectly appreciated the impact geography and weather could have on operations, his main concern was topography—the lay of the land—and how it impacted a battle.

The capture of Winchester gave the initiative in Virginia to the Confederates. The Federals were forced to react to Confederate maneuvers. However, the Confederate advantage did not last long as Jackson was forced to retreat from Winchester less than a week later. Federal control of Winchester returned the initiative to the Federals. Although Abraham Lincoln tried to get his commanders to cooperate and trap Jackson, they failed to do so. The advantage the initiative gave them was wasted.

***

Winchester continued to be a key location later in 1862 when Robert E. Lee decided to move into Maryland. On the 7th of September, ten days before the Battle of Antietam, in a report to Confederate Secretary of War George Randolph, Lee wrote,

> I have the honor to inform you that Lieutenant-Colonel Funk reports that he took possession of Winchester at 11 o'clock on the morning of the 3d instant, the enemy having abandoned the town on the night of the 2d. They blew up their large magazine, burnt an enormous amount of

quartermaster's and commissary stores, and about two squares of the city. Still, a quantity of stores, a large amount of ammunition, some fine guns, medical stores, tents, cooking utensils, &c., were left behind, which have been taken possession of by Colonel Funk. I have directed that he make reports of the captured articles to the proper departments, and I desire that they be secured. As I have directed that Winchester be made a depot for this army, and have sent there our disabled men, horses, batteries, and surplus wagon-trains, in order that they may be recruited and refreshed, I particularly want a good commander for that post, one of energy and experience, who will bring everything into order, give confidence to the community, and take advantage of the resources of the country.[25]

When they realized that they could not defend Winchester, the Federals retreated to Harpers Ferry, where they would later be captured. Winchester's geographic location, accentuated by the road network radiating from Winchester, made it an ideal location for a supply depot. Unfortunately for both sides, it was a location that could not be defended unless a large force was based there, something neither side was willing to do at this stage of the war.

Control of Winchester gave Lee complete initiative in the Virginia theater. The only reason Lee had the advantage before the Confederates gained control of Winchester was that the Federals had given it to him by a combination of lack of activity and incompetence. Lee was only able invade Maryland because he controlled Winchester. Without control of Winchester, his army would have continually been under the threat of being cut off and having to fight their way back across the Potomac. Control of Winchester was essential for any major Confederate move into Maryland or Pennsylvania.

4

Geography and the Second Battle of Winchester

13–15 June 1863

Technology can lessen the impact and influence of geography, but needs to be properly placed and maintained to be effective.

The Second Battle of Winchester was a three-day battle occurring on the 13th, 14th, and 15th of June 1863, although most of the fighting took place on the 14th and the early morning of the 15th. Numerically, the Second Battle of Winchester was the smallest battle in Winchester proper, with 7,000 Federals against 12,509 Confederates (Federal estimates of the attacking Confederates varied from 15,000 to as high as 50,000),[1] with the Confederates having much less than a two-to-one advantage. Although it was the smallest battle in Winchester, this engagement, as for the other battles for Winchester, can only be fully understood when it is considered in context with other events. The Second Battle of Winchester was part of the opening phases of the Gettysburg campaign. Robert E. Lee's only viable route into Pennsylvania was through the Shenandoah Valley, making control of Winchester crucial. The Confederates had to seize control of Winchester if the campaign was to have any chance of success.

As with the other battles for control of Winchester, the Second Battle of Winchester geographically impacted all four levels of command. At the grand strategy level, it allowed the Confederacy to regain territory that had been under Federal control. For the Federals, it created the threat that Confederate forces could now move into Maryland and Pennsylvania. At the strategic level, it placed the Federal Army in the position of needing to guard Maryland, Pennsylvania, and the capital while it opened a number of possible options for the Confederates. At the operational level, it allowed the Confederates to forage from the rich, untouched farmlands of Pennsylvania, while forcing the Federal Army to protect the same. It also gave some relief to those farmers in Virginia whose farms were close to the front lines and subject to raids by Federal forces. At the tactical level, it again showed that Winchester was indefensible, even with fortifications, unless a large garrison was placed there.

Two maps are included that show various details of the battle. Map 4–1 gives an overview of the battle while the second map is from the 1960 publication *Civil War*

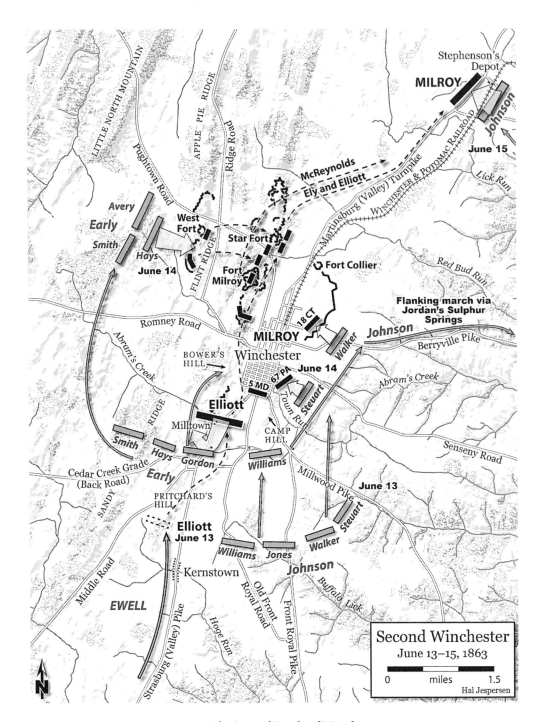

Map 4–1: The Second Battle of Winchester.

Battles in Winchester and Frederick County, Virginia 1861–1865 and shows the battle in relation to 1960 Winchester. Both maps concentrate on the topography, as to be expected, rather than the overarching geography. But at the tactical level, topography will normally supersede geography.

***

4. Geography and the Second Battle of Winchester

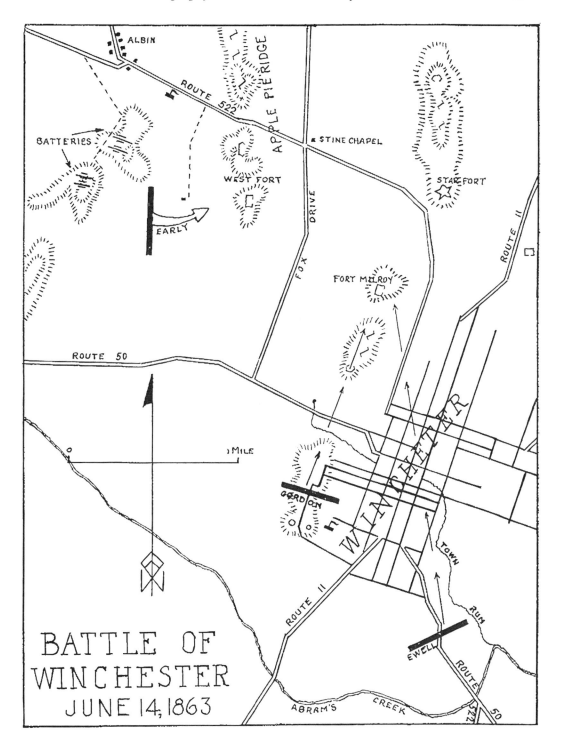

Map 4–2: Second Battle of Winchester showing the location of units in respect to Winchester in 1960 (*Civil War Battles in Winchester and Frederick County, Virginia 1861–1865*, Winchester-Frederick County Civil War Centennial Commission).

Many changes had occurred since the First Battle of Winchester in May 1862 and June 1863. In Virginia, the Federals had been pushed back from Richmond during the Seven Days campaign and then had suffered defeats at Second Manassas, Fredericksburg, and Chancellorsville. However, Lincoln had been able to declare Antietam a victory allowing him to issue the Emancipation Proclamation, which had added an additional perspective to the war. For the Confederacy, this change decreased the possibility of European intervention, and only major decisive victories would bring the possibility of the European nations recognizing the Confederacy.

In the west, the Federals had won at Perryville and had driven back the Confederate attempt to control Kentucky. Then the Federals were able to claim victory at Stones River when the Confederates retreated. Most importantly, the last two Confederate strongholds on the Mississippi River, Vicksburg and Port Hudson, were under siege.

Politically, midterm elections had not gone well for Lincoln as his party had lost seats in the House of Representatives, although it still had a majority with the help of the Union Party. However, in the Senate, the Republicans gained seats. In addition, Lincoln had felt that it was necessary to sign the unpopular Conscription Act to keep up the strength of the Federal armies. But the blockade was still being effective despite Confederate attempts to break it. Overall, except in Virginia, the war appeared to be going well for the North.

For the Confederacy, the outlook was bleak. While Robert E. Lee's army had gone from victory to victory, Stonewall Jackson had died from pneumonia after he had been wounded by his own Soldiers at Chancellorsville. In addition, the trans-Mississippi part of the Confederacy was all but cut off from the rest of the Confederacy. This meant that the crops, cattle, and horses raised there could no longer be sent to the armies and civilians east of the Mississippi River. Even east of the Mississippi River, the stress of the war on the Confederate transportation system along with the blockade had created food shortages in parts of the South. In Richmond, there had been a bread riot in early April that only ended when Jefferson Davis went and made a personal appeal to the rioters. The Confederacy was desperate for foreign recognition and decisive victories.

**

The two opposing generals at the Second Battle of Winchester were Federal general Robert Milroy and Confederate general Richard Ewell. Ewell's corps was the leading element in Lee's movement into Pennsylvania and was expected to clear the way for the rest of the army. Milroy's forces had been placed in Winchester to keep the Confederates from using the Valley as a route to raid the B&O Railroad and the Chesapeake and Ohio Canal, as well as other locations in Maryland and Pennsylvania. Contrary to what Milroy thought, and events proved, he was not strong enough to resist a full-scale movement of the Army of Northern Virginia.

The question of whether Federal forces should even defend Winchester was contentious. General Henry Halleck believed Winchester should not be defended and sent a number of messages to that effect. On the 5th of January 1863, Halleck sent a message to General Robert C. Schenck, VIII Corps commander and Milroy's immediate superior: "No attempt should be made to hold Winchester against a large force of the enemy, but use it simply as an outpost, as advised in our conversation a day or two ago. Isolated posts and columns are too liable to be cut off."[2]

These messages were not considered to be orders; rather, they were interpreted to be suggestions as some of Halleck's messages stated: "I can only repeat the recommendation, so often made to you [Schenck], to mass your troops more in convenient places for rapid and concerted operations, holding railroad bridges only with small detachments, in block-houses, and exposing no large force in advanced positions, where they are liable to be cut off."[3]

Halleck's continued insistence on not defending Winchester, but failing to make it an order, confused General Schenck and his staff. Consequently, Milroy received conflicting orders on whether to defend Winchester or to retreat. On Thursday the 11th of June, Milroy received a message from Lieutenant Colonel Donn Piatt, General Schenck's chief of staff, ordering him "to remove your command from Winchester to Harper's Ferry."[4] Milroy immediately wrote to General Schenck, "I have the place well protected, and am well prepared to hold it, as General Tyler and Colonel Piatt will inform you, and I can and will hold it, if permitted to do so, against any force the rebels can afford to bring against me, and I exceedingly regret the prospect of having to give it up. It will be cruel to abandon the loyal people in this country to the rebel fiends again."[5]

Schenck replied on the 12th of June, one day before the battle would begin, stating Piatt had misunderstood him and ordered Milroy, "You will make all of the required preparations for withdrawing, but hold your position in the meantime. Be ready for movement, but await further orders."[6] Consequently, Milroy believed that he had no option but to defend Winchester until he received orders to withdraw. Milroy then felt it necessary to hold a council of war with his brigade commanders the night of the 14th. At the meeting, it was decided if they did not retreat that night, they would be completely surrounded and forced to surrender. Although Milroy did not know it, the council was unnecessary as Schenck had telegraphed orders to Milroy to withdraw to Harpers Ferry on the 13th of June. Unfortunately, the telegram never arrived because the lines had been cut. All of this came out later at Milroy's board of inquiry, the conclusions of which went to President Abraham Lincoln, who decided "serious blame is not necessarily due to any serious disaster, and I cannot say in this case any of the officers are deserving of serious blame. No court-martial is deemed necessary or proper in the case."[7] Technology can lessen the impact of geographic distance, but only when it works.

Milroy had good reasons for wanting to defend Winchester and presented an excellent case for his actions at his board of inquiry using as evidence a message he sent to General Schenck. Three of his arguments were geographically based, while his fourth (number 3) was a political one concerning civilians. Milroy's arguments were as follows:

1. This place [Winchester] is the key to the Baltimore and Ohio Railroad. Let this point be abandoned, and our forces withdrawn to Harpers Ferry, and no force that it would be practicable for our Government to place at Harpers Ferry, and at points along the Baltimore and Ohio Railroad west of that place, would or could secure it against raids from the enemy occupying this place as a base. That railroad never has been nor never can be kept from destruction while this place is occupied by the rebels.
2. The fortifications on the hill near this place are now perfect, and all approaches to them so well protected by outworks, that I can hold them against five times our number.
3. The Union men and women of this and adjoining counties have been so often disappointed and abandoned to the demons of treason, that they had become very timid and doubtful, but our six months occupation here has begun to give them confidence in, and many of them have come out and taken a decided stand for, the Union, and in both town and country the Union sentiment has recently been rapidly improving. Men and women are coming in daily in large numbers and voluntarily taking the oath of allegiance, and I am told that the leading influential secessionists of this place, in private counsel among themselves, have determined, upon the first serious reverse to their cause in Virginia, to come out boldly and take the stump for reconstruction.
4. There is a large amount of wheat in this and the surrounding counties, of the last two years' crops, still unthreshed, which the rebs would get, if we abandoned the country to them.[8]

Milroy's thoughts were endorsed by General Washington L. Elliott, one of his brigade commanders, who wrote,

With the force under your [Milroy's] command, including that at Berryville, the fortifications commanding the town, and outworks, can be held against two or three times its number.

The loyal sentiment of the inhabitants of the place and vicinity is much stronger than I expected to find, and has increased during the past three months, because of the belief of loyal people that the country would be occupied by our troops, and that they would not again be subjected to the ravages of rebel forces.

From observation and information, I am satisfied that in this vicinity there is a large amount of wheat, the crop of two seasons, not yet threshed; this would afford subsistence to the rebels, should they occupy the country.[9]

General Schenck reinforced the geographic importance of Winchester during Milroy's board of inquiry when he stated,

One of the principle [sic] duties assigned to me was the protection of the Baltimore and Ohio Railroad, not only within the limits of my department proper, but all the way to the Ohio River. My policy was not to permit the railroad to lie along or to constitute the front, toward the enemy, of the country to be guarded, but to keep it in the rear of a strip of country in advance of it, in the direction of the enemy. Thus I would cover and secure my means for the transfer and concentration of troops, and for the transportation of supplies, which I could not do if this line of communication and transportation were in advance of my front and at all times liable to be cut by the enemy. I do not believe that any number of pickets stationed immediately on and scattered along the road itself would insure its protection, and especially against cavalry raids, which we had most and constantly to apprehend. I had no cavalry force in number or condition equal to that mounted force with which the enemy were threatening us, otherwise I might have relied in some greater degree on that resource. These views I consider especially applicable to that portion of the Baltimore and Ohio Railroad most approachable from the Shenandoah Valley, and the valleys of Lost River, Cacapon, Patterson Creek, and New Creek beyond [all of these valleys are in the state of West Virginia] and that part of Loudoun County immediately east of the Blue Ridge. On this account, I always advised, and, so far as my command was concerned, preferred to cover that large bend of the railroad toward the north by a line of occupation to be held with some considerable force, extending along what may be regarded as the chord of that semicircle. For this purpose, I thought there should not along be, as there has constantly been, a pretty strong force kept at New Creek, but that Romney and Winchester, should be occupied, and that as strong a force as General Heintzelman could afford to be kept at Leesburg. These points, and especially Winchester, to the keys to the approaches north.[10]

To these three men, Winchester and its surrounding productive farmland were geographically important and worth defending, besides protecting Federal sympathizers who lived there. Obviously, General Halleck did not feel that Winchester was as geographically important as the local commanders.

The local Federal officers also thought they were better prepared than previously to resist any Confederate attempt to seize Winchester. The reason they felt better prepared was that Federal forces had been in control of Winchester for some time and had built a series of forts protecting the western approaches to Winchester. Although the fortifications had been built on high ground, there was still higher ground farther out. In reality, the forts were simply places of refuge for the Federal units in the city and did not substantially add to its defense.

A major issue was that there were no prepared defenses to the south of the city protecting the approach from the Valley Turnpike, as shown on Maps 4–1 and 4–2. It probably would have been a better option to construct substantial fortifications on the southern approaches to the city, the most likely direction from which a Confederate attack would come, than on its western and northern sides. Bowers Hill and Camp Hill, hills defended by the Federals during the First Battle of Winchester, were both excellent locations for forts. We will never know why this was not done because Milroy was not asked this question. For the Federals, the lack of substantial fortifications covering the southern approaches to the city was a fatal flaw in their defensive scheme.

Although Milroy emphasized in his messages how his units, protected by the new defenses, could defeat a much larger Confederate force, he was not expecting to be attacked by such a large number of Confederates. Milroy believed he would have to deal with only about 7,500 cavalry under the command of Confederate generals William E. Jones and John D. Imboden.[11] He also assumed that General Joseph Hooker, commander of the Army of the Potomac, would "keep General Lee employed while I [Milroy] looked after the enemy's forces in the Valley."[12] Milroy had such confidence that Hooker would let him know if Lee's army was moving against him that he disregarded scouting reports from his own men that indicated a large Confederate force was moving against him. Milroy wrote in his report after the battle,

> I deemed it impossible that Lee's army, with its immense artillery and baggage trains, could have escaped from the Army of the Potomac, and crossed the Blue Ridge through Ashby's, Chester, and Thornton Gaps in concentric columns. The movement must have occupied five or six days, and notice of its being in progress could have been conveyed to me from General Hooker's headquarters in five minutes, for telegraphic communication still existed between Baltimore and Winchester.[13]

Although, not all of Lee's army was across the Blue Ridge at the time of the battle, Milroy's assumption was logical. Unfortunately, Milroy's belief was incorrect and his trust misplaced.

Still, Milroy was not worried about defending Winchester against a more substantial force than 7,500 cavalry because he believed the new fortifications would allow him to defend against a greater number of attacking Confederates. As previously quoted, Milroy informed General Schenck, one day before the Second Battle of Winchester would begin, "I can hold them [the new fortifications] against five times our number."[14] Milroy was not alone is his confidence concerning his fortifications as his assessment was reinforced by three other officers. As previously quoted, Brigadier General Washington L. Elliott, one of Milroy's brigade commanders, informed Milroy on the 12th of June, "The fortifications commanding the town [Winchester], and outworks, can be held against two or three times its number."[15] Lieutenant Colonel Donn Piatt, General Schenck's chief of staff, informed Schenck on the 11th of June, "Just in from inspection of fortifications and troops [at Winchester]. All looks fine. Can whip anything the rebels can fetch here."[16] The most important endorsement came from General Daniel Tyler, an 1816 graduate of the United States Military Academy who stayed in the army until 1834 and was considered an artillery expert. He informed General Schenck on the 11th of June, "Milroy deserves credit for his fortifications; it will take all of Lee's cavalry and light artillery to whip him out."[17] Although some of Milroy's new fortifications would play a role in the Third Battle of Winchester, they only slowed down Ewell's attack, which was conducted by infantry supported by artillery. This was a combination neither Milroy nor Tyler anticipated.

Geography also played a role in the Federal retreat from Winchester. By the time Milroy decided to retreat, Winchester was almost surrounded, and the only real option was to withdraw to the northeast along the Martinsburg Pike. The retreat was to take place at night, and all artillery and wagons were to be abandoned. The problem of retreating with the artillery and wagons was that they would make noise, which would alert the Confederates that the Federal forces were retreating. This could cause them to fire artillery at the retreating Federals. When Captain John Carlin, commander of Battery D, First Virginia Artillery (this was a Federal battery), was asked at Milroy's board of inquiry, "Could you have brought off your battery with as little noise as is made by cavalry and infantry in night marches?" He responded, "Not on that road [Martinsburg Pike]. The road had been traveled a great deal during the winter. It is a stone pike, very much cut up by the wagons, and very rough. The rattling of carriages can be heard in the Valley at night-time for 2 miles."[18]

Captain Carlin's opinion was supported by Lieutenant Edmund D. Spooner, Battery L, Fifth U.S. Artillery, who, when asked at the board of inquiry as to whether "it was practicable to have brought away from Winchester the field guns, or any portion of them," replied, "I do not think it was practicable, because they would have made so much noise as to have attracted the enemy's attention."[19] Noise created by items and accentuated by geography is of concern at the tactical and operational levels of command. It is not something that can, or should, be ignored by commanders.

Beyond the noise the artillery would have made, there were other reasons why it was not possible to have successfully withdrawn the artillery. Major John O. Cravens, Milroy's assistant adjutant-general, when asked as to whether "the roads over which the troops retreated practicable for field guns," answered, "Up to the point of attack on the morning of the 15th, and 2 miles beyond, the roads were practicable for artillery and trains. From that point on we could not have moved our artillery, because we left all roads, and went through the fields and timber, to avoid an anticipated flank movement by the enemy."[20]

There was another related issue with moving the artillery on the Martinsburg Pike—it was blocked by abandoned wagons. General Washington L. Elliot informed the board of inquiry when asked as to whether artillery could "have been drawn off at the time of the retreat,"

> I think it could not. My reason for saying so is that the roads were heavy. We had a hard rain a few days before, after which the roads became blocked up with wagons, the team horses having been taken away. It was with great difficulty that a column of infantry could get through. It would have been impossible to have taken artillery through. The road was a pike road, but was much cut up. The wagons were left in the road after the teamsters had taken the horses from them.[21]

Technology such as macadamized roads can help overcome geographic issues, but if they are not properly maintained and policed, they can become more of a hindrance than a benefit.

One of the big issues during the board of inquiry hearing was the loss of Battery L, Fifth U.S. Artillery. The battery had been posted in West Fort, an advanced position, and was overwhelmed by Confederate forces with geography being a major factor in the loss. When questioned about his opinion on whether the battery was properly posted and supported, Lieutenant Edmund D. Spooner answered,

> The position was not a very good one. Only a portion of the timber in front of the work was cut away, and the enemy could come very near without being seen. The timber in some places

was only 50 yards off. It would have been almost impossible to have withdrawn the guns in a hurry, on account of the hill, which was very steep, and, to get out on the Pughtown road, we would have to pass through a little lane, and ravines were in the way, so that we could not cross with artillery off the road. The work had been commenced a few days before, and was incomplete. If our support had been larger, it would have been better, but we had all that could be spared. What men we had did all they could. Men never fought better than these men did.[22]

The Federals had modified the terrain but had not modified it enough, and the Confederates took advantage of the terrain to overrun the battery.

In the end, the Federal forces had become too dependent on technology and failed to fully plan for the failure of that technology. The railroad from Harpers Ferry to Winchester had not been repaired, the macadamized roads radiating out from Winchester had not been maintained, the telegraph line had been cut, and their fortifications did not provide them the necessary force multiplier they had hoped for. Milroy was not the first general to be frustrated by technology, and he will not be the last.

***

General Lee, having been a military engineer, had an excellent knowledge of geography. One of the main reasons for his desire to move north was due to the need to keep his men and horses/mules well fed. In addition, he wished to give the farmers in Virginia some relief from Federal foraging parties, as well as impressing quality horses from Pennsylvania farmers, horses he could no longer easily obtain in the South.[23] Lee realized the route through the Shenandoah Valley into the Cumberland Valley was the best choice. The majority of the reasons were geographically based, with one being technologically based. The geographic reasons were that the mountains to the east of the valleys would provide protection, both valleys had rich farmlands, and the rivers that would need to be crossed were normally fordable. The technological reason was that the macadamized roads would provide faster movement of troops and supplies than dirt roads. The only fear was that the Federal Army might move against Richmond while Lee's army was moving north, but Lee did not start moving the entire army northward until he was sure that Hooker, the present commander of the Army of the Potomac, was also moving north.

Ewell, now commander of the Second Corps, was given the mission of leading the army into Pennsylvania. His first task was to clear the Federals out of the lower Valley and secure crossings over the Potomac River. To do this, he moved into the Valley and began to move north along the Valley Turnpike. On the 12th of June, there was some skirmishing near Middletown, about 14 miles south of Winchester along the Valley Turnpike, which ended in favor of the Federals. Additional Confederate units moved north, and on the 13th of June, more fighting occurred south of Winchester. This fighting forced the Federal units back into the city. That night, the Federal units withdrew from the south side of Winchester into the forts on the north and west sides of the city. This withdrawal gave the Confederates control of Bowers Hill, one of the hills that the Federals had used to defend the city during the

First Battle of Winchester (shown on Maps 3–1 and 4–2). From Bowers Hill, Ewell and General Jubal Early surveyed the Federal forts. Their reconnaissance identified a hill northwest of Winchester that the Confederates needed to occupy to dominate the city. However, the Federals had constructed West Fort on it, which now had to be taken. Luckily, the reconnaissance also revealed there was a position to the northwest of West Fort where it "might be attacked with advantage."[24]

The Battlefield

The Second Battle of Winchester took place just outside the city with the first day's skirmishing taking place south of the city, the second day's fighting taking place to the northwest, and the third day's fighting taking place to the north of the city. The Confederates approached the city from the south using the Valley Turnpike and the roads from Front Royal and Berryville as their main avenues of approach. The Federals being heavily outnumbered quickly retreated through Winchester and occupied the previously prepared West Fort, Star Fort, and Fort Milroy. All three forts were located on high ground that dominated Winchester, and if Ewell wanted total control of the city, he had to capture these three forts. As with the First Battle of Winchester, the high ground around the city was the key terrain that both sides wanted to dominate. Photographs 4–1 and 4–2 were taken at Star Fort and both show how the high ground to the west of the fort dominates it. Once West Fort was taken, Confederate artillery placed there would have had a height advantage over Federal artillery in either Star Fort or Fort Milroy.

Photograph 4–1: Photograph taken from the interior of Star Fort showing the higher ground to the west of the fort.

Photograph 4-2: Photograph of the interior of Star Fort looking toward the west. The photograph shows the high ground to the west of the fort and how the interior of the fort would have been exposed to artillery fire from that direction.

The third day's fighting took place north of the city and was centered on the Martinsburg Pike, the only viable route of retreat for the Federals. A large part of that battle took place near where the Old Charlestown Road crossed the Winchester and Potomac Railroad. During that fighting, surprise, darkness, and man-made obstacles such as the railroad cut and stone fences played an important part.

The Battle—Phase I: The Fight for the High Ground

After having secured the unfortified high ground south of Winchester late on the 13th, Ewell made a visual reconnaissance with General Early from Bowers Hill on the morning of the 14th. As a result of the reconnaissance, Early was ordered to move three of his brigades and some artillery to the west of Winchester and attack West Fort while keeping enough men and artillery on Bowers Hill to distract the Federals. Early's maneuver was not seen or noticed by the Federals. Twenty pieces of artillery, under the command of Lieutenant Colonel Hilary P. Jones, were placed on the back side of a hill where they were hidden from the Federal units in West Port. An infantry brigade, under the command of General Harry T. Hays, moved under cover into the woods close to the incomplete West Fort with orders to attack "as soon as he should discover that the enemy was sufficiently demoralized."[25] When all of the units were in position, Jones ordered his artillery to move to the top of the hill and open fire on the Federals. The Confederate artillery fire was a complete surprise to the Federals in West Fort, and "in ten minutes after they [the Confederates] opened upon us that it would have been impossible to have taken it [the Federal artillery battery] away. We lost, I [Lieutenant Edmund D. Spooner] suppose, 60 horses, killed and wounded, one caisson and two limbers, blown up by shells from the enemy."[26]

It was a devastating attack. After the Confederate artillery had done its work, General Hays saw the opportunity was right and he attacked, taking the fort with light casualties of 12 killed and 67 wounded.[27] Captain William J. Seymour, one of General Hays's staff officer, wrote after the war,

> Emerging from the woods, our boys had to cross several open fields, jump fences, etc., but so hot was the fire of our artillery that the Yankee infantry had to Keep [sic] so close behind their breastworks that they did not observe us until we had reached an abattis of felled timber some 150 yards from the redoubt. While scrambling through this, our artillery ceased firing and the Yankee infantry opened a brisk fire upon us; but so impetuous was the charge of our men that in a few minutes they were over the breastworks, driving the enemy out in great haste and confusion.[28]

Obstacles, whether man-made or natural, are only successful when any force trying to cross them can be brought under effective fire. This is true no matter if the obstacle is tactical (e.g., an abatis), operational (e.g., a river), or strategic (e.g., an ocean).

The possession of West Fort placed the Confederates on higher ground than the main Federal fort, Fort Milroy (to be renamed by the Confederates as Fort Jackson), as well as Star Fort, allowing Confederate artillery to dominate them. Due to the time required to move and place Confederate artillery into West Fort, the need to build earthworks facing Fort Milroy, and that attacking Fort Milroy required the cooperation of units on the south side of Winchester forced Early to suspend operations because it was late in the day.[29]

While Early was in the process of attacking West Fort, General Edward Johnson's division moved to the east side of Winchester, blocking the Berryville Pike as well as applying pressure on the Federal forces in Winchester. Upon receiving word of Early's success, Ewell, anticipating the possibility of Milroy retreating in the night, ordered General Johnson to move with three of his brigades and a portion of his artillery to a point on the Martinsburg Pike north of Winchester. (As a secondary order, Johnson was told to be prepared to attack the Federal fortifications if they had not retreated.)

The Battle—Phase II: Milroy's Retreat and Fight for Survival

Milroy held a council of war at about 9:00 p.m. the night of the 14th. At the council, it was decided that retreat was the only viable option (the other two being surrender or to continue fighting) and that the division would use the Martinsburg Turnpike. The evacuation began at midnight with teamsters, artillerists (without their artillery), and camp followers riding and leading horses and mules leaving first and the armed units starting at 1:00 a.m. on the 15th.[30] The evacuation could not have started earlier as units had to be informed and the need to organize the column. A geographic disadvantage during the retreat was that it was close to the summer solstice and daylight was substantially longer than the darkness. Sunset was around 8:00 p.m., and sunrise was around 5:00 a.m. However, the night would have been very dark as moonrise was just before dawn, and as it was close to a new moon, there was less than 4 percent visibility from the moon. Consequently, it was dark, but dawn came early, so the retreat had to be done quickly before daylight when the Confederates could see that the city had been evacuated.

Initially, the movement went well as the Confederates did not realize that the Federals were evacuating the city until dawn.[31] There was no confusion in getting the column organized, although some men were not informed of the evacuation and were left behind and captured.[32] Major Alonzo W. Adams, commander of the rear guard and the First New York Cavalry, stated in his report, "At 2 o'clock, the main body of the division having reached the Winchester and Martinsburg turnpike, I marched with a strong rear guard in reverse order, expecting an attack in the rear by the rebel cavalry, and never for one moment anticipating trouble in the front."[33] Although the retreat was well organized, things quickly started to go bad.

As previously stated, General Johnson, whose division was on the right of the Confederate line and east of the city, was given the order after dark to "move by the right flank with three of my brigades and a portion of my artillery to a point on the Martinsburg turnpike, 2½ miles north of Winchester."[34] Night marches are difficult, especially when units must move cross-country off the roads, but Johnson had the advantage of a local guide who knew the area. Johnson reported,

> After moving some distance on the Berryville road, I was informed by my guide that I would be obliged to cross fields over a rough country in order to carry out literally the directions of the lieutenant-general; and, moreover, that near Stephenson's, 5 miles north of Winchester, there was a railroad cut masked by a body of woods, and not more than 200 yards from the turnpike [along which the enemy would certainly retreat], which would afford excellent shelter for troops in case of an engagement.[35]

The extra distance meant that it took Johnson more time to get into position. Still, Johnson was able to get some of his units into position just as the head of the Federal column was passing on the Martinsburg Pike. There was a stone fence along the edge of the railroad cut next to the pike where Johnson placed six infantry regiments. In addition, he was able to place some artillery on higher ground behind the infantry as well as a two-gun section on and beside the bridge crossing the railroad. Johnson placed his units in semicircular formation. He did that due to the need to protect his flanks, as he was outnumbered. Even though the Confederates were outnumbered, they had the advantage of surprise and position as well as artillery.

The fighting was confusing for both sides due to the darkness with the 87th Pennsylvania being fired on by another Federal regiment to their rear.[36] Still, the Federals were able to mount a number of successful attacks and were in the process of outflanking the Confederates when the Stonewall brigade arrived, stopping one of the flanking attacks. Although personal bravery was shown by many of the Federal officers, including General Milroy, the problem for the Federals was, as Colonel J. Warren Keifer, commander of the 110th Ohio Infantry, stated, "there was no concert of action in the conduct of the battle."[37]

After the "hardest fighting" of the battle, which was so fierce that the two-gun Confederate artillery section placed on and beside the bridge had 13 men out of 16 killed or wounded, the Federal forces were broken up and routed.[38] Once the rout began, it was complete. Colonel Keifer stated,

> The cavalry became panic-stricken and, commingling with the mules and horses on which teamsters and others were mounted, all in great disorder took wildly to the hills and mountains to the northwest, followed by infantry in somewhat better order; the mules brayed, the horses neighed, the teamsters and riders indulged in much vigorous profanity, but the most of the retreating mass reached Bloody Run, Pennsylvania, marching via Sir John's Run, Hancock, and Bath. Citizens on Apple-Pie Ridge who witnessed the wild scene describe it as a veritable bedlam.[39]

The completeness of the Confederate victory can be shown by the fact that more Federal soldiers were captured than the number of Confederate soldiers under Johnson.[40] Surprise, the proper use of terrain, darkness, and the timely arrival of reinforcements made the difference.

***

The importance of geography in the Second Battle of Winchester cannot be overemphasized. Whereas geography hurt the Federals, the Confederates used it to their advantage. Schenck and Milroy were correct on the geographic importance of Winchester and the agricultural production around it. However, they were too dependent on technology and modifications to topography. Their technology broke down, and they could not overcome the limitations geography put on them. In addition, their construction of fortifications around Winchester gave them a false sense of security, especially as they were not placed on the most likely avenues of approach to Winchester. In contrast, the Confederates used geography to their advantage. Ewell and his subordinates maneuvered their units to place them in advantageous positions. They did not fall into the trap of attacking the Federal forts blindly; rather, they used geography to attack the Federals at their weaker points. Then Johnson, by using man-made modifications to the terrain, inflicted heavy losses on the Federals, even though he was outnumbered. An appreciation of geography, to include the time of the year, is necessary to completely understand the actions leading up to and during the Second Battle of Winchester.

After the Battle

After the Confederates gained control of Winchester, it became a major supply center for the Army of Northern Virginia. Supplies, such as ammunition, needed by the army were funneled through it, while supplies, such as horses and grain, obtained in Pennsylvania were sent to Winchester. In addition, a number of hospitals were established in its vicinity. However, it did not become a permanent logistic base but rather, a gathering point. General Lee wrote to the commanding officer at Winchester on the 4th of July, when he realized he needed to retreat from Gettysburg, "Upon the arrival of the sick and wounded at Winchester, they will be forwarded to Staunton as rapidly as possible, as also any surplus articles not needed for the army in the field."[41] The reasons Winchester did not become a permanent logistic depot were that the city did not have a railroad connection to the South and was an exposed position that would be difficult to defend. Still, it remained an important logistic base throughout the Gettysburg Campaign.

5

Geography and the Second Battle of Kernstown

24 July 1864

A forgotten battle that gave the initiative back to the Confederates allowing them to make one last major raid into Pennsylvania and forced General Grant to take the threat from the Valley seriously.

The Second Battle of Kernstown is the least known and written about battle for control of Winchester. It is not even mentioned in the pamphlet *Civil War Battles in Winchester and Frederick County, Virginia 1861–1865*. The two opposing commanders, Confederate General Jubal Early and Federal General George Crook, gave it scant notice in their autobiographies. Early covered the battle in only two pages in his *A Memoir of the Last Year of the War for Independence, in the Confederate States of America*. But this is more than Crook, the losing commander, gave as he covered the battle in only four paragraphs in his autobiography. Other individuals who participated in the battle also either ignored or discussed it very briefly. General John Gordon ignored the battle in his memoirs while Henry Kyd Douglas covered it in one paragraph. Fortunately, Jed Hotchkiss left an accurate description of the battle in his journal; there is a short description in Confederate General Armistead Long's article on the 1864 campaign in the *Southern Historical Society Papers*, a number of reports from Federal officers in the *Official Records*, as well as minor references in other sources.

Another issue with obtaining information on the Second Battle of Kernstown is that there is not a period map of the battle in the *Atlas to Accompany the Official Records of the Union and Confederate Armies*. In addition, an internet search of the Library of Congress did not reveal one either. Along with the lack of period maps, reports on the battle in the *Official Records* are scant. This lack of recognition is probably because Second Kernstown was overshadowed by Early's attack on Washington, the burning of Chambersburg, Third Winchester, Cedar Creek, and the bloody battles in Grant's Overland Campaign. This is unfortunate, for the battle was important as will be discussed at the end of this chapter. Map 5–1 was drawn by Hal Jespersen and gives an overview of the battle.

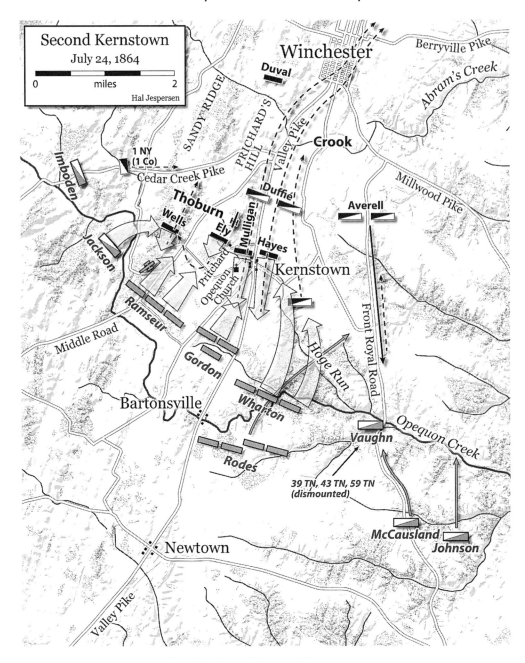

Map 5-1: Second Battle of Kernstown.

The Second Battle of Kernstown was the third largest battle for the struggle to control Winchester. In total numbers involved, it was only exceeded by Third Winchester and Cedar Creek. More troops were involved than in First Kernstown, as well as in First and Second Winchester. It was the most evenly matched battle for Winchester with the 13,000 Confederates only outnumbering the 10,000 Federals by 3,000 men, giving it a difference ratio of 1.3 Confederates for every Federal. Although both First and Second Kernstown occurred on Sunday and on the same terrain with the Confederates attacking from the south and the Federals defending from the north, these are the only actions the two battles have in common. At Second Kernstown, there were about 23,000 men involved in contrast to the less than 13,000 men at First Kernstown. Total losses were greater at Second Kernstown, although the percentage of losses compared to the number of men involved was higher at First Kernstown. At First Kernstown, many, if not most, of the men had never been in battle, and many of their leaders were equally inexperienced. At Second Kernstown, the majority of the men were veterans and were led by experienced, veteran officers, some of whom had fought at First Kernstown. Second Kernstown was also a longer battle than First Kernstown, as it started late morning and the Confederate pursuit did not end until dark, which was much later than at First Kernstown due to the time of the year. Most of the fighting at First Kernstown was on Sandy Ridge, while the fighting at Second Kernstown was centered on Pritchard's Hill. Finally, the results were different in that the Confederates were victorious at Second Kernstown and were able to gain control of Winchester with the Federals conducting a rapid retreat.

The importance of Second Kernstown is that it gave the Confederates control of Winchester and allowed them to make another raid into Pennsylvania. This raid, McCausland and Johnson's raid, which resulted in the burning of Chambersburg, forced Grant to take a definitive response to the Confederate use of the Valley. Because of the Confederate victory at Second Kernstown, geography and politics intersected and resulted in the permanent loss of the Valley as an avenue of invasion for the Confederates.

***

The grand strategy geographic view had not changed for either Abraham Lincoln or Jefferson Davis. Lincoln still wanted the country unified, and Davis still wanted independence for the entire Confederacy. With the presidential election coming soon, Lincoln was worried about the impact Confederate raids into the North would have. This especially included threats to the capital. Since the raids that made the biggest national and international newspaper headlines were those originating in the Shenandoah Valley, Lincoln was very interested in stopping them. This is where grand strategy and strategy intersected.

It had been over a year since the Second Battle of Winchester, and in retrospect, the tide of the war was definitely in favor of the Federal government. Although many events had been in favor of the Federal government, a number of negative events had also occurred. Gettysburg had been a morale-boosting victory along with the opening of the Mississippi River with the surrender of the Confederate garrisons at Vicksburg and Port Hudson. Still, Confederate General John Morgan had been able to raid into Indiana and Ohio although he and most of his men were taken prisoner. Along with Morgan's raid, Confederate irregular forces had sacked Lawrence, Kansas. While Knoxville, Tennessee, had been captured, the Federals had been defeated at Chickamauga, but the victory at Chattanooga had helped to erase that stigma. Another Confederate state capital, Little Rock, Arkansas, had been captured. But there had been major draft riots in New York City, and lesser ones in other cities, that had to be put down by Federal troops. The Federal armies were now united under one commander, General Ulysses S. Grant and his generals would now work in unison. Still, tremendous casualties created by Grant's Overland Campaign had generated a large amount of negative press while William T. Sherman's campaign to take Atlanta seemed to be bogged down in the mountains north of the city. Meanwhile, Grant was also bogged down at Petersburg with no hope of breaking the stalemate in sight. However, the CSS *Alabama* had been sunk by the USS *Kearsarge*, ending the *Alabama*'s destruction of United States' merchant ships. The Federals had been pushed out of the Valley, and Early, after recapturing Winchester, had been able to attack Washington, forcing Grant to transfer troops from Petersburg to defend the capital. Although the war was going well for Lincoln, the importance of the upcoming presidential elections cannot be overemphasized. War wariness was increasing, and it did not appear that the Confederacy was going to be defeated anytime soon.

For Davis, the war was not going well and victories were needed. Davis had been forced to relieve General Braxton Bragg, commander of the Army of the Tennessee, in November 1863 and replaced him with General Joseph Johnston. Then, when Johnston had continually retreated, Davis relieved him in mid–July 1864 and appointed General John Hood in his place. For Davis, finding generals who could produce victories at this stage of the war was difficult. Still, Early had been very successful in the Valley and had threatened Washington, impacting the morale of the voters in the North. The upcoming Federal elections would be key to determining Confederate independence.

At the strategic and operational levels, Grant wanted all Federal armies to attack simultaneously so that the Confederates could not transfer forces from an area where nothing was happening to one where the Federals were advancing. This included the Shenandoah Valley. However, the attempts by Generals Franz Sigel and David Hunter both failed. Sigel was defeated at New Market while Hunter retreated through West Virginia after being confronted by Early at Lynchburg. Robert E. Lee sent Early with his infantry corps to the Valley to oppose Hunter because Lee realized the importance of the major supply depot at Lynchburg and knew it needed to be defended. Retention of Lynchburg was important enough that Lee was willing to send a large number of units to defend it even though he was confronted by a superior number of Federal soldiers. Early's orders were worded so that he was given the discretion to move down the Valley if the opportunity presented itself. Hunter's retreat into West Virginia and away from the Valley allowed Early to advance down the Valley and eventually threaten Washington. This led Grant to transfer units originally designated for Petersburg to Washington, weakening his armies in front of Petersburg.

Weakening the Federal armies opposing him was one of the objectives Lee

5. Geography and the Second Battle of Kernstown

hoped Early would accomplish. Lee's thinking was, if Early could force a greater number of Federal Soldiers to oppose him, it would decrease the force ratio at Petersburg. Grant's view was that he wanted the maximum number of Soldiers to oppose Lee because he wanted to defeat/destroy Lee's army. Thus, any weakening of his force lessened his ability to accomplish this strategic objective. Consequently, Grant initially wanted to send only the minimum force required to stop Early and make him retreat south. In today's terms, Early was performing an economy of force mission, where he was to tie down more resources than he had. Lee summarized his thoughts concerning Early's operations in the Valley in a letter dated 19 July 1864, just prior to Second Kernstown, to James A. Seddon, the Secretary of War:

> In forwarding this report I deem it proper to state briefly for the information of the Department the object of detecting the force under General Early. I think, however, that it would not be prudent to give publicity to this statement at the present time. Finding that it would be necessary to detach some troops to repel the force under General Hunter, which was threatening Lynchburg, I resolved to send one that would be adequate to accomplish that purpose effectually, and, if possible, strike a decisive blow. At the same time General Early was instructed, if his success justified it, and the enemy retreated down the Valley, to pursue him, and, if opportunity offered, to follow him into Maryland. It was believed that the Valley could then be effectually freed from the presence of the enemy, and it was hoped that by threatening Washington and Baltimore General Grant would be compelled either to weaken himself so much for their protection as to afford us an opportunity to attack him, or that he might be induced to attack us. After the retreat of General Hunter toward Western Virginia his pursuit by General Early was attended with great difficulty, owing to the obstacles in the way of supplying our troops. At the same time the presence of General Hunter's forces in the Kanawha Valley endangered important interests in Southwestern Virginia. It was thought that the readiest way to draw him from that region would be to push down the Valley and enter Maryland, and at the same time it was hoped that the other advantages of such an invasion before alluded to might be secured. In addition to these considerations there were other collateral results, such as obtaining military stores and supplies, that were deemed of sufficient importance to warrant the attempt.
>
> General Early's report will explain his operations, and the value of the results obtained need not be further stated at present, as there are yet some to be expected in the future. I may, however, say that so far as the movement was intended to relieve our territory in that section of the enemy, it has up to the present time been successful.[1]

Lee was always thinking aggressively and was willing to weaken his main army opposing Grant for the potential of forcing Grant to weaken his army even more.

Lee's plan worked, to a point, and Grant was forced to send a large number of units to oppose Early when his army was threatening Washington but not enough to allow Lee to attack him. Due to these reinforcements, Early was now outnumbered and retreated to Virginia. Still, Early continued to be active and kept his force as far north as possible. However, due to the large number of Federal forces opposing him and the threat of being outflanked, Early withdrew up the Valley. On the 20th of July, Early moved his army to Newtown, just south of Winchester. On the 21st, he continued his retreat moving to Middletown, and on the 22nd, he moved across Cedar Creek toward Strasburg.[2] While there was fighting during this period, for the most part, the Federal pursuit was very deliberate and relatively ineffective, although Early was forced to retreat. On the 21st, once Early had been pushed south, General Horatio G. Wright, informed General Henry Halleck that

> preparations were accordingly made [to cross the Shenandoah River], and on pushing across on the morning of the 20th, it was found the enemy had retreated during the night, taking the road to Front Royal and Strasburg. Conceiving the object of the expedition to be accomplished, I at once started back, as directed by your orders, and to-night shall encamp on the east side of Goose Creek, on the Leesburg Pike. Two days' easy march will bring the command [Sixth and Nineteenth Corps] to Washington, crossing the Potomac at Chain Bridge.[3]

The reason for the movement of these corps was that Grant wanted them back at Petersburg to strengthen the forces opposing Lee. However, the loss of both of these corps seriously weakened the Federal forces in the Valley and gave Early more favorable odds. Grant's mistake was one of thinking the enemy would do what he hoped they would do.

Federal activity in the Valley did not end with Wright's withdrawal, for as he was withdrawing, Crook was marching his men to Winchester. On the 21st, some of General William W. Averell's cavalry and Crook's infantry occupied the town with Crook arriving on the 22nd.[4] Crook continued to move his units slowly south with the purpose of learning whether Early had already departed or was preparing to leave the Valley. Early had not left the Valley, and one of Crook's cavalry commanders, General Alfred N. Duffié, warned Crook that the Confederates were advancing. However, Crook did not take the reports seriously as he lacked confidence in Duffié. Crook also did not have any confidence in his other cavalry commander, General Averell. Crook reported after the Second Battle of Kernstown, "Our cavalry was of little or no assistance. General Averell was accused of getting drunk during the fight."[5] Still, on Saturday the 23rd, Crook ordered some of his infantry units to Kernstown in preparation for a Confederate attack. Although there was skirmishing and the Confederates were forced back, a major attack did not occur, and the infantry units returned to their camps near Winchester. As a result, Crook's infantry had to march from Winchester to Kernstown when Early attacked his cavalry posted south of Kernstown.

Early was informed on the 23rd "that a large portion of the force sent after us from Washington, was returning, and that Crook and Averill had united, and were at Kernstown, near Winchester."[6] Based on this information, Early decided to attack the Federals and advanced toward Winchester the morning of the 24th using the normal route of advance, the Valley Turnpike, with General John C. Breckinridge's unit in the lead. After driving in the Federal pickets at Bartonsville on Opequon Creek, the Confederate infantry was engaged by Federal cavalry at Kernstown at 10:00 a.m.[7]

The Battlefield

During First Kernstown, the heaviest fighting took place on Sandy Ridge when Stonewall Jackson attempted to outflank the Federals on Pritchard's Hill. During

Second Kernstown, the heaviest fighting took place on or near Pritchard's Hill as the Federals were again concentrated there. Pritchard's Hill was key terrain as it overlooked the Valley Turnpike, and whichever side controlled it also controlled access to Winchester. (Photographs of Pritchard's Hill and the surrounding area can be found in Photographs 2–1, 2–2, 2–3, and 2–4.)

One major geographic difference between First and Second Kernstown was the weather. First Kernstown occurred in early spring and the ground was wet with some of the battlefield being boggy and not trafficable. Second Kernstown occurred midsummer with the ground being dry and fully trafficable. During First Kernstown, Middle Road, the road in the valley between Pritchard's Hill and Sandy Ridge, was not trafficable, but during Second Kernstown, it was. This made a major difference in the battle as the Confederates made use of Middle Road to outflank the Federals on Pritchard's Hill. In addition, at First Kernstown, the foliage was not yet out, while at Second Kernstown, it was. Foliage allowed General John Breckinridge to maneuver his corps to the east with only limited Federal knowledge of the movement.

The ubiquitous stone walls in this part of Virginia also played an important role in the battle. By this time of the war, the Soldiers on both sides were well aware of the importance of stone walls when on the defensive, and the Federal troops quickly made use of them. In addition, many of the Federal units had created temporary breastworks out of wood fences and timber either the day before or built them on the 24th. Most of the men and officers were veterans and had learned by hard experience how to make the best use of the terrain.

One small topographic feature played a prominent role in the battle. Just south of the base of Pritchard's Hill is a very small "knoll." This knoll is over six feet in height and thus blocks the view of individuals on one side from seeing what is happening on the other side. This became important as the two advancing Federal brigades (Joseph Thoburn's and James Mulligan's) became separated by this knoll, which opened a gap in the Federal line. The Confederates were able to take advantage of this gap and used it to penetrate the Federal line. Unfortunately, for the Federals, neither Thoburn nor Mulligan were able to tell what was happening to each other due to the knoll blocking their view. Photograph 5–1 is a picture of this nameless, small knoll and shows that most people would not pay much attention to it.

The Battle

Early's attack was not a total surprise to Crook. Colonel Thoburn, commander of the First Division, Crook's VIII Corps, and commander of the First West Virginia Infantry at First Kernstown, reported after the battle,

> At an early hour on the morning of the 24th, while lying in camp one and a half miles south of Winchester, I received orders to move the First Infantry Division to the front with as little delay as possible, as the enemy was driving in our pickets and reported to be advancing in force. In twenty minutes my command was in motion, and was directed to take position in a

Photograph 5-1: A view of the nameless knoll that separated the two advancing Federal brigades south.

wood to the right and rear of Kernstown. I had occupied this same wood the day before when an attack was expected, and had the front and flanks strongly barricaded with fence rails and logs, greatly improving the strength of the position.[8]

The men, who were veterans commanded by veterans, had created an additional geographic/topographic advantage for themselves. Confederate veterans were equally adept at using the terrain to their advantage. I. Gordon Bradwell, a Soldier in General John Gordon's Georgia brigade, wrote in an article for the *Confederate Veteran* that his unit "was lying flat on our faces in a piece of woodland to avoid the balls of the enemy."[9] As always, at the tactical level, topography is everything, and these veterans had learned how to use it to their advantage.

The Confederate advance came from the south by way of the normal route of the high-speed, all-weather, macadamized Valley Turnpike with the exception of General Stephen Ramseur's division who used Middle Road, located on the western side of the turnpike. The Federals were waiting for the Confederates in a horseshoe defensive formation centered on Pritchard's Hill. But rather than wait, Thoburn's and Mulligan's brigades advanced to meet the Confederates. Then, due to a small knoll, a gap developed in their battle line. The Confederates took advantage of the gap and used it to penetrate the Federal line forcing the Federals to retreat. In addition, due to the terrain, both flanks of the Federal position were vulnerable to being outflanked. This was an opportunity that the Confederates took advantage of.

General Breckinridge, a very experienced officer, observed that the Federal left flank was open. He therefore ordered his units to move to the right and, by using the cover provided by a wooded hill, placed his units in a position where they could attack the Federal flank without being detected.[10] This attack, along with Ramseur's attack on the Federal right flank, forced the Federals to retreat, and every subsequent position they occupied also had its flank turned. However, it took the Confederates some time to outflank each position, giving the Federals time to withdraw before they could be surrounded. Although at the tactical level, both sides made use of the terrain, the Confederates made better use of it. Federal surgeon Alexander Neil wrote in a letter after the battle, "Our troops fought bravely until about 4 P.M. Sunday when the enemy massing a heavy force on our left suddenly flanked us, coming up almost in the rear, pouring into our ranks a galling fire of musketry, grape and canister, our men breaking & running in confusion, the ground literally strewn with our dead & wounded."[11]

Map 5–1 shows how the Confederates outflanked the Federals and how Crook had placed some of the Federal units too far back to influence the battle.

The Federal retreat all but became a rout when some Federal units lost cohesion. Surgeon Neil stated that the "panic commenced about 3 miles from Winchester,"[12] and although Federal cavalry was able to temporarily check the panic in Winchester, "the next day, we arrived at Martinsburg all in confusion, our troops scattered to the four winds & no organized command."[13] Luckily, dark, which happened around 8:00 p.m. (this was before daylight saving time) that time of the year, came, and the Confederates broke off their pursuit. One issue for the Confederates was that it had been a long day for them. They had gotten up early, marched in the heat for over four hours, and then fought a battle. Early informed Lee "he was compelled to halt [the pursuit] from the exhaustion of his men, they having marched twenty-five miles that day."[14] The geographically related heat of a late-July day combined with a long march and a battle had sapped the energy out of Early's men.

After the Battle

Early's victory at Kernstown allowed him to occupy Winchester and order his cavalry to conduct a raid into Pennsylvania. This raid led to the burning of Chambersburg and the destruction of a large part of the Confederate cavalry by Federal cavalry. The losses suffered by their cavalry would impact future events for the Confederates. The raid also forced Grant to take the threat from the Valley seriously. As a result, he put Philip Sheridan in charge of operations in the Valley and gave him an adequate force and the command authority to achieve his missions. In the end, the Confederate victory at Kernstown was, in reality, a pyrrhic victory.

Although Second Kernstown was not a pyrrhic victory in the traditional sense, it directly led to the destruction of Early's force and Sheridan's burning of the middle and lower Valley. If the battle had been a costly Federal victory rather than a substantial Confederate victory, Early would not have been able to occupy Winchester and conduct raids into Pennsylvania and Maryland. With Early continuing to threaten Winchester and the B&O Railroad, Grant would probably still have allocated a large number of units to restrict his movements but not as many as he actually did. Grant would probably have been content with just controlling the lower Valley and stopping Confederate raids into Maryland and Pennsylvania. Stopping the raids was important due to the upcoming presidential election. All of this would have meant that there would not have been a "burning," the Valley would not have suffered the extensive destruction that Sheridan ordered, Sheridan would not have had his decisive victories that helped Lincoln's reelection, and Early's army would not have been destroyed. However, the battle was a Confederate victory, and the subsequent Federal victories helped ensure Lincoln's reelection in November. First Kernstown was a tactical defeat for the Confederates but a long-range strategic victory. Second Kernstown was a tactical victory but led to a strategic defeat. Early's victory at Kernstown had implications well beyond the short-term impact of the battle for both the Valley and the war.

6

Geography and the Third Battle of Winchester

19 September 1864

Once a battle has begun, topography becomes the overriding criteria.

The Third Battle of Winchester was the largest of the six battles for control of Winchester with 15,200 Confederates defending against 39,236 attacking Federals. It was a daylong battle starting before dawn and not ending until after dark. The Confederate Army was still under the command of the proven Jubal Early, while the Federal Army had a new, more aggressive leader in Philip Sheridan. He, along with most of the new Federal commanders throughout the army, had a very different view of how the war should be fought compared to commanders earlier in the war. It was to become a much harder war, a difference that the civilians in the Valley would soon notice.

By this time of the war, mapmaking had become much more professional, and many more maps were being produced. However, Third Winchester, although it was an important and influential battle, did not rate multiple maps. Unfortunately, the official maps are too large and detailed to be included in this book. Three maps (6-1, 6-2, 6-3) were created by Hal Jespersen and show different stages of the battle. A map (6-4) from the 1960 publication *Civil War Battles in Winchester and Frederick County, Virginia 1861–1865* is also included, as it shows a summary of the battle in relation to 1960 Winchester. Unfortunately, neither map shows the monthlong maneuvering that took place leading to the battle. Still, all of the maps are valuable in helping the reader understand how the battle developed.

***

Although it had been only a little less than two months since the Battle of Second Kernstown, a lot had happened by the time of Third Winchester. The siege of Petersburg was tightening even though the attack that followed the mine that had been exploded on the 30th of July under Confederate lines had been a failure. Mobile, Alabama, had been effectively closed as a port for the Confederates, leaving Wilmington, North Carolina, as the only port blockade runners were still able to use. In the west, General Nathan Forrest had temporarily occupied Memphis,

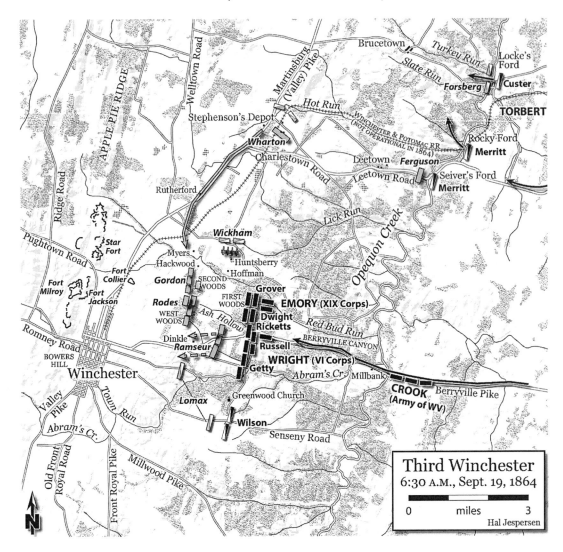

Map 6-1: The Third Battle of Winchester, 6:30 a.m.

Tennessee, and General Sterling Price had begun his movement into Missouri. The biggest news from the west was that General William T. Sherman had captured Atlanta, Georgia. Politically, Abraham Lincoln feared that he would not be reelected while George McClellan had become the Democratic nominee for president.

Things had been busy in the Valley, too. A Confederate cavalry raid into Pennsylvania resulted in the burning of Chambersburg. General Sheridan had become commander of the Army of the Shenandoah and the Middle Military District. As Sheridan outnumbered Early, he moved south and Early abandoned Winchester, which Sheridan then occupied. However, Sheridan found out that he could not be effectively supplied and retreated to Halltown allowing Early to reoccupy Winchester. However, Lee needed additional forces at Petersburg, and General Richard Anderson's corps left the Valley for Petersburg on the 14th of September.

6. Geography and the Third Battle of Winchester

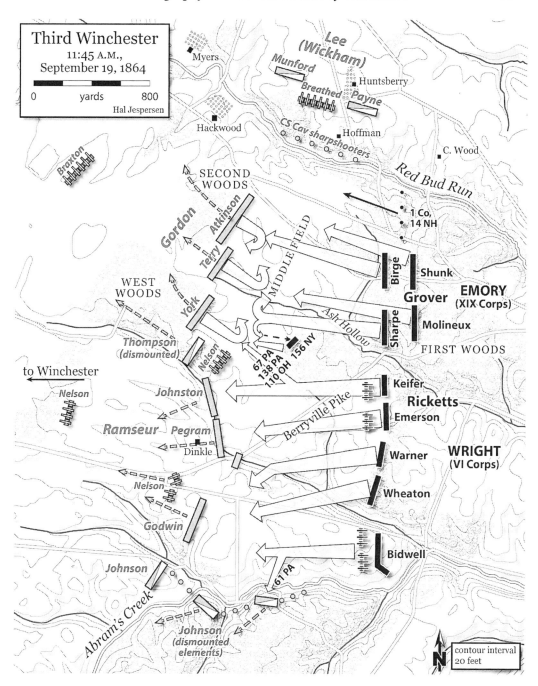

Map 6-2: The Third Battle of Winchester, 11:45 a.m.

Lincoln's overall objective was still unification of the country, and to achieve his goal, he needed to be reelected. He knew that John McCausland and Bradley Johnson's raid into Pennsylvania as well as a repeat of General Early's raid and attack on Washington would make his administration look weak. Additional raids could result in his losing the upcoming 1864 election. It was important for the Federal

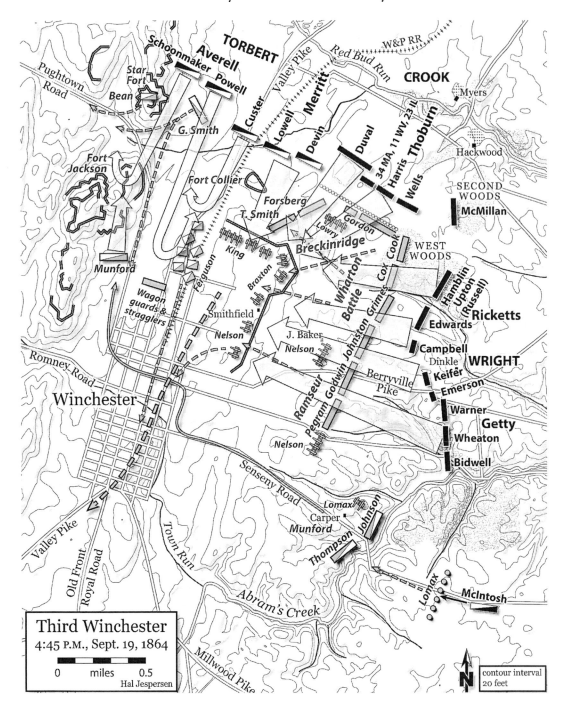

Map 6-3: The Third Battle of Winchester, 4:45 p.m.

government to show that it could protect all of the territory under its control. This was emphasized by Andrew Curtin, Governor of Pennsylvania, and Augusta Bradford, Governor of Maryland, in a letter to President Lincoln: "It seems to us that not merely in this sectional aspect of the case, but in it national relations, the security

6. Geography and the Third Battle of Winchester

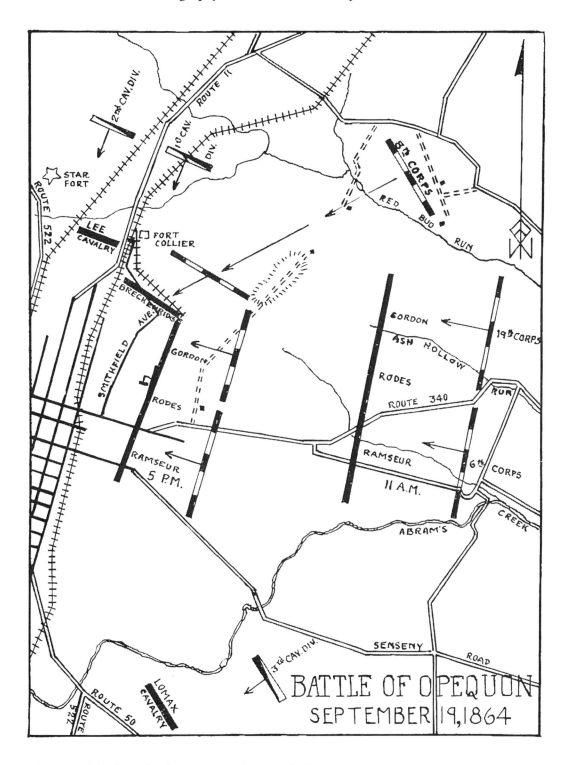

Map 6–4: Third Battle of Winchester showing the location of units in respect to Winchester in 1960 (*Civil War Battles in Winchester and Frederick County, Virginia 1861–1865*, Winchester-Frederick County Civil War Centennial Commission).

of this border line between the loyal and rebellious States is an object justifying and requiring a disposition of a portion of the national force with an especial view to its defense."[1] General Ulysses S. Grant was also aware of the need to protect all of the territory under Federal control and was forced to leave a large number of troops in garrisons across the country. Still, Grant wanted these units to "act directly to their front," which, in his opinion, would "give better protection than if lying idle in garrison."[2]

General Grant, at the strategic level, realized that victory over the Confederacy would only be obtained when "the military power of the rebellion was entirely broken."[3] Grant stated that there were two actions that needed to be accomplished to obtain this goal. The first was to attack all of the Confederate armies simultaneously so that they could not shift troops from a less threatened area to one that was being attacked. Second was to continuously hammer the Confederate armies as well as the resources supporting them.[4] Grant's 1864 campaign had four objectives: the two main Confederate armies east of the Mississippi River, Lee's Army of Northern Virginia and Johnston's Army of Tennessee, and the two cities, Richmond and Atlanta, each army was covering and defending.[5] This was a combination of a moving object and a fixed geographic location. Nothing was stated about Winchester or the Shenandoah Valley. Still, Grant fully supported Lincoln's desire to stop Confederate raids into the North and realized it was up to him to develop a plan to stop them.

To achieve this, Grant's initial orders to Sheridan, after Sheridan was put in command in the Shenandoah Valley, were that he was to drive the enemy south and was to leave nothing that would "invite the enemy to return."[6] To realize the second objective, Sheridan was ordered, "Take all of the provisions, forage, and stock wanted for the use of your command; such as cannot be consumed destroy. It is not desirable that buildings be destroyed; they should rather be protected, but the people should be informed that as long as any army can subsist among them recurrences of these raids [Confederate raids into the North] must be expected, and we are determined to stop them at all hazards."[7] The hope was that this would stop Confederate raids into the North through the Shenandoah Valley by eliminating popular support for the raiders, by forcing people out of northern Virginia, and by destroying agriculture in the Valley.

To help Sheridan achieve these objectives, four military districts (Middle Department, Department of Washington, Department of the Susquehanna, and the Department of West Virginia) were consolidated into the Middle Military District.[8] The purpose of the change was to improve coordination and communication between the districts, especially when Confederate raids were taking place. With Sheridan in command of all four districts, he could direct all of the units in those districts and ensure that proper steps were taken to defeat and stop any attempted Confederate incursion.

The economic and political impact of Confederate raids into Maryland and

6. Geography and the Third Battle of Winchester

Pennsylvania cannot be overemphasized. Geography dictated that one of the easiest routes to cross the Appalachian Mountains was where the Potomac River comes through the eastern part of the mountains. Well before the war, there had been the need to connect the armory at Harpers Ferry to Washington. Consequently, both the B&O Railroad and the Chesapeake and Ohio Canal followed the Potomac River at least up to Harpers Ferry. Thus, it was very easy for the Confederates to raid and destroy portions of either. The economic effect was great enough that General Henry Halleck informed General Grant on the 14th of September 1864,

> It has been represented to me by reliable business men that the long and continued interruption of the Ohio and Chesapeake Canal and Baltimore and Ohio Railroad is very seriously affecting the supply of provisions and fuel for public and private use in Baltimore, Washington, Georgetown, and Alexandria. Unless the canal can be opened very soon a sufficient supply of winter's coal cannot be procured before the close of navigation. The gas companies are already thinking to stop their works for want of coal. The canal and railroad have been several times repaired, and as often destroyed. They, therefore urge the great importance of driving Early far enough south to secure these lines of communication from rebel raids, and that if Sheridan is not strong enough to do this he should be reinforced. I respectfully communicate the substance of these representations for your consideration.[9]

The political impact of another defeat in the Valley was something Sheridan was well aware of. In his autobiography, he stated,

> The difference of strength between the two armies [Sheridan's and Early's] at this date [end of August 1864] was considerably in my favor, but the conditions attending my situation in a hostile region necessitated so much detached service to protect trains, and to secure Maryland and Pennsylvania from raids, that my excess in numbers was almost canceled by these incidental demands that could not be avoided, and although I knew that I was strong, yet, in consequence of the injunctions of General Grant, I deemed it necessary to be very cautious; and the fact that the Presidential election was impending made me doubly so, the authorities at Washington having impressed upon me that the defeat of my army might be followed by the overthrow of the party in power, which event, it was believed, would at least retard the progress of the war, if, indeed, it did not lead to the complete abandonment of all coercive measures, Under circumstances such as these I could not afford to risk a disaster, to say nothing of the intense disinclination every soldier has for such result; so, notwithstanding my superior strength, I determined to take all the time necessary to equip myself with the fullest information, and then seize an opportunity under such conditions that I could not well fail of success.[10]

However, Grant was under political pressure and decided to visit Sheridan to determine what his plans were. In one of his general reports, Grant stated,

> The two armies [Sheridan's and Early's] lay in such a position—the enemy on the west bank of Opequon Creek, covering Winchester, and our forces in front of Berryville—that either could bring on a battle at any time. Defeat to us would lay open to the enemy the States of Maryland and Pennsylvania for long distances before another army could be interposed to check him. Under these circumstances I hesitated about allowing the initiative to be taken. Finally, the use of the Baltimore and Ohio Railroad and the Chesapeake and Ohio Canal, which were both obstructed by the enemy, became so indispensably necessary to us, and the importance of relieving Pennsylvania and Maryland from continuously threatened invasion so great, that I determined the risk should be taken. But fearing to telegraph the order for an attack without knowing more than I did of General Sheridan's feelings as to what would be the probable

result, I left City Point on the 15th of September to visit him at his headquarters, to decide, after conference with him, what should be done.[11]

Grant, wanting action, had his own plan with him in case Sheridan did not have a plan or had a plan that was not acceptable. Fortunately for Sheridan, Grant approved his proposal and he never showed his plan to Sheridan. Thus, Grant was able to keep his vision at the higher strategic level. If Grant had become too involved in operational plans and issues, he would have taken the initiative away from his subordinate commanders and neglected his higher level responsibilities.

If Sheridan had not acted or had been defeated, there was a strong possibility that Grant would have relieved him. Although Grant kept men he did not know in command positions, he was willing to relieve them if they did not perform up to his expectations. Anyone he relieved was replaced by someone he knew and trusted. Grant also gave this same authority, to relieve and replace individuals who were not performing to their expectations, to his commanders.

Although Confederate military strategy had changed due to circumstances during the war, Jefferson Davis's overall strategy of achieving independence for all of the seceding states remained constant. Therefore, he wished to retain control of as much territory as possible while forcing the Federal government to recognize the independence of the Confederacy.[12] Robert E. Lee's views on what he wanted Early to accomplish in the Valley were much more specific. Lee wanted Early to defeat General David Hunter's force and, if possible, destroy it. Once that was accomplished, Early was to move down the Valley in hopes of crossing the Potomac River and, if feasible, threaten Washington.[13] Lee was continuously worried about supplies. Consequently, when Early reached Winchester, he received a message from Lee directing him to remain in the lower Valley until everything was in place to cross the Potomac River. Once Early crossed the Potomac, he was to "destroy the Baltimore and Ohio railroad and the Chesapeake and Ohio Canal as far as possible."[14] One reason for the delay was to thresh and grind enough wheat to supply Early's troops. Lee informed President Davis on the 29th of June 1864 that Early's "general plan of action is in conformity to my original instructions and conversations with him before his departure. I still think it is our policy to draw the attention of the enemy to his own territory. It may force Grant to attack me, or weaken his forces. It will also, I think, oblige Hunter to cross the Potomac or expose himself to attack. From either of those events I anticipate good results." Lee went on to state, "To retain [Early] there inactive would not be advantageous." Still, Lee's greatest concern was to "secure regular and constant supplies."[15]

Unfortunately for the Confederates, delays, some of which were geographic in nature, stopped Early from capturing Washington. The main delays were the Battle of Monocacy (9 July 1864) and then the march from Monocacy to Washington. This march was conducted in hot weather and dusty conditions, causing some of the men to develop sunstroke. Because of these delays, Early's army did not reach

Washington until the 11th of July. This gave enough time for units from the Army of the Potomac to reach and reinforce the Washington defenses.

Lee's desire for ensuring adequate supplies for his men can be seen in his message to Early on the 11th of July, that if he was forced to come back into Virginia, he should march through Loudoun (County) as it would "facilitate the procurement of provisions, forage, &c., for your command."[16] Although Loudoun County was just to the east of the Blue Ridge and thus not in the Valley, Lee's desire for Early to retreat through it and collect supplies demonstrates the fact that Confederate forces in the lower Valley did not need to receive food and forage from Richmond. By doing this, Early would ease the logistic burden on the Army of Northern Virginia. Lee was also concerned about making the maximum use of his available troop strength. He informed President Davis on the 23rd of July that he had told General Early if he could not detain the forces he had driven across the Shenandoah River, it would be necessary for him to return to the main army.[17]

Both Lee and Grant were testing each other as to who would and could send units from their respective armies to Early and Sheridan in the Valley. Both men, through a variety of means—prisoners, deserters, newspapers, and scouts—kept close watch on whether any units of the opposing side had left the front for the Valley. Lee was hoping that "General Grant, rather than weaken his army, would have attempted to drive us from our position. I fear I shall not be able to attack him to advantage, and if I cannot I think it would be well to re-enforce General Early. In that way it would oblige him further to diminish his force."[18] Lee reinforced Early when he was forced to retreat up the Valley after Sheridan took command. However, Early did not have to retreat very far because Sheridan was worried about his left/eastern flank due to all of the passes through the Blue Ridge Mountains. Sheridan's concern was justified when reinforcements from Lee attempted to outflank him through the Blue Ridge Mountains. The threat was serious enough that Sheridan retreated down the Valley. However, as he retreated, Sheridan ordered his units to destroy all forage and subsistence so that the returning Confederate units would need to go farther to get these items. It was another "race" up and down the Valley, one that had been done a number of times already during the war. There was one major difference: Sheridan did not leave the Valley. To protect his force, Sheridan had his men build fortifications around Halltown, just outside of Harpers Ferry, where he could threaten any advance Early made across the Potomac River. Sheridan had decided on using Halltown as his defensive line prior to engaging Early. Before Sheridan began his campaign, he consulted with officers who had spent time in the Valley and conducted a map reconnaissance of it. Sheridan stated in a report, "I at once looked over a map of the Valley for a defensive line—that is, where a smaller number of troops could hold a greater number—and could see but one. I refer to that at Halltown, in front of Harper's Ferry. Subsequent experience has convinced me that no other really defensive line exists in the Shenandoah Valley."[19]

Early's problem was whether he had enough men to make another raid into the north and/or successfully battle Sheridan's forces. Early's difficulty was when Sheridan retreated, he was reinforced by units he had left behind to guard his supply line. In addition, at Halltown, Sheridan had an excellent defensive position and was well supplied. Early also knew he either had to make use of the reinforcements from Lee or send them back. Sending the reinforcements back to Lee was what both Sheridan and Grant were hoping as Grant informed Sheridan,

> I telegraphed you [Sheridan] that I had good reason for believing that Fritz Lee had been ordered back here [Petersburg]. I now think it likely that all troops will be ordered back from the Valley except what they believe to be the minimum number to detain you. My reason for supporting this is based upon the fact that yielding up the Weldon road seems to be a blow to the enemy he cannot stand. I think I do not overstate the loss of the enemy in the last two weeks at 10,000 killed and wounded. We have lost heavily, mostly in captured, when the enemy gained temporary advantages. Watch closely, and if you find this theory correct push with all vigor. Give the enemy no rest, and if it is possible to follow the Virginia Central road, follow that far. Do all the damage to railroads and crops you can. Carry off stock of all descriptions, and negroes, so as to prevent further planting. If the war is to last another year, we want the Shenandoah Valley to remain a barren waste.[20]

It was a situation where both sides wanted superiority in the Valley, but they were equally worried about maintaining pressure on each other's main army entrenched around Petersburg and Richmond.

***

For both Sheridan and Early, beyond the political implications of their actions, the most important item was the geography of the lower Valley north of and around Winchester. As previously stated, Early was dependent on the agriculture around Winchester to feed his men and animals. However, Sheridan had begun the destruction of that support during his mid–August retreat.

> In compliance with instructions of lieutenant-general commanding [Grant], you [Brigadier General Torbert] will make the necessary arrangements and give the necessary orders for the destruction of all the wheat and hay south of a line from Millwood to Winchester and Petticoat Gap. You will seize all horses, mules, and cattle that may be useful to our army. Loyal citizens can bring in their claims against the Government for this necessary destruction. No houses will be burned, and officers in charge of this delicate, but necessary, duty must inform the people that the object is to make this Valley untenable for the raiding parties of the rebel army.[21]

Sheridan reinforces this view in his autobiography: "In war a territory like this [the Shenandoah Valley] is a factor of great importance, and whichever adversary controls it permanently reaps all of the advantages of its prosperity."[22] "Death is popularly considered the maximum of punishment in war, but it is not; reduction to poverty brings prayers for peace more surely and more quickly than does the destruction of human life, as the selfishness of man has demonstrated in more than one great conflict."[23] The war had changed to one in which the destruction of the enemy's resources for its army and civilians had become legitimate objectives.

Early's army, when it first returned from Maryland and before it had to retreat up the Valley, was able to obtain what they needed "principally from the lower Valley and the counties west of it, and the money which was obtained by contributions in Maryland was used for that purpose."[24] Although it is questionable how voluntary the contributions were, most likely the Virginia farmers were very pleased to be paid in U.S. money. However, the drain Confederate military manpower requirements put on the population around Winchester (as well as the people who had been arrested by Union authorities) forced Early to detach men to thresh and grind the wheat. This reduced his fighting strength as these men continued making bread during battles.[25] When Early returned to Winchester, after Sheridan had retreated to Halltown, he was forced to obtain flour from the upper Valley. In addition, his horses and mules were only able to graze on grass and had no oats to eat.[26] This would have lessened their overall strength, making them less able to pull heavy loads or, for cavalry horses, to run at their top speed. This gave Union cavalry, whose horses were fed grain, a distinct advantage. The need to detach men was also an issue for Sheridan because he was forced to assign units away from his main force to guard various locations. Both men had drains on their fighting strength with Early's army probably being the most impacted as his fighting strength was less to begin with than Sheridan's.

There were geographic features that would impact the upcoming campaign. The first was the weather, which remained dry and allowed for easy movement of the armies. Although there was a wide variation of the terrain throughout the lower Valley, for the most part it was a good place for maneuvering because the majority of the terrain consisted of rolling hills and open ground. There were a number of waterways with the three biggest being the Potomac River, Shenandoah River, and Opequon Creek. The Potomac and Shenandoah Rivers were fordable at numerous locations. The Potomac River was mainly an obstacle for Confederate forces since it helped channel any movement into the North to specific crossings. The Shenandoah River was a potential obstacle for both sides, but for the upcoming campaign, it would not be a stumbling block since it mostly ran very close to the Blue Ridge Mountains on the eastern side of the Valley. Besides, it was not a major obstacle for the Union Army as it was already across the river at Halltown. Opequon Creek was a different matter; it ran south to north, paralleling the Shenandoah River. As such, it helped protect the Confederate Army, while being a major obstacle for the Union Army since Winchester and the Confederate Army were west of it while the Union Army was east of it. The creek was an obstruction because its banks were very steep, and there were only a limited number of fords. Whereas infantry and cavalry could cross the creek at locations other than the fords, artillery and wagons could not. Consequently, it made a good defensive line for the Confederates. Sheridan was well aware of this. He informed General Grant that "Early still holds his position on west bank of the Opequon Creek, near Jordan Springs. It is exceedingly difficult to attack him in this position. The Opequon Creek is a very formidable barrier; there are various crossings, but all difficult; the banks are formidable. I thought it best to remain on the defensive until he detaches, unless the chances are in my favor."[27] Closer to Winchester, once the high ground surrounding the town had been taken, the town became indefensible. The most obvious and best route for Sheridan to attack the town from Harpers Ferry was from the north, along the Winchester and Potomac Railroad. If he took this route, his army would have a number of potential fords across the Opequon Creek and would have open ground near Winchester. However, Early had concentrated his army at Martinsburg, which was due west of Harpers Ferry and along the B&O Railroad. This would place Early on Sheridan's flank if he advanced on Winchester from the north. Still, the most direct route between Winchester and Halltown/Harpers Ferry was along the railroad, through Charlestown, and across the Limestone Ridge where Summit Point was located.

The difficulty Sheridan faced was that he wanted to decisively defeat Early and not merely have another race up and down the Valley. If he moved up the Valley without a decisive defeat of Early or, better, destroying Early's army, he would probably have to retreat again as his line of communications would lengthen. This would force him to leave units behind to guard his line of communications while Early's line of communications would shorten, along with the strong possibility he would receive reinforcements from Lee. Thus, attacking Early by the most direct route would allow Early to easily disengage and retreat. This was not a feasible option since Sheridan, Grant, and the administration wanted and needed a decisive victory in the Valley. As a result, most of the infantry fighting during the Third Battle of Winchester took place east of the town, the main cavalry action was north of the town, and for Sheridan, a disappointing cavalry action south of the town. The question for historians and researchers is, why did Sheridan make his main attack from the east when there were more obstacles on that side of the town and it was not the most direct route from Halltown to Winchester? The answer is, Sheridan was hoping to achieve the most elusive of victories—complete annihilation of the enemy. Sheridan wanted to achieve this during his first advance up the Valley as he tried to place his army in Early's rear and right flank, forcing Early to attack him. However, Early anticipated Sheridan's maneuver and was able to retreat before Sheridan could get south of him.[28]

Both Sheridan and Early were aggressive commanders and confident in their abilities. Both were also well aware of the disadvantages of attacking an entrenched enemy. After retreating down the Valley, Sheridan used the fortifications at Halltown for protection and waited until he was sure of victory. He deliberately did not place many troops at Martinsburg in hopes that Early would move north and cross the Potomac River. As Sheridan informed General Grant on the 20th of August, "I left everything in that direction [north to the Potomac River] for them, but they have not accepted the invitation as yet."[29] Sheridan had informed Grant the previous day, "They [the Confederates] have made no attempt to pass down the Valley to Martinsburg, which I hold with a small force of cavalry. If they cross the Potomac they expose their rear and I will pitch into them."[30] Both Sheridan and Grant were being

6. Geography and the Third Battle of Winchester

very cautious since they did not want a Confederate victory too close to the upcoming election. Grant ordered Halleck, on the 12th of August, to inform Sheridan that "it is now certain two divisions of infantry have gone to Early, and some cavalry and twenty pieces of artillery. This movement commenced last Saturday night. He must be cautious and act now on the defensive until movements here force them to detach to send this way. Early's force, with this increase, cannot exceed 40,000 men, but this is too much for Sheridan to attack."[31]

Grant continually kept Sheridan informed when he learned about any transfer of troops from Lee to Early or from Early to Lee.

Early was in a very different situation than Sheridan. Lee's instructions to him on the 26th of August were,

> Your [Early's] letter of the 23d [August] has been received, and I am much pleased at your having forced the enemy back to Harper's Ferry. This will give protection to the Valley and arrest the travel on the Baltimore and Ohio Railroad. It will, however, have little or no effect upon Grant's operations, or prevent re-enforcements being sent to him. If Sheridan's force is as large as you suppose, I do not know that you could operate to advantage north of the Potomac. Either Anderson's troops or a portion of yours might, however, be detached to destroy the railroad west of Charlestown, and Fitz Lee might send a portion of his cavalry to cross the Potomac east of the Blue Ridge, as you propose.... I am in great need of his [Anderson's] troops, and if they can be spared from the Valley, or cannot operate to advantage there, I will order them back to Richmond. Let me know.[32]

Although Grant would have liked to have many of the units under Sheridan sent to the Petersburg area, it was far from being as critical as it was for Lee. Consequently, Early's operations were more constrained than Sheridan's. After the war Early wrote,

> The relative positions which we occupied rendered my communications to the rear very much exposed, but I could not avoid it without giving up the lower Valley. The object of my presence there was to keep up a threatening attitude towards Maryland and Pennsylvania, and prevent the use of the Baltimore and Ohio railroad, and the Chesapeake and Ohio canal, as well as to keep as large a force as possible from Grant's army to defend the Federal Capital. Had Sheridan, by a prompt movement, thrown his whole force on the line of my communications, I would have been compelled to attempt to cut my way through, as there was no escape for me to the right or left, and my force was too weak to cross the Potomac while he was in my rear. I knew my danger, but I could occupy no other position that would have enabled me to accomplish the desired object. If I had moved up the Valley at all, I could not have stopped short of New Market, for between that place and the country in which I was there was no forage for my horses; and this would have enabled the enemy to resume the use of the railroad and canal, and return all the troops from Grant's army to him.[33]

Early was very aware of how geography, especially forage for his horse, beyond the constraints imposed by Lee, limited his options. Early also knew how open the terrain was around Winchester and how this could be used to the Federal cavalry's benefit as it was far greater in size than his cavalry.[34]

Sheridan, in preparation for the upcoming battle, placed his army to the northeast of Winchester from Clifton (halfway between Berryville and Summit Point) to Berryville. He also had units occupy Summit Point to protect his right flank and his communications with Harpers Ferry.[35] In his autobiography, published 23 years after the war, Sheridan stated he wanted to make his attack a surprise to General Early. He knew if Early became aware of when the attack would take place, he would concentrate his army and ask that the units that were on their way back to Petersburg be returned to him. To assist in making the attack a surprise, Sheridan used his cavalry, which had become superior to the Confederate cavalry, to control about six miles between the lines. This allowed him to move his men into position for attack without Early's knowledge. Sheridan made his attack after he was confident General Richard Anderson's force, whose main strength was General Joseph Kershaw's infantry division, had left and were far enough on their way back to Richmond that they could not quickly return and influence the battle. Sheridan also learned that Early had sent two infantry divisions to Martinsburg. Once Sheridan learned this, he decided to attack at once in hopes of destroying Early's army piecemeal. However, Early learned about Sheridan's meeting with Grant and concluded that Sheridan would soon attack. Consequently, he kept his units in supporting distance of each other.

The Battlefield

The battlefield for the Third Battle of Winchester was very large, too large for anyone to be able to see the entire battlefield from one location. This in itself makes it different from most of the other battles for control of Winchester. North to south, the battlefield goes from Stephenson's Depot to Abrams Creek for about 5½ miles. East to west, the battlefield goes from Berryville Canyon to Star Fort for about 4½ miles. Thus, the battlefield covers about 25 square miles. Due to the distances involved, once the battle began, neither Sheridan nor Early could see, much less direct, events on most of the battlefield. In addition, the size of the battlefield encompasses a wide range of geography breaking the battlefield into a number of different topographic features to include man-made ones.

Based on the location of Sheridan's army and his desire to destroy Early's army, the best approach for Sheridan was from the east along the Berryville Turnpike. The problem was that right after the turnpike crossed the Opequon, it went through the Berryville Canyon.[36] The canyon was about two miles long, and Ash Hollow Run flowed through it. James E. Taylor, a reporter and artist, described the canyon (as shown in Drawing 6-1) as "a broad cheerless ravine of a mile and a half extent between timbered slopes through which a nameless brooklet loitered on its way amid boggy soil sown with silver bark saplings."[37] Photograph 6-1 shows the Berryville Canyon as it looks today on the route Sheridan's men would have marched. Today, the canyon is a divided four-lane highway, but it is still possible to visualize how it would have looked in 1864. It would have been a very constricted avenue of approach, and if the exit from it had been fortified and well manned, it would have become a trap for the Federals.

6. Geography and the Third Battle of Winchester

Drawing 6-1: The Berryville Canyon (drawn by James E. Taylor, The Western Reserve Historical Society, Cleveland, Ohio).

Photograph 6-1: Berryville Canyon.

Although Sheridan's orders to his subordinates for the upcoming battle were very brief, consisting of five short paragraphs, he included some geographic/topographic locations. One reason Sheridan probably kept his initial orders brief was that he knew that as soon as contact was made with the enemy, "developments which may occur cause other dispositions to be made."[38] Sheridan made the Berryville Pike his main avenue of approach As soon as his leading infantry unit, the Sixth Corps, reached open country beyond the Opequon Creek, they were to form a line of battle.[39] Sheridan also made use of his cavalry to open up the Berryville Canyon for his infantry when he ordered Brigadier General James Wilson's cavalry division to lead the advance through the canyon with instructions to "drive in the enemy's cavalry on that pike [Berryville Pike] and follow them up."[40] After clearing the canyon for the Sixth Corps, Wilson's cavalry division was to move south, with the purpose of cutting the Valley Turnpike south of Winchester, as this was Early's only viable route of retreat.

Although Wilson's cavalry was able to secure the western end of the canyon, problems occurred in getting the infantry through it due to an ammunition wagon train blocking it. However, once Sheridan's leading infantry units advanced through the Berryville Canyon, the ground opened up and mainly consisted of open fields with some standing corn.[41] Sheridan also made use of the Berryville Pike to guide James Ricketts's division in their advance. For Sheridan's cavalry, maneuvering to the north (the Confederates' left flank), the ground became open and favored their movement once they crossed Opequon Creek. In his autobiography, Sheridan stated, "The ground which Breckenridge was holding [on the Confederate left flank north of Winchester] was open, and offered an opportunity such as seldom had been presented during the war for a mounted attack."[42]

Berryville Canyon continued to be a bottleneck for Union units throughout the battle. General George Crook, commander of the Army of West Virginia, reported after the battle that when his unit was ordered to leave its reserve position on the east side of the Opequon Creek, he found it blocked by "ammunition wagons, battery wagons, forges, ambulances, and stragglers going to the rear."[43] His progress was delayed, and his artillery was delayed an additional hour. Beyond Berryville Canyon, there were other geographic issues Sheridan's units had to confront.

The problem for the Federals was that Berryville Canyon sat at the bottom of a *V* with the two sides being creeks, which restricted movement. Abraham's Creek was to the south, and Red Bud Run was to the north. Although Abraham's Creek was not swampy like Red Bud Run, many of its banks were very steep, almost cliff-like, making it an obstacle to north-south movement. Red Bud Run was a slow-moving creek consisting of relatively steep banks with a wide and swampy bottom with a heavily timbered morass, which was very difficult to cross. Photograph 6-2 shows Red Bud Run in the vicinity of where the main Confederate line met it. It is a significant obstacle, and the Confederate infantry depended on it to guard their left flank. There was also a few Confederate cavalry and horse artillery units on the northern side of Red Bud Run who were able to fire across the run at the Federal units attacking the left flank of the Confederate main line (where Gordon's division was located). Even today, Red Bud Run is a substantial obstacle at the tactical level. However, Photograph 6-2 does not show the depth of the run and that the bottom and most of the banks are boggy. It is a tactical obstacle that even modern military units with all of their equipment would have to take into consideration. This would be especially true if they had to cross it under fire, as the Federal infantry had to in 1864. Until strong Federal units crossed Red Bud Run, Confederate units on its north side were protected by the run and caused significant casualties to a number of Federal units. Thus, due to the topography, Federal units initially had a very restricted maneuver zone.

The Confederate view of the geography of the battlefield was different. First, Early had only one good route of retreat. This route was to the south along the Valley Turnpike. If a strong Union force was able to get south of his army across the Valley Turnpike, he would be forced to fight his way through them. Early was well aware his route of retreat was vulnerable. He stated in his autobiography that during the afternoon of the battle when there was a temporary pause in the fighting,

> The enemy was still to be seen in front in formidable force, and away to our right, across Abraham's Creek, at the junction of the Front Royal and Millwood roads, he had massed a division of cavalry with some artillery, overlapping us at least a mile, while the country was open between this force and the Valley Pike, and the Cedar Creek Pike back of the latter; which roads furnished my only means of retreat in the event of disaster.[44]

As a result, Early was compelled to weaken his forces on his left flank, which was under pressure from both Federal cavalry and infantry, to reinforce his more critical right flank.

Early's challenge was that he had too few troops to accomplish all of his assignments but too many to remain idle. If he concentrated his forces to defend the Berryville Canyon and the crossing points north and south of it along the Opequon Creek, he would not have enough units left to interfere with the reconstruction

Photograph 6–2: Red Bud Run looking east.

and operation of the B&O Railroad or the Chesapeake and Ohio Canal. Both his northern/left and southern/right flanks also needed to be adequately protected. If he retreated up the Valley, as he had previously done, his army would no longer be a threat to Washington or Pennsylvania, and Sheridan would be able to send units back to Petersburg. This would also allow Sheridan to continue the destruction of the agricultural resources of the lower Valley. All of this forced Early to stay near Winchester with its network of roads. This network allowed Early to continually maneuver his forces hoping Sheridan would make a mistake, allowing him to defeat Sheridan or a portion of Sheridan's army. With Sheridan out of the way, Early could then conduct raids into the North. Any Confederate success would cause additional concerns with voters and could possibly result in politicians favoring peace to be elected. In both Lee's and Early's opinions, the risks were worth the potential gains. In the end, no matter what their orders or desires were, geography limited both Sheridan's and Early's options.

***

At the tactical level, a commander's view of geography becomes all but topographic in that he was more interested in the lay of the ground rather than the geographic importance of the site. Still, he should be interested in the weather and how it impacted the battlefield as well as sources of water for his men, along with water and forage for his animals. A commander's view of geography also depends on the type of unit he commands and on whether he is defending or attacking. An attacking infantry commander would want the terrain to be such that his unit could get close to the enemy without being seen. At the same time, he would not want the terrain his unit is passing through to restrict movement or break up his unit's formation. In defense, an infantry commander would want his unit to be on higher ground with adequate cover for his men but have an open field in front that the enemy would need to cross. In contrast, a cavalry or artillery commander would want open ground in front of them, which would allow for a massed cavalry charge, or open fields of fire for the artillery whether they were defending or attacking. When reading the reports of infantry, cavalry, and artillery commanders, they all mention the same various topographic features. Part of the reason may be that they were using the topographic features to help explain their movements and also mention them to help explain any difficulties that impacted their unit's performance.

Officers who were involved in the tactical level of combat at Third Winchester made frequent mention of topographic features in their reports. Some examples are the reports by Lieutenant Colonel Edward L. Campbell, Colonel Charles H. Tompkins, and Lieutenant John T. Grant. Campbell, commander of the 15th New Jersey Infantry, who was temporarily commanding the First Brigade, First Division, Sixth Army Corps, mentions Berryville Turnpike, a wooded hill, open ground, the crest of a hill, a ravine, cornfield, and a dwelling house in his report.[45] Tompkins, commander of the First Rhode Island Light Artillery, mentions Berryville Pike, a ravine, a cornfield, a ridge, woods, and a brick house in his report.[46] Grant, commander of the Fifth New York Battery, mentions Opequon Creek, woods, dense undergrowth, and a deep ravine in his report.[47] No matter the type of unit, topographic features were frequently mentioned in the reports of officers who were commanding units at the tactical level.

Higher ranking officers, who were also involved in the tactical level, also mentioned topographic features in their reports. An example of this can be found in the report of General George Crook, commander of the Army of West Virginia. In his report, he stated,

> The road to be passed over [Berryville Turnpike] led through a narrow defile, whose sides were covered with a dense undergrowth of pine, rendering it very difficult to move along, except on the pike, and that was so blockaded by ammunition wagons, battery wagons, forges, ambulances, and stragglers going to the rear that the progress of the infantry was greatly impeded and the artillery was unable to come up for an hour after, having been compelled to halt at almost every step by the press in the road.[48]

Later, in the same report, General Crook continued,

> Colonel Duval [Isaac H. Duval, commander of the Second Infantry Division, Army of West Virginia], after getting squarely around, charged the enemy in flank and found him strongly posted behind a stone wall with his left flank resting on an almost impassable morass, named Red Bud Run, which it was necessary for him to cross. The rough and uneven ground, the tangled thickets on the bank of this slough, and the great difficulty experienced by the men in crossing, as it was very deep and miry in places, broke the lines completely and mingled the men of the different regiments and brigades into one great throng.[49]

General Crook in his report does mention other topographic features beyond Red Bud Creek and stone fences. Crook's comments were not an exception as General Emory Upton, commander of the First Division, Sixth Army Corps, in his report on the battle mentions woods, fences, a stone wall, Berryville Pike, and a brick house.[50] Also, General Wesley Merritt, brigade general, commander of the First Cavalry Division, in his report on the battle mentions Seiver's Ford, Opequon Creek, Locke's Ford, a railroad cut, rail barricades, the crest of a hill, and a brick house.[51] Even Sheridan was directly impacted by topography/geography during the battle. When General Emory Upton was making his attack on the Confederates, Sheridan, due to trees, did not have any idea of the effectiveness of Upton's attack until a messenger informed him.[52]

In autobiographies and letters, the view of the battlefield became even more topographic. In his autobiography, Captain French Harding (Confederate States of America) discusses his experiences during the Third Battle of Winchester. He wrote that when his company was on the left of General Stephen Ramseur's division, he could see the extensive plain west of Winchester on which Union cavalry would make the charge that broke the Confederate left and forced the Confederate Army to retreat. Lemuel Abbott, a captain in the Tenth Regiment Vermont Volunteer Infantry, mentioned the Opequon Creek, Berryville Canyon with its "second growth or scrub oak and ash trees and underbrush coming close down its scraggy abrupt banks," a belt of timber, ravines, open fields, as well as the lack of cover.[53] For these men, topography was everything.

The Battle

Although the battle covers a large area, it can be broken down into two different geographic areas—a center section, which was an infantry and artillery fight, and a northern section, which was Federal cavalry and horse artillery against a mixed force of Confederate infantry, cavalry, and artillery. The southern part of the fight involving James Wilson's cavalry division is not included in this analysis as that part of the battlefield remained relatively stable with limited action.

In the center, the fighting began when General Wilson's Federal cavalry division pushed through the Berryville Canyon before dawn, followed by the infantry of the Sixth Corps under General Horatio Wright, followed by the 19th Corps under General William Emory with General George Crook's Army of West Virginia in reserve.[54] For the Confederates, General Stephen Ramseur's division was covering the road from Berryville, General Robert Rodes' division was at Stephenson's Depot, General John Gordon's division was at Bunker Hill with orders to march to Stephenson's Depot at daylight on the 19th, and General John Breckinridge's was at Stephenson's Depot.[55] Wilson's cavalry very quickly cleared the Confederates away from the entrance to the Berryville Canyon, but the Federal infantry and its accompanying artillery were slow in getting through the narrow canyon—geography had immediately impacted the battle. If the restriction of the canyon had not slowed the Federal deployment, Ramseur's division of about 2,000 men would have been facing two Federal corps of about 26,000 men—tremendous odds.[56] It was not until 11:40 a.m. that the two Federal corps were lined up and ready to advance—a delay of over five hours. This delay gave Rodes's and Gordon's division enough time to reach the battlefield and ruined Sheridan's hope of engaging only part of Early's army rather than all of it.[57]

Once the Federal advance began, it was successful but immediately ran into strong Confederate resistance. Still, a number of Confederate units were forced to retreat with some being routed. One Federal brigade, Henry Birge's, chased Gordon's retreating men and outran the supporting units to their left and right but were right behind the Confederates. Once the Confederates and Federals passed through Second Woods, the Federals entered an excellent artillery killing zone. However, their closeness to the retreating Confederates protected them until the Confederates were out of the way of their supporting artillery. The seven guns of Major Carter Braxton's battalion firing double canister were able to completely stop the Federal charge and force them to retreat. Photograph 6–3 shows the ground where the Federal charge took place and where they were stopped by Braxton's artillery. Braxton could not have asked for a better killing ground, as it was open with no cover for the Federals. This was the perfect topography for artillery to show its destructive power.

6. Geography and the Third Battle of Winchester　109

Photograph 6–3: The artillery killing ground.

Unfortunately, for the Federals, due to their advance, their once-continuous line began to develop gaps in it. One problem was, as previously mentioned, that Berryville Canyon was at the bottom of a *V* and that the farther the Federal infantry advanced from it, the wider the front it had to cover. In addition, Confederate resistance, which slowed some units down, as well as the broken terrain contributed to the development of the gaps. The Confederates, being veterans, were quick to notice and exploit the gaps and their attack drove the Federals back. However, there were not enough Confederates to completely defeat the Federals, and the lines of both sides stabilized.

Around 12:00 p.m. Crook was ordered to move his troops forward to the battlefield.[58] However, as previously discussed, the blockage caused by the Berryville Canyon delayed his progress for a number of hours—a geographic problem of trying to put too much through a very limited space. Sheridan had originally planned to place Crook's units on the left flank so that they could cut the Valley Pike, Early's route of retreat.[59] However, Confederate pressure on his right flank caused him to order Crook to the right. An issue facing Crook was that the Confederate left flank was anchored on Red Bud Run—"an almost impassable morass."[60] Crook's Second Division crossed the run behind the Federal line without opposition. They then advanced westward until they were on the left flank of the Confederates. Consequently, it was not until about 4:00 p.m. that Crook's units were able to make a coordinated and successful attack.[61] Crook's Second Division had trouble recrossing Red Bud Run, as "this creek and the rough ground and tangled thicket on its banks was in easy range of grape, canister, and musketry from the rebel line. A very destructive fire was opened upon us, in the midst of which our men rushed into and over the creek."[62] However, they were successful due to the fact that at the same time, the Federals on the other side of the creek were also attacking. Then, about the same time that the Federal infantry were attacking, the Federal cavalry on the northern part of the battlefield were also making an attack.

As Sheridan was concentrating on the infantry attack in the center, the northern part of the battlefield was controlled by General Alfred Torbert, Sheridan's chief of cavalry. General Wesley Merritt's division was ordered to cross the Opequon Creek at Seivers' and Locke's Fords while General William Averell's division was to cross the Opequon north of those fords and advance on Winchester by the Winchester and Martinsburg Pike.[63] Merritt's crossing was opposed, but his men were across the creek before sunrise.[64] The Confederates fighting Merritt were forced to retreat again around 1:30 p.m. when Averell's division, coming from the north, got behind them. The two cavalry divisions then reunited on the Winchester and Martinsburg Pike in the vicinity of Stephenson's Depot. By this time, Breckinridge's infantry had been ordered to reinforce the main Confederate line, seriously weakening the far Confederate left flank. The weakness of the Confederates facing Torbert's two cavalry divisions, along with the topography, gave the Federal cavalry an opportunity not seen in the war.

The open and relatively flat country north of Winchester gave the Federal cavalry the terrain it needed to make a massive charge against the Confederate left flank. Geography came into play as the ground was dry, and Early had only one feasible route of retreat. If it had been very wet that month, the terrain would have been boggy, and any cavalry charge would have had trouble rapidly traversing the terrain. The fact that Early had to transfer troops to his right flank to protect his line of retreat also played a major role in the success of the Union cavalry. If Early had a different or multiple lines of retreat that were in locations inaccessible to Union forces, he could have kept his left flank strong and possibly defeated the Union cavalry charge. It was this charge in the late afternoon that decided the battle. Without this successful charge, the Confederates would probably have held out until nightfall and then made an orderly retreat. The cavalry charge at Winchester is the only time during the Civil War in which a cavalry charge decided a major battle. It was the most successful large cavalry charge during the war, and the topography/geography around Winchester made it possible.

Photograph 6-4 shows the interior of Fort Collier, one of the main anchors for the Confederate left flank, while Photograph 6-5 shows the ground to the immediate north of Fort Collier. There is a famous painting of the charge by artist Thure de Thulstrup that was completed in 1880. Although it is a very dramatic and quality painting, it is not historically correct. Fort Collier was located on a small hill, which gave it a height advantage over the surrounding countryside. Photograph 6-5 shows how the ground to the north of Fort Collier slopes away. Unfortunately, due to the trees and the industrial buildup in the area, it is difficult but not impossible to envision the charge, as the ground is still flat to the north of the fort.

6. *Geography and the Third Battle of Winchester* 111

Photograph 6-4: The interior of Fort Collier.

Photograph 6-5: Looking north from Fort Collier.

Regrettably, many people gain their knowledge of the terrain fought over during Third Winchester from paintings and drawings done well after the event and/or by people who have never visited the site. The only way to truly appreciate a battlefield's terrain is to visit it and hope that it has not been significantly changed since the battle.

***

The successful Federal cavalry charge along with the coordinated Federal infantry attack ended the battle with the Confederate defenses breaking down late afternoon around 4:30 p.m. It had been an all-day battle with some of the Federal Soldiers being up for about 18 hours. For the Confederates, darkness saved them from greater losses, as it became dark a little past 6:00 p.m. and the Federal pursuit ended at dark. Geography had worked for and against both sides. The narrow Berryville Canyon and Opequon Creek had delayed Federal deployment, while the open and flat ground north of Winchester had allowed the Federal cavalry to make a massive charge only seen once in the war.

After the Battle

Sheridan's decisive victory at Winchester on the 19th of September and his subsequent victory at Fisher's Hill on the 22nd of September gave him the opportunity to destroy the lower Valley's ability to provide supplies to the Confederates as ordered by General Ulysses S. Grant in August: "Do all the damage to railroads and crops you can. Carry off stock of all descriptions, and negroes, so as to prevent further planting. If the war is to last another year, we want the Shenandoah Valley to remain a barren waste."[65] Sheridan ensured that his troops carried out those orders. As a result, the destruction was extensive. He informed General Grant on the 7th of October that the destruction included "2,000 barns, filled with wheat, hay, and farming implements; over 70 mills, filled with flour and wheat, have driven in front of the army over 4,[000] head of stock, and have killed and issued to the troops not less than 3,000 head of sheep."[66]

Although Sheridan's numbers may be inflated, the destruction of the farms in the Valley had an impact on Confederate operations. Prior to the Battle of Cedar Creek, 19 October 1864, Early was unable to remain at Fisher's Hill for the want of forage.[67] Early stated in his report to General Robert E. Lee, concerning the Battle of Cedar Creek, that he halted his army's advance due to the large number of men who had stopped to plunder the Union camps.[68] Although Early's statement was disputed by some former Confederates, with the most notable being General John Gordon, there are a number of personal reminiscences and letters, including Henry Kyd Douglas's reminiscences, that state that a large number of Confederates stopped to plunder the Union camps.[69] Hunger is a tremendous motivator, and with the Confederates being short of food, the temptation to eat the food abandoned in the Union camps would have been too great to resist. Thus, the lack of food for the men and horses in Early's army played a major role in the Battle of Cedar Creek, which will be discussed in Chapter 7.

Even after the Battle of Cedar Creek and after Lee had recalled a large part of Early's army, the devastation of the Valley impacted Confederate operations although the remaining force was small. Early informed Lee in early October 1864, "He [Sheridan] has laid waste to nearly all of Rockingham and Shenandoah [Counties], and I will have to rely on Augusta [Augusta County, Virginia] for my supplies, and they are not abundant there. Sheridan's purpose, under Grant's orders, has been to render the Valley untenable by our troops by destroying the supplies."[70]

Early's situation did not improve with time, as in November, he informed the Confederate government, "The supplies are so limited in the Valley that unless they are kept here [the Shenandoah Valley] my troops cannot be subsisted. I have, therefore, directed that all supplies be stopped unless by your special permission."[71] Sheridan had destroyed the lower Valley's ability to support a large Confederate force as well as the ability of the upper Valley to send supplies to Richmond. Geography had made the Valley an important source of supplies for the Confederacy as well as an avenue of invasion of the North. It became necessary for the Union to destroy its agriculture in order to cut off support for the Confederate armies and to eliminate its use by Confederate forces to invade or raid Maryland and Pennsylvania.

Beyond influencing the Valley's ability to supply Confederate forces, the destruction also, as one of its unintended consequences, impacted Union forces. However, the effect on Union forces was not as serious as it was to the Confederates because the Union Army was well supplied from Harpers Ferry. But due to the destruction, there was a limit as to how far a Union army could move up the Valley. Sheridan stated in his report on the campaign that he was confident his transportation could not supply him farther than Harrisonburg, about 75 miles south of Winchester but about 100 miles from Harpers Ferry, Sheridan's main supply base.[72] Sheridan's statement is reinforced by General John D. Stevenson's (commander of the Military District of Harpers Ferry and responsible for the supply depot located there) message to Secretary of War Edwin Stanton: "No army [Sheridan's army] of such magnitude relying upon its rear for supplies can be maintained for a greater distance than 100 miles without either water or railroad transit."[73] Sheridan's statement is further reinforced by Charles A. Dana, assistant secretary of war. Dana informed General John A. Rawlins, Grant's chief of staff, on the 29th of October after visiting the Shenandoah Valley and Sheridan,

> Besides, the devastation of the Valley, extending as it does for a distance of about 100 miles, renders it almost impossible that either the Confederates or our own forces should make a new campaign in that territory; and when Sheridan has completed that same process down the Valley to the vicinity of the Potomac, and when the stores of forage which are yet to be found in Loudoun County and in some parts of Fauquier, and the animals that are still there are all destroyed or removed, the difficulty of any new offensive operations on either side will have been greatly increased.[74]

Dana went on to state, "The opening of the Winchester railroad to this point—an affair of not more than eight or ten days—will render it possible to supply the garrison with safety and economy; and this line of railroad communication can be defended with a less force than is now required to escort the wagon trains which supply Sheridan from Martinsburg and Harper's [sic] Ferry."[75]

Sheridan's concern for supplies was such that he informed General Halleck on the 29th of October, ten days after the Battle of Cedar Creek, that he wanted the railroad repaired between Harpers Ferry and Winchester as his horses were suffering very much, and he could not be supplied by wagon.[76] An additional geographic problem, beyond receiving adequate supplies, was that the farther south Federal forces went, the greater the danger of a flank attack through one of the passes in the Blue Ridge Mountains. This was a threat Sheridan was well aware of as the possibility of being outflanked was the major reason for his retreat down the Valley from Strasburg to Halltown in mid-August 1864.

The destruction of the farm supplies in the Valley also impacted future operations of Sheridan's forces. After he had defeated and dispersed Early's army, Grant wanted Sheridan to cross the mountains and destroy the Central Railroad, which connected the Shenandoah Valley to Richmond. However, Sheridan informed Grant, "It will be exceedingly difficult for me to carry the infantry column over the mountains and strike at the Central Road. I cannot accumulate sufficient stores to do so, and think it best to take some position near Front Royal, and operate with cavalry and infantry."[77] Sheridan was fortunate he had proven himself as an aggressive and successful leader, for if someone other than Sheridan had informed Grant that he could not comply with his orders, they most likely would have been replaced. Still, Sheridan was probably correct in telling Grant he could not accomplish what Grant wished. One reason is that it may have been possible for Lee to detach a large enough force from Petersburg/Richmond to defeat Sheridan, who would have been a long way from any supporting units, before Grant could react. Such a defeat, just prior to the upcoming presidential election, could have had a very negative impact on Lincoln's reelection.

The Confederacy's inability to retain control of Winchester led to other disasters. In December 1864, Federal forces were finally able to make a successful attack on Saltville. The success of the raid was directly due to the Confederacy's inability to adequately protect the Valley and its resources. The loss of Winchester was a direct reflection of the fact that Confederate manpower requirements could no longer be met. Winchester was like the "canary in a mine," and its death/loss showed that the cause was doomed.

***

Geography dictated that Winchester would be an important town during the Civil War, and because it was indefensible (unless it was manned by a very large garrison), control of the town would change numerous times during the war.[78] The location of the city in the lower Valley was the point the Union needed to control to stop Confederate forces from using the Valley as a highway to the North. For the Confederacy, control of Winchester gave it many options of taking the war to the north as well as being able to keep a large force supplied with food and forage. These two factors increased the city's importance to the Confederacy well beyond its importance as an urban center. While geography dictated the importance of Winchester, topography was important at the lower levels of command. Topography became important when the city was to be defended or attacked, and the value of various topographic features varied depending on the individual's level of command. The importance of geography to the conduct of a war cannot be overemphasized, and anyone wishing to understand a war or battle needs to appreciate the impact geography had on that event.

7

Geography and the Battle of Cedar Creek

19 October 1864

Sheridan's destruction of the agriculture in the middle and lower Valley had an immediate benefit for him, more than he realized.

Although it was not the last battle in the Valley, the Battle of Cedar Creek was the last major battle fought for control of Winchester and was heavily influenced by geography before, during, and after the battle. Before the battle, the destruction of the agricultural resources south of Cedar Creek directly impacted General Jubal Early's options. At the same time, the destruction and defeats the Confederates had suffered gave the Federal forces a false sense of security. Consequently, the disposition of the Federal forces at Cedar Creek, which was based on the area's geography and topography, gave the Confederates an opportunity to attack the weakest flank of the Federal camp. During the battle, the creek, fog, soil conditions, Valley Turnpike, and topography greatly influenced how it was fought. After the battle, as the Confederates were retreating, a bridge became blocked, and because the creek was unfordable for vehicles in that area, many of the artillery pieces and wagons were captured along with many of the men being killed or captured. One small geographic feature can have an impact well beyond what would seem reasonable.

The Battle of Cedar Creek was the second largest battle numerically in the struggle for Winchester with 15,265 Confederates attacking 31,944 Federals. However, a northern newspaper report gave the Confederate's a strength of 30,000, a number of men that Early probably wished he did have.[1] This battle, like Third Winchester, lasted an entire day. Initially, the Confederates enjoyed a massive early success, but the Federals recovered and inflicted a substantial defeat on the Confederates. The result of the battle was that it ended Confederate attempts to regain complete control of the Valley.

Two maps are included that cover the Battle of Cedar Creek. Each of the maps shows different aspects of the fighting, and both need to be viewed to get a full understanding of the battle since no single map can adequately convey all of the details of a location or event. Map 7–1 was created by Hal Jespersen and gives an

7. Geography and the Battle of Cedar Creek 117

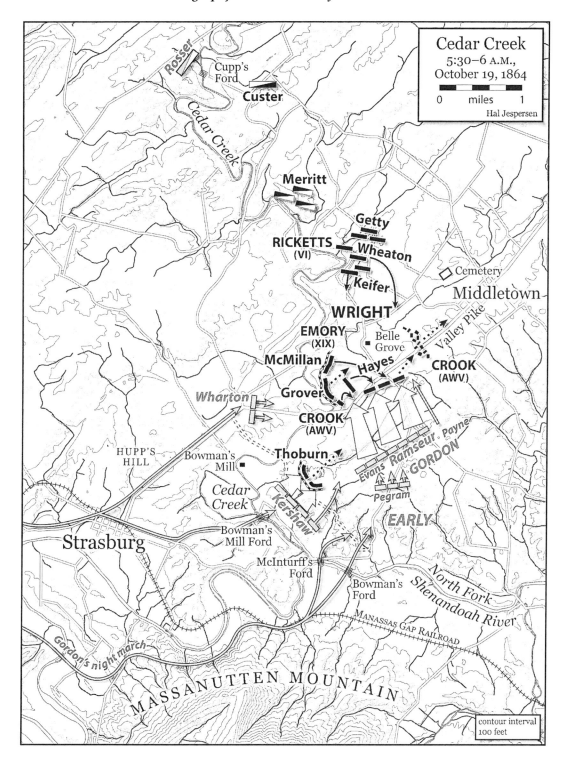

Map 7-1: The Battle of Cedar Creek.

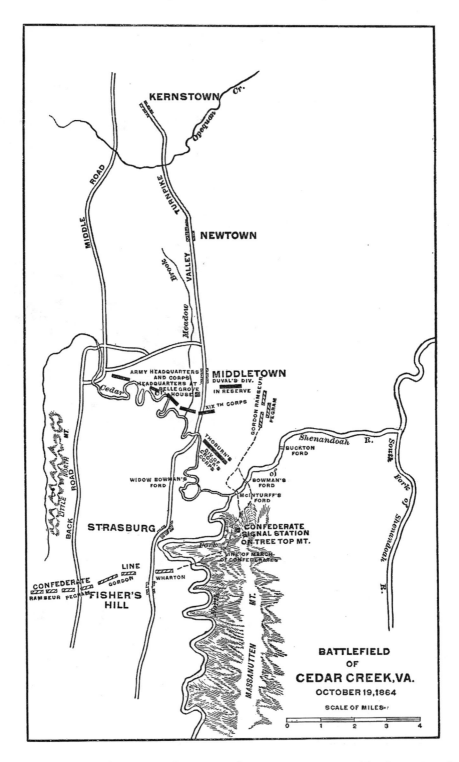

Map 7-2: Battlefield of Cedar Creek, Virginia (by Henry A. Du Pont, *The Campaign of 1864 in the Valley of Virginia and the Expedition to Lynchburg*, National Americana Society, New York, 1925).

overview of the initial Confederate attack. Map 7–2 is from Henry A. Du Pont's autobiography and shows how the Federal forces were aligned just prior to the battle.

***

There was only a month between the Third Battle of Winchester and the Battle of Cedar Creek, but even during that short time, there had been a number of significant actions. The siege at Petersburg continued with a Federal victory at Fort Harrison along with the extension of the siege lines farther south. This extension put additional pressure on the available manpower in the Army of Northern Virginia forcing Lee to consider decreasing the number of men under Early unless he could be more successful and tie down additional Federal forces. Sterling Price's raid into Missouri continued and appeared to be very successful.

In the Valley, Early was defeated at Fisher's Hill, and Sheridan's men began "the burning" of agricultural resources in the middle and lower Valley. The Confederate cavalry suffered an embarrassing defeat at Tom's Brook. This defeat highlighted the superiority the Federal cavalry now had over the Confederate cavalry. Once Philip Sheridan was satisfied with the destruction his army had carried out, he moved it back to Cedar Creek. A positive for the Confederates was that a Federal attack on Saltville, Virginia, with its vital salt industry, was repulsed.

***

For both Abraham Lincoln and Jefferson Davis, their respective geographic grand strategies had not changed. Lincoln wanted the country reunited, and Davis wanted an independent Confederacy, mutually opposing views. For Lincoln, Sheridan's victory at the Third Battle of Winchester and his follow-up victory at Fisher's Hill solved a number of problems. First, it severely restricted opportunities for the Confederates to make raids into Maryland and Pennsylvania. Second, it helped Lincoln's reelection efforts. It would have appeared to the casual viewer in the North that the Confederate threat from the Valley had finally been crushed. For Davis, Sheridan's victories were a blow to Confederate morale, especially since Atlanta had been taken a few weeks before the fall of Winchester. The loss of Confederate territory and resources was continuing at a rapid pace.

Grant viewed Sheridan's victory at Winchester as an opportunity to gain reinforcements for Petersburg from units in the Valley. Both Sheridan and Grant assumed Early was no longer capable of offensive actions due to his defeats at Winchester and Fisher's Hill and the losses he had sustained at each. Consequently, General Horatio Wright's VI Corps was ordered to leave the valley and return to Petersburg. Both Sheridan and Grant badly miscalculated Early's and Robert E. Lee's aggressiveness and willingness to take risks. Lee fully understood the impact a major Confederate victory in the Valley would have on Northern morale and the upcoming election. However, with the Federals now in control of Winchester, Lee had lost the initiative and was forced to react to Federal moves rather than the

Federals reacting to his. Consequently, he had to order General James Kershaw's division, which was on their way to Petersburg, to return to the Valley. Lee needed Early to continue tying down Federal forces in the Valley as well as causing enough of a disruption that it would impact the upcoming election. Lee felt the potential gain was worth the risk.

Sheridan's victories at the Third Battle of Winchester and Fisher's Hill (22 September 1864) allowed him to gain control of the lower and middle parts of the Valley. Then from the 6th of October until the 10th of October, as his army retired (I use the word *retired* as Sheridan was not forced to retreat) down the Valley back toward Winchester, Sheridan set his men to work destroying as much of the agriculture in the Valley as they could.[2] The destruction went from Harrisonburg to Cedar Creek. Sheridan reported that he "stretched the cavalry across the Valley from the Blue Ridge to the eastern slope of the Alleghanies [sic], with directions to burn all forage and drive off all stock, &c., as they moved to the rear, fully coinciding in the views and instructions of the lieutenant-general [Grant], that the Valley should be made a barren waste."[3] While Sheridan's final report on the total amount of destruction may have been exaggerated, the destruction met its goal of there not being enough food and forage for any sizable Confederate force to sustain itself in the middle or lower Valley for any length of time. Consequently, Early was forced to attack or retreat. Sheridan's destruction directly impacted Early's options.

Although today, it may seem odd to us that the lack of forage would impact Early's operations, it must be remembered that horses and mules were the "engines" of the day. They provided personal transportation, were used by the cavalry, and pulled the wagons and artillery. Today, fuel is the largest, bulkiest, heaviest class of supply used by the military. If our engines do not get the required amount of fuel, they cannot operate. It was a similar situation when horses and mules were the "engines." Adequate forage was essential, and without it, an army could not efficiently operate. As stated earlier, a horse was authorized 26 pounds of food a day with that being a mixture of grain and grass/hay. The problem for both sides was that it was mid–October, and the grass in the local area would have not been plentiful, and what grass there was would have been quickly eaten by the animals. Also, the armies had been campaigning in this area for a long time and what forage had existed was probably already consumed. The challenge for both sides was transporting enough forage to the camps for the horses and mules. Sheridan's army was able to accomplish this, but Early's was not. By this stage of the Civil War, the Confederacy was running out of horses and mules, while the Federals could still provide their forces with an adequate number, although their generals probably wanted more. This, along with better firearms (such as the Spencer repeating carbine), training, and aggressive officers, allowed the Federal cavalry to finally overwhelm the now less numerous Confederate cavalry who, all too often, were riding weaker horses.

***

For Early, the reinforcements Lee sent to him gave him the ability to conduct offensive operations, and with those units, Lee told Early, "The enemy must be defeated, and I rely upon you to do it."[4] Early was aware that part of Sheridan's forces were being sent to reinforce Grant. Consequently, on the 13th of October, he placed artillery on Hupp's Hill (which is north of Strasburg and south of Cedar Creek along the Valley Turnpike) and bombarded the Federal camps across Cedar Creek. In response, the Federal First Division of VIII Corps was ordered to cross the creek and attack the Confederate artillery. Since Early had two divisions in the area, the Federal attack failed. However, the failure alerted Sheridan to the possibility of a Confederate assault, and he ordered the Sixth Corps, which was on its way to Petersburg, to return to Cedar Creek. Although Early's attack had achieved its purpose, it was a hollow victory because it caused the Federal army he wanted to attack and possibly destroy to be reinforced by the Sixth Corps, who would play an important role in stopping Early's attack at Cedar Creek.

When Sheridan departed for his trip to Washington on the 16th of October, he left General Horatio Wright, commander of the VI Corps, in command and took most of the cavalry, under Brevet Major General Alfred T.A. Torbert, as they were to conduct a raid to Charlottesville after they crossed the Blue Ridge Mountains.[5] The cavalry units with Sheridan were Torbert's First Division under Brigadier General Wesley Merritt and the Second Division under Colonel William H. Powell.[6] On the night of the 16th at Front Royal, Sheridan received a message from Wright that information had been intercepted stating that James Longstreet's forces were in the process of reinforcing Early with the idea of crushing Sheridan. Wright also stated, "If the enemy should be strongly re-enforced in cavalry, he might, by turning our right, give us a good deal of trouble. I shall hold on here until the enemy's movements are developed, and shall only fear an attack on my right, which I shall make every preparation for guarding against and resisting."[7] The message had been sent by the Confederates knowing the Federals would intercept it. The idea behind the message was that it would retain Federal units in the Valley so that they would not be transferred to Petersburg, but Sheridan did not know this. Although Sheridan decided to continue on his trip, he also decided to "give to General Wright the entire strength of the army."[8] Accordingly, he ordered Merritt's division to return to Cedar Creek while Powell remained in his camp at Front Royal. Again, these were reinforcements that would play an important role in the Federal victory.

When Merritt arrived, his division was placed on the western (right) flank of the Federal Army with the rest of the cavalry—the flank Wright was most worried about. This left all of the picketing duties to the infantry on the Federal eastern/left flank. However, the infantry units only posted pickets close to their camps, as this was their normal procedure, and failed to post more distant pickets.[9] Captain Henry Du Pont stated in his autobiography that it seemed to him "that our left flank was very inadequately protected."[10] His fear was that if the left flank was turned, "it would be extremely difficult, if not impossible, to withdrawal the pieces [his artillery guns]."[11] Du Pont was told that Powell's cavalry was protecting the left flank, but when Du Pont rode out to find them, he could not. No cavalry was on that flank because it was assumed by many that the Federal left flank was safe due to geography/topography, a mistaken assumption.

A general posting of the Federal Army before the battle can be seen on Map 7–2. Most of the army was to the west of the Valley Turnpike with the units to the east of the Turnpike pushed forward due to the bending of Cedar Creek. The problem was that the Federals had grown complacent. General Wright stated in his post battle report,

> About 9 o'clock of the evening [18th of October] I was called upon by Major-General Crook, commanding the Army of West Virginia, who reported that the reconnaissance of a brigade sent out by him that day to ascertain the position of the enemy had returned to camp and reported that nothing was to be found in his [the Confederate] old camp and that he had doubtless retreated up the Valley. It should be borne in mind that the destruction of all supplies by our forces between our position at Cedar Creek and Staunton had made it necessary for the enemy to supply his force from the latter place by wagons, and consequently we had been expecting for some days that he would either attack us or be compelled to fall back for the supplies, which it was believed he could not transport in sufficient quantity by his trains. This view of the matter, which is still believed to be sound, lent the stamp of probability to the report of the reconnoitering party.[12]

Wright, being cautious, ordered out additional reconnaissance parties for the 19th "to place the truth of the report beyond a doubt."[13] However, in all probability, the men in Crook's units had heard about the results of the reconnaissance on the 18th and felt that there was no threat from the Confederates. As a result, they let down their watchfulness.

The Battlefield

The Valley is about four miles wide where Cedar Creek joins the North Fork of the Shenandoah River. Cedar Creek is a winding creek with a narrow channel and steep banks making passage of it difficult. Just to the south of the creek, on the east side of the turnpike is the northern end of Massanutten Mountain. Whereas Hupp's Hill, on the west side of the turnpike, was an excellent observation post and artillery position for the Confederates (as previously mentioned), Signal Knob on Three Top Mountain offered a panoramic view of the Valley north of Massanutten to include a superb opportunity to examine the Federal camp along Cedar Creek. It was from Signal Knob that General John Gordon, General Clement Evans, Major Robert Hunter, and Captain Jed Hotchkiss viewed the Federal camp and its defenses. General Gordon wrote after the war that they could see

> not only the general outlines of Sheridan's breastworks, but every parapet where his heavy guns were mounted, and every position of artillery, every wagon and tent and supporting lines of troops, were in easy range of our vision. I could count, and did count, the number of his guns. I could see distinctly the three colors of trimmings on the jackets respectively of infantry, artillery, and cavalry, and locate each, while the number of flags gave a basis for estimating approximately the forces which we were to contend in the proposed attack.[14]

7. Geography and the Battle of Cedar Creek

It was a rare opportunity for an army during the Civil War to have such intelligence on their opponent. This reconnaissance allowed Hotchkiss to create a map of the Federal positions and for the men on the reconnaissance to develop the plan that would be adopted by Early to attack Sheridan's army. Photographs 7-1 and 7-2 were taken from Signal Knob. The view of the lower Valley from that point is spectacular, and Gordon, Evans, Hunter, and Hotchkiss would have had an excellent view of the Federal camp.[15]

The major problem with the plan was how to get a large enough force to attack the relatively unguarded Federal left flank when the route was blocked by Massanutten and that the Shenandoah River flowed at the base of Massanutten. General Gordon, General Stephen Ramseur, and Captain Hotchkiss made a reconnaissance and found a route that was then improved by pioneers under Hotchkiss's command. Then three divisions of infantry had to quietly ford the cold (it was mid–October) Shenandoah River, march along a narrow path within hearing distance of Federal pickets, and cross the cold Shenandoah River again to make their attack. All of this had to be done at night. Their route of march can be seen on Maps 7-1 and 7-2. Captain William J. Seymour wrote after the war,

> A little after dark the first named Divisions [Gordon's and Pegram's—Seymour does not include Ramseur's division as it also made the march] were put in light marching order, the men being divested of their canteens & everything that could rattle or make a noise so that they could get as near as possible to the enemy before the movement could be detected. Gen. Gordon, who commanded this portion of the expedition, led his men far around to the right

Photograph 7-1: View of the lower Valley from Signal Knob.

Photograph 7-2: Looking down onto the location where the Federal camp would have been from Signal Knob.

of the enemy & for a considerable distance over a mountain path which was so narrow that the men had to march single file.[16]

It was an audacious movement that had to overcome a number of geological obstacles.

The majority of the battlefield was relatively open ground with rolling hills, although it was broken up by stone fences and ravines. In addition, the Federals had constructed fortifications. Another man-made feature that would come into play was the town of Middletown, as it was an obstacle and provided protection to the retreating Federal troops. Once the early morning fog had lifted, there was no problem with both sides seeing each other's deployments.

The Battle

The start of the fighting varies depending on the individual, but all would have agreed that it started before dawn with most of the men in the Federal Army still asleep. The Federal Army was taken by surprise. E.A. Paul, a reporter for the *New York Times*, stated in his article about the battle,

> One thing is certain; the command of Gen. CROOK [sic] was taken entirely by surprise; so complete, indeed, was it that few or no men were in the line of earthworks; in fact, they could have made but a poor defence [sic] had they been there, for a galling fire was poured in upon their flank. The panic that followed it is impossible to describe. Officers present at the

time can give only a meagre account of it. They heard the whistle of innummerable [sic] bullets, the yelping of the enemy, but could not see exactly where they were, or from what point attacked.[17]

Although it would be easy to discredit the conduct of these men, I would challenge anyone who does to wake up under a surprise attack by an enemy that is supposedly defeated, that is being conducted in the dark and fog, when you do not know where the enemy is, how many enemies there are, your unit in disorder, and not have a panic occur.

All participants commented on the dense fog that, combined with the smoke from the artillery and rifles, made it difficult for Federal forces to know where the Confederates were coming from and for the Confederate commanders to know what was happening. The fog was a geographic phenomenon created by the combination of the water in Cedar Creek, the temperature, and lack of wind. Federal captain Henry Du Pont, when informed shortly after the attack that one of his artillery batteries was ready to fire with canister but no enemy could be seen, ordered the battery to fire as it was "very important that everyone should understand that a general engagement had begun."[18] When then asked where to fire, Du Pont ordered them to "fire to the left in the direction of the sound."[19] The fog also created a problem for the Confederate commanders. Early stated in his postwar memoirs, "There was now a heavy fog, and that, with the smoke from the artillery and small arms, so obscured objects that the enemy's position could not be seen."[20] Still, the fog probably had a greater effect on the Federals as it accentuated their confusion while the individual Confederate Soldiers knew exactly what they needed to do.

Fog was not the only geographic problem the Federals faced. The terrain created problems for an orderly withdrawal for those units that were still organized. Crook stated in his post-battle report, "The ground to be passed over was one succession of hills and ravines, so that it was impossible for troops to make a rapid retreat in anything like good order."[21] Even the modifications the Federals had made to the terrain with their entrenchments did not help, as Gordon's units were able to outflank them and force the Federals to retreat. As always, modifications to geography/topography are only effective if properly placed for the situation.

For the Confederates, the Valley Turnpike, although it had been used for part of their movement to Cedar Creek, became an obstacle to the rapid advance of their artillery. The turnpike was important for the Confederate artillery as it was not possible for them to follow the infantry in their cross-country movement. However, the artillery had to wait until the battle had begun due to the "fear of attracting the attention of the enemy by the rumbling of the wheels over the macadamized road."[22] Technology can modify geography but comes with its own set of constraints.

The fog began to dissipate approximately four to five hours after the battle began, around 9:00 a.m., and both sides could now see each other clearly. The lifting of the fog helped the Federals as they could now see where the Confederate attacks were coming from and the number of men involved. However, the Confederates were still able to push the Federal units back, but the rate at which the Federals were retreating slowed. The continued resistance of the Federal VI Corps, which had not been attacked by the Confederates in the initial assaults, was the key to the Federal defense. The VI Corps was strongly posted, and Early wrote in his postwar memoirs, "Discovering that the 6th corps could not be attacked with advantage on its left flank, because the approach in the direction was through an open flat and across a boggy stream with deep banks."[23] However, Confederate artillery and the threat of being outflanked forced the Federals to retreat, but they retreated in an orderly manner.

The Confederate initial offensive ended around noon for a variety of reasons. First, overconfidence on the part of Early that Federals had been broken and demoralized and would retreat. Wright was still in command—although he was not the charismatic leader Sheridan was—and he and his corps had not been defeated. Still, a significant number of the Federal Soldiers thought the battle had been lost and were retreating in disorder to Winchester along with many of the supply wagons. However, more than enough men remained, and their officers had been able to reestablish control of their units. The Federal Army was not going to retreat any further unless forced to.

Second, with the fog having dissipated, the Federal forces could now see the Confederates and could see that they outnumbered them, which boosted their spirits and emboldened their resistance. In addition, the country became more open farther away from Cedar Creek, and the concentrated Federal cavalry became a threat to the Confederates. The small number of Confederate cavalry could not contain the numerically superior Federal cavalry, and having seen what happened when the massed Federal cavalry charged at Winchester, Early and his men were extremely worried about the situation.

Third, the Confederates had been up all night and had been fighting since before dawn. They were tired and hungry. This led to men leaving the ranks for food. Sheridan's destruction of the ability of the middle Valley to supply enough food for Early's men provided an unintended consequence that helped the Federals. The lack of food resulted in a significant number of the Confederate Soldiers leaving the battle line to look for food in the overrun Federal camps. Early claimed that this event helped lead to the Confederate defeat. Although some individuals, General John Gordon being the most prominent, disputed Early's claim, there is ample evidence to support it. D. Augustus Dicket, a company commander in Kershaw's brigade, wrote that at the beginning of the battle,

> the smoking breakfast, just ready for the table, stood temptingly inviting, while the opened tents displayed a scene almost enchanting to the eyes of the Southern soldier, in the way of costly blankets, overcoats, dress uniforms, hat caps, boots, and shoes all thrown in wild confusion over the face of the earth. Now and then a suttler's [sic] tent displayed all the luxuries and dainties a soldier's heart could wish for. All this fabulous wealth of provisions and clothing looked to the half-fed, half-clothed Confederates like the wealth of the Indies. The soldiers broke over all order and discipline for a moment or two and helped themselves.[24]

After the morning fighting had ended, Dicket wrote, "But the halt was fatal—fatal to our great victory, fatal to our army, and who can say not fatal to our cause. Such a planned battle, such complete success, such a total rout of the enemy was never before experienced—all to be lost either by a fatal blunder or the greed of the soldier for spoils. Only a small per cent comparatively was engaged in the plundering, but enough to weaken our ranks."[25]

I. Gordon Bradwell, a Soldier in General Gordon's old brigade, wrote after the war that after the initial assault, only one other man was with him, and

> I suggested to my comrade that we go and help the few men who were still keeping up the fight against the routed enemy, but he said "No, let's go down the line of works and fill our haversacks with meat and crackers left by the Yankees, and then we will go." We did accordingly, and when we came to our men holding the front there were only a handful of them there, and no effect was being made to bring up the stragglers or strengthen our position, while one piece of artillery that had not fallen into our hands was keeping up a game fight.[26]

Hunger is a tremendous motivator. With the Confederates being hungry and poorly clothed and with winter approaching, the temptation to eat the food left in the Union camps and gather clothing would have been too great to resist. Thus, the lack of food for the men and horses and clothing for his men played a role in Early's defeat at Cedar Creek.

Sheridan's famous ride from Winchester to Cedar Creek, though dramatic, did not stop the Federal retreat since the retreat had already stopped, and Wright had the army well under control. Still, Sheridan's presence inspired the men, and many of the men who were still retreating either voluntarily returned to the ranks or were forced to return by Sheridan's staff and cavalry escort. Sheridan, for all of his faults, was an inspirational leader and his men believed in him. Sheridan's ride and the subsequent defeat of the Confederate Army are very interconnected and have become legendary. Fortunately for Sheridan, Winchester is not far from Cedar Creek, and the Valley Turnpike was an excellent road. Even when the turnpike was blocked by wagons and retreating Soldiers, the fields were open enough for Sheridan to ride around any blockage. Distance, technological improvements, and geography made Sheridan's famous ride possible.

Geography helped the Federals in their counterattack. The Confederate infantry was holding firm until the Federal cavalry was able to overwhelm the Confederate cavalry and attack the Confederate left flank. They were able to do this as the terrain favored cavalry action. The impact the Federal cavalry had on the victory cannot be overstated. If Merritt's cavalry division, which contained about 40 percent of the Federal cavalry involved in the battle, had not returned but had instead conducted the raid on Charlottesville, there is a strong possibility the Confederates would have been able to retreat in good order.[27] If this had happened, the battle would not have been a decisive victory for Sheridan, and Early's army would have remained a major greater threat. Early stated in his memoirs, "As the enemy's cavalry on our left was very strong, and had the benefit of an open country to the rear of that flank [the Confederate left flank]."[28] In his post-battle report, Early stated, "A terror of the enemy's cavalry had seized them [his men], and there was no holding them. They left the field in the greatest confusion."[29] Weary after being up all night, fighting all day, and then being threatened by a strong force of cavalry took their toll on the Confederates. They also knew they were fighting with Cedar Creek and the Shenandoah River to their backs, geographic obstacles that would impede their withdrawal.

Although geography helped the Federals, it also hurt them. Sheridan ordered the counterattack to begin at 4:00 p.m.[30] The problem was that sunset was at 5:15 p.m. on that day, and there was no moonlight until 9:00 p.m.[31] This gave the Federals only 75 minutes before it would become dark. Darkness took away the ability of the Federal cavalry to conduct a sustained pursuit. Although the darkness helped the Confederates, it also hurt them as units were not able to stay together, men got lost, and when the turnpike got blocked, men panicked. All of this led to the Confederates losing irreplaceable men, wagons, artillery, and horses. The darkness was a double-edged sword.

A small bridge on the Valley Turnpike crossing a small stream, which in normal circumstances would not have caused a problem, played an important role in the Confederate retreat. The problem was that the bridge became blocked by wagons.[32] The darkness, confusion, and fear of the Federal cavalry did not allow anyone to take control and clear the blockage. This resulted in all of the wagons and artillery behind the blockage being abandoned, as they could no longer cross the bridge. A small geographic feature that had been overcome by technology (the bridge) but blocked by technology (wagons) became an impediment to the Confederate retreat. Geography's influence on events at all levels cannot be ignored and needs to be appreciated before a full comprehension of an event can be understood.

After the Battle

Sheridan's victory at Cedar Creek came about three weeks before the presidential election and was an additional boost to Lincoln's reelection effort. If it had been a defeat, it would, in all probability, have had a major negative effect with the possibility of Lincoln losing the election. Confederate forces in the Valley were reduced after the battle, as Robert E. Lee needed reinforcements at Petersburg. As a result, the Confederates gave up trying to retain control of the entire Valley and only worked to preserve their hold on the upper Valley. The loss of Winchester meant the Federals now held the initiative in the Virginia theater of war, an initiative Grant would not give up. The loss of Winchester meant the loss of the Valley, and the loss of the Valley meant the loss of Virginia. The struggle for control of Winchester was over; the Federals now firmly controlled the key to the Shenandoah Valley.

8

Control of Winchester

The side that controlled Winchester held the key to the Shenandoah Valley and the initiative in the Virginia theater of war.

Although the Battle of Cedar Creek left the Federal Army firmly in control of Winchester and the lower Valley, who would dominate Winchester had been heavily contested. As previously stated, it is estimated that Winchester changed hands at least 72 times during the Civil War. Even though it was difficult for either side to permanently occupy Winchester, holding the city was vital to both sides. Whichever side controlled the city held the initiative in the Virginia theater of war. By initiative, I mean that the side that controlled the city was able to dictate events in Virginia. It does not mean that the occupying side was always attacking. Rather, it had the ability to determine where and how the armies would meet or how to disrupt the opponent's plans. This, of course, depends on a commander's willingness to take the initiative. This chapter is not meant to describe every time Winchester changed hands but to link changes in control to other events happening in the Virginia theater of war.

Loss of Control of Winchester by the Confederates in the Spring of 1862

The Confederates held Winchester from the beginning of the war until early March 1862. Until late winter 1862, the Confederates held the initiative in Virginia. Although Federal forces did attack during that period, the Battles of Ball's Bluff and the First Bull Run/Manassas were defeats for them. However, for a variety of reasons, the Confederates did not follow up their victories. Still, the Confederates did take advantage of having the initiative and placed a number of batteries along the Potomac River, effectively cutting Washington off from the Chesapeake Bay. In addition, General Stonewall Jackson advanced against Federal positions in western Virginia, but his efforts were eventually thwarted by politics.

By the winter of 1862, the buildup of Federal strength created armies much larger than opposing Confederate forces. Consequently, in early March 1862, Joseph Johnston retreated from Manassas, south to the Rappahannock River, and abandoned the gun batteries on the Potomac. Jackson was also forced to retreat from Winchester on the 11th of March, allowing Federal troops to occupy the city. Northern Virginia and the lower Shenandoah Valley were now controlled by the Federals, and the initiative went to the Federals. George McClellan's Peninsula Campaign was one of the results of the Federals gaining control of Winchester.

The Battle of Kernstown on 23 March 1862 Caused a Major Disruption in Federal Plans

The Federals retained the advantage until the Battle of Kernstown. Although the Confederates were defeated, the perceived threat resulted in the retention of Nathaniel Banks' division in the Valley and the return of the brigades that were already east of the Blue Ridge Mountains. It also temporarily ended the planned movement of General Irvin McDowell from Fredericksburg toward Richmond in support of General McClellan's movement up the peninsula to Richmond. In addition, it resulted in the transfer of General Louis Blenker's 10,000-man division from McClellan's army to General John Fremont's command in the mountains west of the Valley.[1] A failed attack by fewer than 4,000 Confederates, which threatened the control of Winchester, resulted in a major disruption of Federal plans. Although Jackson was not able to gain control of Winchester, by his actions, Jackson was able to psychologically dominate the Federals and force them to change their plans. Often, psychological domination is just as effective as physical occupation.

The First Battle Winchester on 25 May 1862, Part of Jackson's Valley Campaign, Caused Further Disruption in Federal Plans

When Jackson defeated General Banks at Winchester, the Federal government took immediate measures to counter Jackson's threat. The measure that had the most impact on the military situation was the order to retain General McDowell's corps at Fredericksburg and not allow him to advance on Richmond. This reaction provided relief to the outnumbered Confederate forces defending Richmond from General McClellan's army. McClellan used the loss of McDowell's corps as one of his excuses for his defeat. If McDowell had been allowed to move south, his corps would have protected McClellan's right flank and forced the Confederates to defend against an additional threat. That being said, if McDowell had protected McClellan's right flank and if McClellan would still have been defeated, he would have probably found another excuse for his defeat.

Jackson's control of Winchester, though brief, made the Federal government fear for the safety of Washington. The reason is that Winchester is located north of Washington, and from Winchester, in theory, Jackson could have crossed the

Potomac River and attacked Washington. Winchester's geographic position made it an ideal location for the Confederates to move into Maryland and Pennsylvania.

When Jackson retreated from Winchester, the initiative passed back to the Federals. Once they controlled Winchester, they unsuccessfully tried to trap Jackson. In addition, their advance on Richmond continued, but McClellan retreated even though he substantially outnumber Lee. Then a new Federal Army was created in northern Virginia under General John Pope. Lee was still reacting to movements by the Federals.

Federals Lose Control of Winchester on the 2nd of September 1862

Although the Army of the Potomac under McClellan had been pushed back to the James River and the new Army of Virginia under Pope was cautiously advancing into central Virginia, the Federals still held the initiative. However, McClellan exhibited excessive caution and failed to cooperate while Pope was overconfident and outmaneuvered. As a result, the Federals suffered a devastating defeat at Manassas. Although one side has the advantage, if generals fail to take advantage of the situation, it means nothing. In contrast to his opponents, Lee was not the type of general who failed to take the initiative.

On the night of the 2nd of September 1862, Federal forces evacuated Winchester without a fight, and the Confederates occupied it the next day. Lee needed to control Winchester, for without it, any movement by the Army of Northern Virginia into Maryland could be threatened by a strong Federal force based there. Lee directed "Winchester be made a depot for this army, and have sent there our disabled men, horses, batteries, and surplus wagon-trains, in order that they may be recruited and refreshed."[2] The Federals now had to react to the movement of Lee's army.

After the Antietam campaign, when Lee retreated across the Potomac River, Winchester lost some of its importance. Nevertheless, Jackson's corps remained there until late November. Lee had allowed Jackson's corps to remain in Winchester because "your remaining in the valley was based upon the supposition that, by operating upon the flank and rear of the enemy, you might prevent his progress southward, and, so long as you found that this could be effected, I considered it advantageous; but, when this cannot be accomplished, the sooner you make a junction with Longstreet's corps the better."[3] Lee went on to state, "Your presence, then, in the valley seems to be too distant from his [General Ambrose Burnside, the current commander of the Army of the Potomac] line of operation to affect his movements, should you remain quiescent."[4] Lee was also worried about the oncoming winter weather and that Jackson's "detention there, until the occurrence of bad weather and deep roads, might so break down your command as to render it inefficient for further operations, should they become requisite elsewhere."[5] Again, geography and distance directly impacted military operations.

With the departure of Jackson's corps, only a few Confederate units remained to defend the city. Although Federal forces could have easily occupied and held the city after Jackson's departure, they did not, and there was a continual change of control. One reason the Federals did not take control of Winchester was logistic, the bane of all commanders. General John Geary, commander of the Second Division, 12th Army Corps, made a reconnaissance to Winchester during the first part of December and occupied the city for part of a day. In his report, he stated,

> Another subject worthy of comment is the destruction of the Harper's [sic] Ferry and Winchester Railroad and of the property of the people, who have been bereft of nearly all the necessities of life. Devastation of a painful character is noticeable over all the section visited by the troops of Jackson and Hill. Cattle and hogs have nearly all been taken, and throughout a vast area there is not enough provender to maintain a troop of cavalry in any one neighborhood for a single week.[6]

The lack of a working railroad between Harpers Ferry and Winchester would cause problems for General Robert Milroy as he occupied the city, and it would not be repaired until 1864 after General Philip Sheridan captured the city.

It was during this period of uncertainty for the residents of Winchester that General Ambrose Burnside moved the Army of the Potomac to Fredericksburg and made his disastrous attacks against strong Confederate positions. Lee wanted to counterattack, but the terrain and the strong Federal artillery made it unfeasible. In reality, neither side really had the initiative. Although Confederates were too strongly entrenched to be attacked again, they were not strong enough and not adequately provisioned to maneuver. The winter weather had also made the dirt roads all but impassable as Burnside found out during his infamous "Mud March."

23 December 1862, Federal Forces Occupy Winchester until 14 June 1863

General Benjamin F. Kelley assumed command on the 16th of December 1862 "of all the forces on the Upper Potomac," which included "the defense of the Baltimore and Ohio Railroad west."[7] Kelley was an aggressive commander, and on the 22nd of December, he informed General Milroy, "I intend to occupy and hold Winchester as soon as practicable."[8] General Gustave P. Cluseret, commander of the First Brigade in Milroy's division, occupied Winchester on the 23rd. On the 1st of January, General Milroy with the rest of his division arrived, and a harsh occupation of the city began. From then until the beginning of the spring campaign season, the Virginia theater of operations was relatively quiet. Although the Federal Army of the Potomac and the other Federal forces in Virginia heavily outnumbered the Confederates, the winter weather halted all major operations. Lee was so desperate for supplies that he sent General James Longstreet and two divisions to southeastern Virginia to besiege the Federal garrison at Suffolk and gather supplies in that part of the state. Because of this, Longstreet's force would not be available for the Battle of Chancellorsville.

When spring arrived, Lee was forced to react to General Joe Hooker's maneuvers. However, Lee did not react as Hooker expected, and the decisive Battle of Chancellorsville in early May 1863 gave the initiative to General Lee. In reality, the Army of the Potomac was still larger and better equipped than the Army of Northern Virginia, but the Federal Army withdrew from the battlefield and did not renew its offensive. The Federals could have retained the initiate, but General Hooker squandered it and gave it to Lee. There was a debate on whether Lee should send units to assist General Joseph Johnston in Mississippi or to take the war into Pennsylvania. Although the decision was for Lee to move north, it took some time for his army to start the campaign because horses were weak from the lack of forage over the winter, and the army had to be reorganized due to the death of General Jackson.

Once Lee felt everything was ready, he knew the Valley was his best avenue into Pennsylvania. To gain control of the Valley, he had to defeat the Federal forces defending Winchester and recapture the city. This was accomplished by General Richard Ewell's corps, and Winchester again became a major logistic depot for the Army of Northern Virginia. However, with the Confederate retreat after the Battle of Gettysburg and the movement of the Army of the Potomac on the east side of the Blue Ridge Mountains, all major Confederate units departed the lower Valley, leaving only a few units to defend Winchester and the lower Valley.

August 1863 to the 1st of May 1864, Winchester Continually Changes Between Confederate and Federal Control

During these nine months, neither side could gain the initiative. Although there was the Mine Run campaign and other actions, decisive victories were elusive. Both armies were also weakened because they had sent a large number of units to Tennessee. Neither side had the strength needed to continually control Winchester since both armies needed to remain concentrated in the event their opponent made an aggressive move. Still, it could be argued that the Army of the Potomac had sufficient forces to occupy Winchester and the lower Valley and to conduct offensive operations against the Army of Northern Virginia. General George Meade asked General Henry Halleck in late July 1863 if he should reoccupy the Shenandoah Valley. The response was, "I see no advantage in the reoccupation of the Shenandoah Valley. Lee's army is the objective point."[9] A few days later, Meade clarified his question by stating, "The only object in reoccupying the Valley of the Shenandoah would be to prevent the enemy from having the benefit of the incoming crops, which last year, I understand, he employed his army in gathering, and sent to the rear for winter use."[10] Halleck's reply was substantially the same as before: "The occupation of the Shenandoah is now a matter of little importance."[11] These are statements Halleck probably regretted after General Jubal Early occupied Winchester, moved into Maryland, and threatened Washington. Early's actions would completely change the opinion of the Federal high command on the importance of controlling Winchester and the lower Valley.

Federals Reoccupy Winchester on the 1st of May 1864, Evacuate the City in Late June, Reoccupy It on the 20th of July, Evacuate It on the 24th of July, Reoccupy It on the 12th of August, and Evacuate It on the 17th of August

During these few months, control of the city continually changed between Confederate and Federal. It was during this time that the Federal government finally realized how important it was to the Federal cause to retain control of Winchester. The continual change of who held the city was also a reflection of the stalemate between the Army of the Potomac and the Army of Northern Virginia during the Overland Campaign. Neither side could gain a decisive advantage, and a stalemate ensued.

The Federal reoccupation of Winchester was part of General Ulysses S. Grant's plan to simultaneously attack the Confederates everywhere so that they would be unable to reinforce a threatened area with troops from a region that was inactive. General Franz Sigel was responsible for the Shenandoah Valley and was initially successful, but he was defeated at New Market, and General David Hunter took command. Again, General Hunter was initially successful, but he was defeated by General Early and retreated west into West Virginia rather than down the Valley. This left the Valley open for General Early to advance north. Once the few Federal units in the Winchester area learned of Hunter's defeat and his retreat into West Virginia, they abandoned Winchester. This allowed General Early to occupy Winchester with little resistance. Then, from Winchester, his units continued to move north into Maryland and eventually threatened Washington before returning to Virginia. Early's actions caused General Grant to react, and he transferred two of his corps to counter Early's corps. Again, control of Winchester forced the Federals to react to Confederate moves.

The Confederates retained control of Winchester until the 20th of July, when they were forced to retreat, but returned on the 24th after defeating General George Crook at Kernstown. Control of Winchester again allowed the Confederates to raid into Maryland and Pennsylvania. The most famous raid was General John McCausland's burning of Chambersburg, Pennsylvania, in retaliation for General Hunter's burnings in the Valley. This raid caused Grant to rescind his "orders for the troops to go out and destroy the Weldon Railroad, and directed them to embark for Washington City."[12] The continual raids were an embarrassment to President Abraham Lincoln, especially with the imminent election, and he met with Grant to determine what needed to be done. It was decided to consolidate some of the military departments and put General Philip Sheridan in command of the forces opposing Early.

On the 12th of August, Federal units again occupied Winchester as the Federal

Army of the Shenandoah, under General Sheridan, moved south and began the destruction of the Valley's agricultural resources. Sheridan was not able to complete the destruction as Lee, who was now forced to react, sent reinforcements to Early. This forced Sheridan to retreat to his Halltown defenses. From then until the Third Battle of Winchester, the Confederates retained control of Winchester.

Confederates Control Winchester from the 17th of August until the 19th of September

Control of Winchester allowed General Early to tie down many more Federal troops than he had in his command. Sheridan did not want to attack Early until he was confident of victory, for another Federal defeat in the Valley would be bad for Lincoln's chances for reelection. Therefore, he waited until Confederate units were ordered to leave the Valley and rejoin Lee at Petersburg. Once that happened, Sheridan attacked and won a decisive victory. Sheridan's victories continued in the Valley and allowed him to destroy the Valley's ability to sustain any sizable force, Federal or Confederate. Winchester stayed under Federal control for the remainder of the war as Lee's options slowly dwindled. By that time, the Confederacy no longer had the strength to fight for control of Winchester. Losing that ability foretold the permanent loss of the initiative in the Virginia theater of war.

9

Geography and History

Technology can mitigate the impact of geography but can never eliminate it.

Geography, as previously stated, is more than topography (the physical layout of the land), for it also deals with climate, natural resources, vegetation, along with a variety of other things. As a consequence, geography has had an impact on history by dictating where it is possible for people to live and, when a suitable location is chosen, how people live. Geography, along with the available technology, also dictates the number of people living in any location. Technology allows for a greater concentration of people in an area than that location can support naturally. Where and how people decide to live is not a random decision but a rational one that considers the surrounding geography and available technology.

The vast majority of cities prior to the advent of the steam engine and the railroad were located along rivers navigable by large ships of the time period. This was crucial since water transportation was the only effective means of transporting bulky, heavy items. It needs to be remembered that many rivers that we would not consider to be navigable today were navigable centuries ago when rivercraft were smaller and had a shallower draft. There were some notable exceptions to this rule such as Jerusalem, Timbuktu, and Mexico City. With the exception of Mexico City, these cities were located along major international trading routes. Geography had an important role in determining where these trading cities were located since trading routes were dictated by various or specific geographic items such as sufficient drinkable water, available grazing for livestock, and defensible terrain. Mexico City, although it is located in a region known for its earthquakes and volcanic activity, is different because it was built on a large navigable lake with the adjacent countryside capable of growing enough crops to support a large population. Still, as a rule, large cities are located where adequate resources to support the community exist and at a major transportation hub.

Geography and technology were, and are, the two major items that determine where and how large a city will become. The size of ancient Rome was determined by how much fresh, drinkable water was available. Without the numerous aqueducts the Romans built, Rome could not have grown as large as it did. The advent of the railroad allowed for large, inland cities to be built such as Denver and Dallas.

Railroads provided an easy, fast means of transporting people and production to and from these inland cities. Prior to the railroad, steam engine–powered ships allowed cities located along navigable rivers to grow. Some examples are Saint Louis, Cincinnati, and Pittsburgh. However, overdependence on a technology can prove to be devastating to a city when that technology is superseded by a new technology or is displaced. The loss of industry has had a major impact on both Detroit and Cleveland. Unfortunately, both of these cities were heavily dependent on heavy industry which either needed fewer workers due to newer technology or lost their dominance due to competition.

House construction has also been geographically dependent. Prior to the advent of central heating and air conditioning, people constructed the buildings they lived and worked in based on geography. First, locally available natural resources determined the building material to be used. This affected building design because buildings constructed from clay bricks will have a very different structure than buildings constructed from rock or timber. Second, climate was a determining factor in how the buildings were designed. In hot, arid climates, buildings were designed and constructed to achieve maximum cooling, while buildings constructed in cold climates were made with the idea of retaining heat. The few exceptions to this rule were buildings of cultural importance. Today, much of this has changed due to technologies such as air conditioning and central heating. However, geography continues to have an impact as buildings constructed in earthquake zones or heavy snow fall regions are constructed with consideration for the effect local geography has on structures.

Geography also played a role in determining which animals were available for use by the people living in a region. People living in open, grassy plains made greater use of horses than those people living in rugged mountains. One consequence of this was that the plains people became superior horsemen. However, one would not expect plains people to become open water sailors as did people living beside an ocean. Nor would one expect to find fish to be a major source of food for people living far away from the ocean, a river, or a very large lake. Animals become genetically adapted to their environment, and people adapt to the animals living in their environment. Cultures that do not adapt, such as the Norse in Greenland, die out.[1]

Cod is an example of the impact animals can have on history.[2] Cod was such a valuable resource that men have fought over the right to fish for it in the cold, dangerous Northern Atlantic.[3] It is a nutritious fish that can be preserved by drying or salting. Either method extends its shelf life, making it an excellent source of food for long ocean voyages. In fact, it is believed the Basques and other fishermen had been catching and preserving cod off North America years before Columbus's famous voyage. When New England was colonized, cod trade became one of the mainstays of its economy. The significance of the cod trade to the New England colonies caused the lowly cod to appear on some official crests and coins, and a carved gilded cod hung in the Boston town hall. Access to cod was considered so important that the right for Americans to fish on the Grand Banks off the coast of Canada was one of the terms agreed to in the peace treaty after the American Revolution.

There have been three "cod wars" since World War II over the right to fish for cod in the waters around Iceland, mainly between Iceland and Great Britain. During these "wars," ships were rammed and nets cut. Fortunately, no lives were lost or ships sunk during these "wars." These events occurred because of geographically determined fishing grounds.

Jared Diamond's book *Guns, Germs and Steel* gives an extensive discussion of the effect of geography on history. He concludes that there are four major sets of environmental differences that have impacted history.[4] The first is continental differences in plant and animal domestication. The second is the rate of diffusion and migration of domesticated plants and animals as well as ideas within connected land masses such as Eurasia. The third is the difficulty of transferring domesticated plants, animals, and ideas between areas disconnected by oceans or other barriers, such as deserts. The fourth, and last difference, is the available area in which a large population can be supported. This is a relative size, as the Norse could not compete in Greenland against the relatively larger Eskimo population whose culture was better adapted to the climate. However, Diamond's book does not fully discuss the impact of geographically placed minerals and other natural resources, items that have had a major impact on history.

Geography determines the placement of other natural resources because it takes a specific set of natural occurrences to create them. The natural resources available to a group of people will have a tremendous impact on their lifestyle. Although some natural resources are always crucial, such as water and sources of food, the importance of minerals on which society places high value also have an influence. Gold and silver have been two minerals that societies have placed a high extrinsic value on throughout the centuries. The wealth and power of ancient Athens was, in large part, determined by its access to the Lavrion silver mines. The silver produced at these mines provided the money Athens needed to create its empire by funding the building of its navy. Without access to the Lavrion silver mines, Athens may very well have succumbed to the power of Persia because they may not have had enough ships available to defeat the Persian fleet.

The Roman Empire was self-sufficient in metals for its technology, but this should not be too surprising considering the extent of the empire. However, transportation of metals overland during that period, unless it was an especially valuable metal, was cost prohibitive. The Romans were fortunate that a large part of their empire had access to the Mediterranean Sea or the Atlantic Ocean and other parts had access to navigable rivers. Thus, bulk shipments of metals could be carried by galleys. The Romans also had access to gold mines and were able to produce enough of this precious metal to pay for mercenaries or buy off barbarians when needed.[5] Loss of gold and silver mines have negatively impacted a country. The Carthaginians felt this impact when they lost Spain to the Romans. The loss of Spain was more than a loss of territory and population since they also lost access to the Spanish gold and silver mines. This loss of a valuable source of revenue was made worse as their enemies, the Romans, gained control of the mines.

Still, the importance of natural resources is dependent on the technology currently in use. Timber was important to the shipbuilding industry, and the governments of those countries for which navies were crucial made tremendous efforts to ensure they had ready access to the necessary timber. However, those natural resources for which there is little or no need are disregarded until a change in technology dictates a need for the resource. For example, the placement of coal had little impact until the advent of the steam engine and the need for a source of energy, other than timber, to heat the water used in the engines.

The placement of timber and other naval stores have influenced history. The Venetian Arsenal, which was responsible for the construction of war galleys for Venice, was very concerned about its domestic supply of timber. The reason was that the arsenal used oak to build the galleys, beech to make the oars, fir to make the masts, and larch (a tree of the pine family) to line the interior of the galleys. To ensure supplies, it was given control of a number of large forests. These forests were guarded and replanted by officials from the arsenals. However, this policy was disastrous for private shipbuilders because villagers deliberately cut down any sapling of the desired wood to ensure that the arsenal would not confiscate their land because of its wood. As a result, private shipbuilders were forced to buy foreign ships, leaving the arsenal as the only place Venetian shipwrights could find work.[6]

Great Britain's dependence on the Royal Navy for its security was one of the determining factors in its overseas geographic political policies. Consequently, Great Britain's need for naval stores is one of the keys to understanding its policies in the age of sailing ships. Naval stores, in its broadest definition, consisted of all of the materials used to construct and repair these wooden ships such as hemp, pitch, tar, lumber, and tall straight trees. Thus, Great Britain's need for geographically dependent naval stores helped dictate foreign policy.[7] Still, the end of the era of sailing warships did not lessen the impact the Royal Navy had on Great Britain's overseas policy.

The change from wooden sailing ships to steam-powered steel ships changed only what was critical; it did not change the need for access to strategic materials. Due to the limited range of ships dependent on coal for propulsion, naval stations had to be built in strategic locations. These naval stations had to meet certain geographic conditions such as a good harbor that could be defended, be within easy cruising distance from at least one other naval station, and have the ability to provide fresh water and provisions to the ships. Nations that did not have a good source of quality coal were at a distinct disadvantage during this era. The transition to fuel oil from coal did not change the Royal Navy's geographic dependence as sources of oil, such as the Middle East, became very important. One of the major reasons Japan went to war with the United States, Great Britain, and the Netherlands during World War II was because the economic embargo, which had been imposed on them, cut

Japan off from the strategic materials necessary for war and its economy. This especially impacted Japan's access to the oil fields in the Dutch East Indies (Indonesia). Consequently, Japan had to submit to the demands from the United States, Great Britain, and the Netherlands or go to war.

Gunpowder is another, and older, example of an item crucial to the military yet geographically dependent.[8] It was the first non-natural force created by humans. Gunpowder, or black powder, is a mixture of niter, also known as saltpeter, charcoal, and sulfur. Although the percentages of each of its ingredients can vary, gunpowder is, by weight, about 75 percent niter, 15 percent charcoal, and 10 percent sulfur. European powers had been manufacturing charcoal for years, and it was relatively easy for them to find sulfur. However, niter was much more difficult to find in Europe, especially northern and western Europe. As a result, many nations established saltpeter beds using decaying organic material and gave monopolies to individuals to collect the needed material. But it took about 18 months before a bed would produce saltpeter. During the 1600s, high-quality saltpeter was being exported from India, and those countries having access to this trade slowly disestablished their saltpeter beds. The problem was that this made them dependent on either controlling the source in India or remaining friendly to the power that did—eventually, Great Britain.

A more current example is the Cold War. During this time, the United States and its allies had serious concerns about selected strategic minerals. Some of these minerals were manganese, chromium, cobalt, and platinum, which were concentrated in South Africa and the former Soviet Union.[9] The issue was that these minerals are used in the production of superalloys, which are utilized in various weapon systems as well as in the production of high-quality steel. Unfortunately, no adequate substitute was found for them. The United States therefore stockpiled these minerals to ensure that it had an adequate supply in case of war. The critical need for these minerals also helps explain the friendly attitude the United States displayed to South Africa even though it disagreed with many of its domestic policies.

Even a mineral, such as phosphate, which most people would not consider vital, can easily become a contention between nations.[10] Phosphate is used as a fertilizer throughout the world and is crucial in producing high crop yields. Only a few countries in the world are self-sufficient in phosphate, and those that are not must import this mineral. Today, Morocco is the largest exporter of phosphate. But large reserves of phosphate were found in Western Sahara, so Morocco was afraid Western Sahara would become a competitor. Today, Morocco controls Western Sahara, a territory that no country, except Morocco, recognizes as part of Morocco. Spain had previously controlled Western Sahara since the late 1800s and wanted to keep control once it was discovered how extensive the phosphate reserves were. However, most of the world considered Western Sahara to be a Spanish colony, and they were forced to give independence to the region. Both Morocco and Mauritania, which adjoin Western Sahara, wanted control when Spain left. But the local population wanted independence. Morocco was able to gain control but has had to fight a war against Polisario, a nationalist organization advocating independence for Western Sahara. Currently, this struggle is ongoing, although both sides have been observing a cease-fire. For the United States, the issue was that Polisario was supported by Algeria who, in turn, was supported by the former Soviet Union. Accordingly, the United States backed Morocco fearing if Morocco was not able to maintain control of Western Sahara, the moderate regime of Hassan II would fall to left-wing socialists and become part of the sovietization of the region. With the fall of the Soviet Union, both it and the United States are no longer actively involved, but this may change if extreme Muslim groups become active in Western Sahara or Morocco. An understanding of geopolitics is important for a full understanding of actions that governments make.

Today, new strategic minerals have been added to the list with one being "rare" earth elements. These elements are used extensively in electronics, high-performance magnets, catalysts, and alloys. Although these elements are not really rare, economical concentrations are limited. Today, China is the largest producer of rare earth elements. They have been perceived as using their production as a political/economic weapon (something other countries have done throughout history). As a consequence, many countries are creating strategic stockpiles of these elements, and it has forced the search for other economically viable sources. Our increasing technological demands have increased our dependence on limited supplies of many other natural resources. Technology will change, but there will always be a limited supply or, at least, limited access to strategic materials. These limitations have caused conflict in the past and have the potential of causing conflict in the future.

Diseases can also be geographically dependent. Diseases, like any other organism, need a certain environment in which to live. Although some diseases are more mobile than others, provided their host environment is more mobile, some are dependent on hosts that only live in a selected environment. Malaria is one example as it was unknown in the Americas until infected individuals and the *Anopheles* mosquito were brought to the Americas. On the other hand, geographically dependent diseases can be advantageous. For example, the diseases in the interior of Africa kept the central portion of Africa from being exploited by Europeans for a number of years.

Geography has also had other, more subtle influences on history. Prior to the advent of steam power, ships were dependent on manpower through the use of rowers or wind using sails. Ships propelled by rowers are limited in size due to the relationship between the number of rowers needed and the amount of food and water that must be carried to sustain their efforts.[11] Consequently, long-distance ocean voyages, which remained out of sight of land, were not common until the advent of an effective sailing ship that required a smaller crew and, thus, needed to carry less food and fresh water. However, the sailing ship was dependent on the prevailing winds as well as ocean currents, both of which are geographic phenomena. One only needs to consider the impact on history if the prevailing winds and ocean currents in the Atlantic Ocean had not allowed Europeans to easily sail from Europe to the Americas and then return to realize their importance.

Technology can mitigate the influence of geography but cannot eliminate its impact. The development of the internal combustion engine and the automobile changed how we live and view the world. At the same time, it increased our dependence on oil and made regions of the world that had been previously unimportant critically important. Politicians and generals had to go from worrying about where to find horses and the fodder to feed them to where to find iron deposits to build the vehicles and the oil necessary to fuel them. Unfortunately, the by-products created by the increased use of oil has impacted our atmosphere. There are always unintended consequences associated with any technology.

Another technological transition occurred when railroads replaced canals as the prime means of moving bulky, heavy items within a country. Railroads were more versatile, quicker and less expensive to build, and able to move freight and people faster and cheaper. Railroads changed our perception of geography and, at the same time, were affected by geography. Railroads decreased the amount of time required to move products from one region to another. This allowed natural resources located in one region to be quickly transported to a different region that needed them. Chicago would not have become a national meat packing industrial center without the railroad. The ability to easily transport natural resources, finished products, and people allowed for the growth of larger cities with greater populations. However, locomotives needed fuel and a supply of clean water. In those regions of the country lacking either one of these, the railroad companies had to ship in and stockpile the needed items. Trains were also limited in their ability to climb mountains and needed bridges to cross rivers and ravines. Plus, certain types of land, such as swamps, increased the cost of construction. For this reason, the route any railroad took was carefully surveyed. At the same time, the railroads had to go where they were needed. Railroads helped solve certain geographic problems, such as allowing the creation of large interior cities, but in turn, had their own set of geographic challenges.

Great Britain was the first country to experience the Industrial Revolution, partly due to its geography. The safety provided by the English Channel and enforced by the Royal Navy allowed Great Britain to avoid the worst of the upheavals created by the continual wars in Europe. This security allowed its industry and farming to develop without the fear of destruction. Great Britain was also blessed with an accessible source of fine-quality coal and numerous rivers that could be used to supply power to industry. These same rivers provided a base around which a navigable canal system could be built. All of these items, along with political considerations, directly contributed to the establishment of the first Industrial Revolution in Great Britain. But the loss of any one of these items could have slowed or even stopped this process.

Invasion routes have also been geographically dependent, although many people view invasion routes only through the lenses of topography. Topography is important, but an excellent invasion route during one time of the year may not be acceptable during a different time of the year. Before the advent of the internal combustion engine, navigable waterways that could be used to transport supplies determined many invasion routes. Food for the horses used for transportation and fighting and the cattle herds accompanying the armies were other crucial factors. If the grass supply was not adequate, it mattered little if the topography was favorable. The creation of the fully motorized army changed these needs but at the same time made the trafficability of the terrain very important. Sometimes an indirect approach will be better than a direct approach if the terrain on the direct approach is boggy or soft sand. Technology can only modify, not eliminate, the effects of geography.

Numerous more examples can be cited to demonstrate the impact geography has had on history. Geography's influence has been wide and constant. Still, the impact of geography can be mitigated by technology but never eliminated. Geography and technology are interrelated. An item may be invented in one region of the world due to a geographic need. Then it may take years before the same item is accepted in a less geographically favorable region, if ever.[12] The question still remains: what, if any, impact has geography had on war?

10

Geography and War

Modern warfare has only increased the need for an understanding of geography.

Many military philosophers have discussed geography, but in reality, they have only described topography. One of the earliest military philosophers, Sun Tzu, discussed six types of terrain (accessible ground, entangling ground, temporizing ground, narrow passes, precipitous heights, and positions at a great distance from the enemy) in addition to rivers and mountains. Sun Tzu wrote about the impact each type of terrain had on an army and a battle. However, the only real discussion of geography was when he briefly mentioned lines of supply and depriving an enemy army of food or water.[1] During Sun Tzu's life, over 2,500 years ago, the technology used by armies was much simpler and not as geographically dependent as it is today. Still, it is surprising that Sun Tzu did not at least mention the need to control good farmland unless, of course, he did not consider it crucial to military success or, possibly, too obvious to discuss.

This trend continued, as centuries later, geography was not considered important knowledge for the education of a military commander. Niccolò Machiavelli (1469–1527) in his book, *The Art of War*, does go further than Sun Tzu, as he discussed the importance of maps.[2] Machiavelli also included an aspect of geography in his list of the sinews of war when he stated, "Men, arms, money, and provisions are the sinews of war, but of these four, the first two are the most necessary."[3] Unfortunately, he puts provisions, a geographically dependent resource, in the second tier.

The importance of geography for the education of an officer, and in the writings of military philosophers, increased with the advent of the Industrial Revolution. Carl von Clausewitz (1780–1831) in his book *On War* discussed the impact geography had on supply, but he was mainly interested in food for the Soldiers and forage for the horses. Clausewitz did not discuss geography, broadly defined, because he did not discuss the impact geography had on industry and technology. He probably did not bother with the impact of geography on these two items since in Northern Europe it was not a problem. Fortuitously, Northern Europe had adequate sources of iron, wood, and most of the ingredients for gunpowder, the most important military raw materials during the time period. In addition, the full impact of the Industrial Revolution was only beginning to be felt during Clausewitz's life.

However, a contemporary of Clausewitz, Antoine-Henri Jomini (1799–1869), whose writings were more influential during the 19th century than Clausewitz's, discussed the impact of geography much more extensively than Clausewitz. In his book *The Art of War*, Jomini had a section on military statistics and geography. However, he conflated geography and topography. Later, when discussing military institutions, Jomini stated, "Nothing should be neglected to acquire a knowledge of the geography and the military statistics of other states."[4] Jomini contended that there are two classes of objective points, one being points of maneuver and the other, geographic objective points. When discussing geographic objective points, Jomini stated, "The geographical position of the capital, the political relations of the belligerents with their neighbors, and their respective resources, are considerations foreign in themselves to the art of fighting battles, but intimately connected with plans of operations."[5] This appears to be the first written acknowledgment of the importance of geographic resources by a military theorist. Jomini continued this trend when he discussed depots of supplies and stated, "A general should be capable of making all the resources of the invaded country contribute to the success of his enterprise."[6] However, Jomini was only referring to food for the men and horses, not minerals such as iron and coal, although food is a very important geographically based resource. Jomini stated that there are two types of reconnoissances. One type is to gather information about movements of the enemy and the other being topographic and statistical. Topographical and statistical reconnoissances include gaining "a knowledge of a country, its accidents of ground, its roads, defiles, bridges, &c., and to learn its resources and means of every kind."[7] It was also during this time, in 1836, that the first book entirely dedicated to military geography was written by Théophile Lavallée, titled *Géographie physique, historique et militaire*.[8] Since then, many more articles and books have been written about military geography, and it is studied at most centers of military education.

Field Marshal Helmuth Graf von Moltke was a prolific writer on the topic of war. As with previous military writers, he had a tendency to conflate geography and topography. One reason for this may be that the wars he directed against Austria in 1866 and France in 1870–71 were short. Thus, the need to control strategic geographic resources did not become a determining factor. Still, he wrote, "One must distinguish between the *object of the war* and the *object of the operation* of the attack. The former is not the army, but the land mass and the capital of the enemy, and within them the resources and the political power of the state. It comprises what we desire to hold or that for which we will subsequently trade" (italics in the original).[9] This statement shows that Moltke was aware of the importance of resources, but short wars are dependent on military material that is on hand, not future production. I suspect that Moltke would have placed a greater emphasis on natural resources if he had been involved in long wars requiring uninterrupted access to natural resources vital to conducting war.

The geography in which a country expects to fight determines the composition of a country's armed forces. In the past, countries that consisted mainly of plains would have large numbers of cavalry in their army. An excellent example of this is the cossacks who were famed cavalrymen. In contrast, countries that are very mountainous and do not have good grazing land for horses tend to be weak in cavalry but strong in infantry. The Swiss, with their famous mercenary pikemen and halberdiers, are but one example. Today, the same is true, as a country will create military units that match the geography in which they expect to fight. The Swiss, planning on a defensive fight for their mountainous country, do not need large numbers of heavy armor units while the Finns, Swedes, and Norwegians have a large number of ski units. Other countries located in Northern Europe need and have numerous heavy armor units due to the geography of their countries.

Geography also impacts naval warfare. Unfortunately, again, naval theorists combine topography with geography. Alfred Thayer Mahan (1840–1914), one of the most famous naval theorists, discussed geography but, for the most part, mixed geography and topography. Mahan did discuss the importance of harbors, ease of access to the ocean, and the impact climate has had on whether a nation is self-sufficient or needs to use ships to transport material to sustain itself. Mahan also mentioned natural resources but does not go into detail. For example, he discussed the need for coal to fuel ships but did not discuss the need to control the sources of coal.

War is seldom declared to conquer wastelands because the economic value of a territory has always been important. It is doubtful whether the Spanish and other Europeans would have put as much effort into conquering and colonizing the Americas if no gold or silver had been found. Douglas Porch in his book *Wars of Empire*, published in 2013, discussed the impact of geography on the European efforts to conquer colonies throughout the world. Mosquito-borne diseases, such as malaria and yellow fever, took a heavy toll on European troops, while the lack of water and fodder killed many of the horses. Porch quotes the German governor of South West Africa, when complaining, in 1894, about how deficient the country was in water and pasture for even a small force of men: "We would be defeated not by the people, but by Nature."[10]

Poison gas, first used extensively during World War I, is very geographically dependent. Wind and rain can disperse it, while extreme cold and heat can impact its effectiveness. During that war, the Allies had an advantage over the Germans because in Western Europe, the winds normally blow from west to east. However, both sides experienced shifting winds that either drove the poison gas back on their own men or made it drift where they did not want it. Some gases, such as mustard gas, can linger for a long period when the conditions are right. My grandfather, who was a corporal in the Royal Engineers in World War I, told me about the time he was on a work detail and he took off his helmet and laid it on the ground. While his helmet was on the ground, mustard gas impregnated the leather head strap in his helmet. Then, when he put his helmet back on, he inadvertently gave himself mustard gas burns around his head. All weapons are affected by geography, and the users must be fully aware of the impact if they are to get the maximum effectiveness from their weapons.

Communications, especially space or airborne communications, are also geographically dependent. Atmospheric conditions along with terrain obstacles can disrupt radio communications. A greater threat to radio communications are electromagnetic pulses. These pulses can be generated from a number of sources with nuclear blasts and solar flares being the best known. Solar flares have the potential of temporarily knocking out radio communications and, if powerful enough, permanently damaging electronic equipment. Although solar flares will normally only damage unhardened electronic equipment, they have the potential to damage hardened equipment including satellites. So today, space weather is a factor that must be considered, and it has become necessary to have an early warning system in place that can give timely warning of any potentially dangerous solar flare.

Mud, an item that most people would consider very mundane, has influenced many campaigns and battles. It is a geographic element having tremendous variations depending on its composition and the weather. Civilizations have tried to lessen its impact through technology by the creation of all-weather roads, such as macadamized roads, and all-terrain vehicles.[11] However, its impact has never been eliminated. There are many historical examples of the effect mud has had with the Battle of Waterloo and the German invasion of Russia in 1941 being two. The rain, which fell just prior to the Battle of Waterloo, turned the battlefield into a quagmire, forcing Napoleon to delay the start of the battle and lessening the impact of his artillery. The churned-up fields also slowed down the charges of the French cavalry as well as the final attack by Napoleon's Old Guard. A dry battlefield may have resulted in a French victory and allowed Napoleon to continue his reign. In Russia, the German army's advance in the autumn of 1941 was halted due to the Russian muddy season, an event that should not have surprised them. This delay was one of the factors contributing to their failure to capture Moscow in 1941. The Russian muddy season continued to impact their operations twice a year, once in the autumn and once in the spring. The war in Russia would have been very different if the two muddy seasons did not exist.[12]

The importance of topography cannot be overlooked because it plays a critical role in campaigns and battles, as it funnels navies and armies to certain locations. In reality, they are only funneled there because of a need to control some geographic attribute. Technology has changed how the military views topography, but at the same time, it has increased the importance of geography. Years ago, the military only needed reliable access to food, livestock, wood, iron, and the components of gunpowder. Today, due to the increased complexity of technology, the military requires dependable access to those same items as well as oil, numerous other metals such as magnesium and titanium, in addition to uranium. Major General J.F.C. Fuller stated in 1941 in his book *Machine Warfare*, "Not so very long ago, as Napoleon said, an army marched on its belly. To-day it rolls into battle on oil. Were oil suddenly to vanish every organized nation would collapse. Oil is the life-blood of the modern world."[13] The geographic distribution of these new materials has made leaders, at the grand and strategic levels, more aware of the impact and importance of geography to the success of their plans.

When a nation controls the seas, it means that the nation can safely use the ocean to transport supplies and military forces. It does not mean that it controls 100 percent of the ocean because it is a waste of resources to dominate an empty sea. European naval forces have always been interested in controlling topographic choke points such as Gibraltar and the Danish Straits, to name two. Today, navies are interested in dominating the same choke points as well as protecting geographic features such as offshore oil fields. Ships, especially submarines, have always been impacted by geography. For submarines, water density and temperature play an important part in their safety. Even aircraft carriers are influenced by geography because their air operations are very weather dependent. Any naval strategist must always keep geography in mind when planning any operation.

Tides, wind, and storms have all played major roles in naval and amphibious operations. Storms, to include the famous kamikaze "divine wind" typhoon, helped the Japanese fight off an invasion by the Mongols. The English benefited from the "Protestant winds," which drove many of the ships in the Spanish Armada onto the coasts of Scotland and Ireland. Modern military operations have been equally impacted. The date of the allied invasion of Normandy was determined by the phase of the moon and the time of the tides, while the landings at Inchon were dependent on the tides. Other types of weather can also have an influence. John Connor proposed in his article "Climate, Environment, and Australian Frontier Wars: New South Wales, 1788–1841" that there was a strong correlation concerning drought and the wars fought between the British and Aborigines due to the pressure the drought caused on farming and grazing.[14] This correlation should not be surprising as any extreme change in climate will disrupt society and, in all likelihood, will lead to war.

During the age of sailing ships and oar-powered galleys, the vast majority of major naval battles occurred near land. Large fleets searched for each other but rarely found the other in the open ocean; however, they often found their opponent at choke points or close to a harbor. One example is when Admiral Horatio Nelson pursued a French fleet in 1805 across the Atlantic to the West Indies and back to Europe without being able to bring them to combat. Eventually, he was able to meet the combined French and Spanish fleet in combat at the Battle of Trafalgar close to Cádiz, Spain, gaining one of the most decisive naval victories in history. There are very few exceptions to sailing fleets fighting battles out of sight of land. One of those rare times was the engagement between the English and French at the Battle of the

First of June in 1794. However, in this case, the French fleet of over 20 warships was escorting a convoy of over 100 merchant ships loaded with food. One reason the British were able to find the French was that the convoy and warships covered a very large area, making them easier to locate. The first naval battle in which ships from either fleet did not see the enemy was the Battle of Coral Sea in 1942. Airplanes from both fleets conducted searches and were responsible for locating the opposing fleet. However, identification errors by the pilots and confusing radio messages negated much of their efforts. All of the damage done to both sides was inflicted by aircraft. Still, both fleets were relatively close to land, and cloud banks helped hide some of the ships at critical moments.

Geography also impacts air forces. Planes are affected by cold, heat, sand, visibility, and "currents" (jet stream) in the atmosphere along with other geographic items. Even though technology has lessened the impact of certain geographic features, such as radar's impact on visibility, the effect of additional geographic features has not diminished. During World War II, the jet stream had a tremendous negative impact on the effectiveness of high-altitude bombing of Japan. The planes crossing the Himalaya Mountains during World War II had to worry about the extreme cold, strong winds, as well as all too frequent limited visibility. Carl H. Fritsche, who was a B-24 pilot during World War II, flew supply missions over the Himalayas and stated that during one mission in January 1945, they lost 33 aircraft. Also, during their flight to India across the Middle East between Cairo, Egypt and Abadan, Iran, one B-24 was lost because the pilot waited to take off from Cairo and arrived at Abadan after 10:00 a.m. Unfortunately, during that time of year, there are frequent sandstorms that start late morning that hide the airfield from view. Due to this geographic phenomenon, the late pilot could not see the airfield and crash-landed killing everyone on board.[15] Even today, with all of our modern technology, weather still impacts aircraft travel and can be the cause of crashes. Geography has an exceptionally invasive reach and must be considered by all military units.

Modern warfare has only increased the need for an understanding of geography. When the horse was the main means of transportation, providing fodder for them was crucial. The problem is that in order to perform hard work, horses need to be properly fed. If an army was going to a location where fodder was limited, wagons must be used to haul the necessary food. As previously discussed, the problem is that after so many miles, which will vary depending on the terrain, a team of horses will need to consume everything they are carrying in the wagon. The same is true for modern military vehicles. During the week of 20–26 August 1944, the First and Third U.S. Armies were consuming over 800,000 gallons of motor fuel per day. The next week saw the Third Army reporting a fuel deficiency while the First Army had less than a day's reserve. The lack of an adequate amount of fuel had such an impact that it became impossible for the First and Third Armies to maintain the momentum of their pursuit of the retreating Germans. The issue was not the amount of fuel available in the theater of operations; rather, it was the inability to transport it to the front. During this period, the famous "Red Ball Express" trucks were using more than 300,000 gallons per day.[16] Even their efforts were not enough to feed all of the vehicles needing fuel.

Many modern military operations have been impacted by the availability or nonavailability of fuel. During World War II, German petroleum sources were a high-priority target for Allied bombers. The military's incessant need for fuel explains Adolf Hitler's desire to overrun the Russian oil fields in Baku as well as Germany's concentrated heavy antiaircraft defenses around the Romanian oil fields. The oil fields in Baku were so important that Winston Churchill ordered plans to be developed for British bombers to attack and hopefully destroy the Baku oil fields in order to keep the Germans from gaining control of them. This plan came close to being implemented when it appeared that the Soviet Union would be defeated in late 1941.[17] Even though Russia maintained control of the Baku region, it was not self-sufficient in oil for a large part of the war. In response, the Western allies shipped 2,113,449 long tons (a long ton is an imperial ton and is equal to 2,240 pounds) of petroleum products to Russia mainly through the Persian Corridor.[18] Japan was also anxious to control a reliable supply of oil and deny it to the Allies. Possession of the Indonesian oil fields helps explain why Japan invaded Indonesia. However, Japan's oil supply line was vulnerable to interdiction by Allied submarines, and submariners on both sides considered oil tankers an important target. The United States was the only major country during World War II that was not dependent on foreign sources of oil, although it needed to transport petroleum products around the world to its widely dispersed military units as well as numerous allies.

There are many other natural resources beyond oil that are vital to the operation of a modern economy and military. During World War II, the trucks, tanks, and aircraft given to the Soviet Union were the most publicized items sent to them. However, there were items of equal, if not more, importance that were transported to the Soviet Union at high risk. A partial list would include aluminum, manganese, and coal.[19] All of these minerals are vital to the production of modern military equipment, and Russia was in need of them to replace sources that were now under the control of the Germans. Very few countries are completely self-sufficient for all of their mineral needs. Thus, it is important for countries to control the sources either through peaceful trade or treaties or, as a last resort, military action.

Geography also impacts the design of military equipment. During World War II, the United States had arguably the best long-range transports and bombers. Part of this was due to the United States being a continental country, and thus large aircraft were designed to fly long distances. Ships are not exempt from this as ships in the U.S. Navy were designed to operate for a long time, far away from support bases, while ships in the British navy were not because Britain had major supply bases around the world. Heavy armor vehicles are especially susceptible to the influence of geography. During World War II, Russian tanks had broad treads that allowed them to more easily traverse the often boggy ground of northern Russia, while German tanks with their narrow treads had difficulty. Vehicles used by the United States were designed so that they could be easily transported by ships and landing craft since all of its equipment had to be moved overseas. Today, this trend of adaptation due to geography continues, as those countries whose armor vehicles are expected to operate in a desert climate need to be air-conditioned if their crews are expected to operate at peak efficiency.

Climate has played a major role in many military campaigns. During World War II, fighting took place in the extreme climates of the Artic, jungles, and deserts. All of these climates demand different logistics and equipment. The Axis (German/Italian) experience in North Africa is but one example. The geographic problems confronting the Axis forces in North Africa were numerous. First, all of the supplies they needed had to be shipped from Europe. In Europe, many necessary logistic items could be obtained locally but not in North Africa. Second, the ports they used were small due to geography and could not handle the necessary volume of supplies. Third, their supply line from the ports to the front was extremely long. The front eventually moved so far from the ports that a large percentage of the fuel being hauled was needed for the vehicles hauling it. The British, who had similar problems, made extensive use of railroads and pipelines both of which are more efficient than vehicles. In the end, geography assisted the Allies, as they were able to use technology to better mitigate the geographic issues than were the Axis.[20]

**

Throughout history, there have been a number of locations that have had more than their share of battles. Two locations in Europe are Adrianople (today's Edirne, Turkey) and Belgium, the "Cockpit of Europe." Geographically, Adrianople is a funnel point for armies moving either from or to Eastern Europe and the territory north of the Bosporus and Dardenelles Straits. It is a strategic location that gives the side holding it more freedom of movement. The case of Belgium is similar as it is the best route between Northern Europe and France. A number of armies have clashed in both locations, and in most cases, the victor in that battle went on to win the war.

**

Geographic errors can and will inevitably occur at all levels of command. One excellent example of an error at the grand strategy level is imperial Germany's decision to construct a high seas fleet. The policy to create a large battle fleet was initiated by Emperor Wilhelm II in the late 1800s as part of his desire to increase German influence throughout the world.[21] However, imperial Germany's army was considered the strongest in the world, and its economy and manufacturing base were also considered the largest in Europe.[22] These strengths, along with Germany's increasing population, made Great Britain nervous when imperial Germany's fleet increased to a size where it began to threaten Great Britain's naval dominance of the North Atlantic and the safety of the island nation. The new imperial German fleet became a threat to the geographic safety of Great Britain, while not increasing the geographic safety of imperial Germany.

As a result of Wilhelm's actions, Great Britain was forced to become allied with its longtime enemy, France. As part of the alliance, it was agreed that the French navy would guard the Mediterranean while the British navy guarded the North Atlantic. It is highly probable that without Great Britain's entry in World War I, on the side of the Allies, imperial Germany would have defeated both France and Russia. Thus, Emperor Wilhelm II's policy to build a large navy was directly responsible for his country's defeat in World War I—a fleet that did not make his country any safer. However, if the war had been short and the British blockade did not have enough time to take effect, Wilhelm's error would not have had much of an impact. However, it was a long war and the British blockade had a tremendous impact. It is estimated that 750,000 German civilians died from starvation, almost as many who died due to Allied bombing in World War II, while thousands of others in countries allied to German also died from starvation.[23] The blockade was very effective, and beyond the civilian deaths, the inability to import vital raw materials directly impacted German manufacturing.

Decisions made at the tactical level can also have far-reaching effects, but only if at the grand strategy level these events are allowed to get out of control. Although the assassination of Archduke Franz Ferdinand of Austria started World War I and can be used as an example, there is an earlier one. In 1754, George Washington was instructed to establish a fort where the Allegheny and Monongahela Rivers meet to form the Ohio River. However, the French were able to chase away the Virginians who were building the fort and proceeded to build their own. Additional Virginia militia units, under the command of George Washington, were sent to force the French out. Washington, believing that the French were too strong for his force, established a fort at Great Meadows. While there, Washington learned that a small French unit was camped near his location. He took a portion of his command along with some allied Indians to contact the French unit. After Washington and his men had surrounded the French, a shot was fired, which caused all of his men to fire their muskets. The surviving French soldiers surrendered, but then the French commander, Ensign Joseph Coulon de Jumonville, was killed after the surrender. One French soldier escaped and reported the attack. The French retaliated by attacking Washington's "army" at Fort Necessity, forcing Washington to surrender and sign a document stating that he was guilty of the assassination of a French officer, Jumonville. This minor incident at the tactical level started the world on the path to what is considered the first world war and is known by many different names. The one most familiar to Americans is the French and Indian War, which is better known in Europe as the Seven Years' War.[24]

This flash point incident occurred in a part of the world that most European leaders could not have found on a map. However, there were grand strategy/policy issues that allowed it to become the flash point. The European war prior to the

Seven Years' War was the War of Austrian Succession, which ended with the Peace of Aix-la-Chapelle in 1748. The peace treaty was more of a truce than a lasting peace. The problem was that the treaty left many of the disputes that started the war unresolved. Consequently, both Great Britain and France, along with Austria-Hungary and Russia, waited for an incident that they could use to justify a new war. The conflict between Great Britain and France, over who would control the area where the Allegheny and Monongahela Rivers meet to form the Ohio River, was the needed flash point. So even though a decision made at the tactical command level actually initiated the war, decisions made at the grand strategy command level allowed it to have more significance than it deserved.

Problems can also arise if one level of command interferes with another. If higher level leaders interfere with the plans or operations at lower levels, the levels will be compressed. If compressed too tightly, there will be an implosion, which will often lead to disaster. The opposite is true. If leaders at a lower level make decisions that impact operations or plans at higher levels, these decisions will, if left unchecked, result in an explosion and, at worse, a disaster and, at best, a disruption of plans. Examples of both can be found during the Civil War and will be discussed in other chapters.

***

A knowledge of geography and the impact technology has on it is essential for all political and military figures. This is especially important on the effect geography has on logistics. A weak or misleading knowledge will lead to disaster. It must be remembered that the level of command will influence the view an individual has. For example, at the higher levels, the concern is what type of supplies are needed, while at the lower level, the concern is how to get the supplies to where they are needed. Consequently, the study of history directly related to the impact of geography is essential as many of the problems are similar. The geographic issues faced by Scipio Africanus and his Carthaginian opponents in 210 BC and how both sides solved or did not solve them are still good lessons for today. This is not to belittle strategy or tactics, as a knowledge of geography is essential to both. However, if the logistic support is not sufficient, it will directly impact both. Geography is all encompassing, and a lack of knowledge about it will eventually lead to failure.

11

Geography and Command Decisions During the American Civil War

Geography influences all levels of command but impacts each one differently.

There are many different definitions of grand strategy, strategic command, operational command, and tactical command. The definitions I will be using are as follows:

- Grand strategy are decisions made at the highest possible level and determines which wars to fight, how to generate the necessary resources for that war, including popular support, and what the goals of the war are.
- Strategic command determines how the available resources are to be allocated, how the war is to be fought, and what objectives need to be controlled to achieve the goals of the war.
- Operational command determines which battles to fight and the objectives for each battle.
- Tactical command determines how the battle is to be fought.

As previously stated, there is degree of overlap between each of the levels. However, the amount of overlap has changed over time as technology has increased the distance between each level. In ancient times, Alexander the Great controlled all four levels. But as technology advanced and the size of armies and the distances involved increased, separation began between the four levels. By the time of the Civil War, the separation between the four levels had developed to the point we know them today. Abraham Lincoln, for the most part, was involved in the two highest levels of command while Ulysses S. Grant's level of command changed from tactical to operational and finally strategic as his rank and authority increased. Still, when he became the commander of the Federal armies, Grant dealt with both the strategic and operational levels. On the Confederate side, Jefferson Davis, like Lincoln, involved himself mainly with the two highest levels. Although Davis had military advisors, there was no commander of the Confederate armies until Robert E. Lee was appointed to the position very late in the war. Prior to that, Lee concentrated on the Virginia area of operations, although he did give advice to Davis when asked.

One technological change that increased Lincoln's and Davis's ability to be actively involved in strategic and operational issues was the telegraph. It allowed both men to quickly send written messages to their commanders and to receive information from them reducing the twin obstacles of time and distance. It also allowed newspaper reporters to quickly send information, which could be positive or negative, to their papers. Being in constant and quick communication with subordinates became so important that the Federal Army created the Military Telegraph Service. The service followed all of the armies, and at times, commanders in the field felt that it restricted their independence. One example is when General William T. Sherman was worried about the possibility of his March to the Sea being recalled until he was no longer in telegraph communication with Washington.[1] The ability to quickly contact a subordinate decreased their independence and showed that any technological tool is double sided and has both positive and negative aspects.

***

Control of a geographic location(s) has been a major objective in many wars. Wars have been fought to control Alsace-Lorraine, the Caribbean sugar islands, as well as Russia's quest for a warm water port and the United States' drive to go from the Atlantic Ocean to the Pacific Ocean "Manifest Destiny." The list goes on. The American Civil War was no different as both sides' objectives can be viewed through the lens of geography.

For Lincoln, at the grand strategy level, the geographic objective of the war was unification of the country. This is not to say that other objectives did not exist but that geographic unification of the country was one of his major objectives. Lincoln emphasized his geographic objective a number of times, with none more forcibly than in August 1862 when he sent a letter to Horace Greeley, owner of the *New York Tribune*, concerning an editorial that Greeley had placed in his paper about Lincoln's policy toward emancipation of the slaves. In his letter, Lincoln stated,

> As to the policy I "seem to be pursuing" as you say, I have not meant to leave any one in doubt. I would save the Union. I would save it the shortest way under the Constitution. The sooner the national authority can be restored; the nearer the Union will be "the Union as it was." If there be those who would not save the Union, unless they could at the same time save slavery, I do not agree with them. If there be those who would not save the Union unless they could at the same time destroy slavery, I do not agree with them. My paramount object in this struggle is to save the Union, and is not either to save or to destroy slavery. If I could save the Union without freeing any slave I would do it; and if I could save it by freeing some and leaving others alone I would also do that. What I do about slavery, I forbear because I do not believe it would help to save the Union. I shall do less whenever I shall believe what I am doing hurts the cause, and I shall do more whenever I shall believe doing more will help the cause.[2]

Lincoln kept his principal goal in mind whenever he had to deal with problems. During the Trent Affair in late 1861, he reluctantly gave in to the British demand that the United States release the two Confederate diplomats, James Mason and John Slidell, who had been taken off the British mail packet RMS *Trent* by Captain Charles Wilkes, commander of the USS *San Jacinto*. A few years later in 1865, when visiting General Grant and his armies in Virginia, Lincoln stated in regard to the Trent Affair: "We [Lincoln and his cabinet] gave due consideration to the case, but at that critical period of the war it was soon decided to deliver up the prisoners [Mason and Slidell]. It was a pretty bitter pill to swallow, but I contented myself with believing that England's triumph in the matter would be short-lived, and that after ending our war successfully we would be so powerful that we could call her to account for all of the embarrassments she had inflicted upon us."[3]

Confederate president Davis had a similar geographic grand strategy except his was the independence of the states in the Confederacy. During the winter of 1865, after the failure of the Hampton Roads conference, General Robert E. Lee spoke to Davis about the possibility of negotiating a peace with the Federal government. After his meeting with Davis, Lee informed General John Gordon that President Davis believed the Confederacy could not obtain terms acceptable to the Confederacy, as independence was its primary goal.[4] This is what made the war so terrible since the war aims for both sides were mutually exclusive, only permitting one side to achieve its grand strategy goal.

Lincoln's experience with the military had been limited before the Civil War to serving as a militia company commander during the Black Hawk War where he saw no combat. Consequently, Lincoln initially limited his involvement in military affairs and mainly gave suggestions rather than orders. But when his commanders did not achieve success and failed to adequately communicate with him, Lincoln studied books on military operations and became more involved at both the strategic and operational levels. As previously discussed, a relatively new piece of technology, the telegraph, allowed Lincoln to quickly communicate with the vast majority of his commanders and to see all of the messages they were sending to Washington.

One of Lincoln's first major attempts to control and coordinate Federal armies was during the 1862 Shenandoah Valley campaign. During this time, General George McClellan was the commander of all the Federal armies. However, he failed to adequately perform the job because he concentrated on the Army of the Potomac, the army he directly commanded. McClellan should have been acting at the grand strategy and strategic levels, but he disregarded those levels and concerned himself with the operational level. As a result, when General Stonewall Jackson began his 1862 Valley campaign, there was no military officer who could adequately command and coordinate Federal efforts to defeat him. Lincoln felt forced to fill the void and began sending orders to Generals McDowell, Fremont, and Banks. Lincoln realized that the geography of the Valley gave his armies the opportunity to trap Jackson and then destroy his army. However, his plan collapsed, mainly due to failures on the part of his generals.

Most of Lincoln's lower level supervision was concentrated in the eastern theater of operations due to his proximity to it and the continual threat to the capital. Still, he kept track of events in the western theater and would give orders to the commanders there as needed. One example of this is Lincoln's messages to General

11. Geography and Command Decisions During the American Civil War   157

Ambrose Burnside at Knoxville. General William Rosecrans had been defeated at the Battle of Chickamauga, and his army had been bottled up in Chattanooga. During this crisis, Lincoln repeatedly sent Burnside telegrams ordering him to march to the relief of Rosecrans. Although General Henry Halleck was the nominal head of the Federal armies, he refused to take responsibility and issue orders. Thus, Lincoln was forced to take command. Luckily for Lincoln and the Federals, once General Ulysses S. Grant took command of all of the Federal armies, Lincoln realized he now had a general who would follow his grand strategic plan and keep him well informed.

Lincoln also gave commands when political issues became involved. One example is when Lincoln wanted eastern Tennessee under Federal control due to its large pro–Federal population. A second example is when he wanted to stop Confederate raids into Maryland and Pennsylvania from the Shenandoah Valley. A good example of an action taken at a lower level impacting higher levels of command was when General John C. Fremont issued a proclamation in August 1861. The proclamation included a statement emancipating all slaves owned by anyone who had taken an active part in the rebellion against the government.[5] Since neither the country, especially the border states, nor Lincoln was prepared for such a step so early in the war, Lincoln was forced to order Fremont to revise his proclamation. This upset the northern abolitionists but reassured the border states. One reason Lincoln ordered Fremont to revise his proclamation, beyond the principle that Fremont did not have the authority to issue such a proclamation, was that he was worried about losing Kentucky to the Confederacy. Lincoln later wrote to Orville Browning,

> No doubt the thing [Fremont's proclamation] was popular in some quarters, and would have been more so if it had been a general declaration of emancipation. The Kentucky Legislature would not budge till that proclamation was modified; and Gen. Anderson telegraphed me that on the news of Gen. Fremont having actually issued deeds of manumission, a whole company of our Volunteers threw down their arms and disbanded. I was so assured, as to think it probable, that the very arms we had furnished Kentucky would be turned against us. I think to lose Kentucky is nearly the same as to lose the whole game. Kentucky gone, we can not [*sic*] hold Missouri, nor, as I think, Maryland. These all against us, and the job on our hands is too large for us. We would as well consent to separation at once, including the surrender of this capitol.[6]

Lincoln was politically and geographically astute and fully realized the importance of controlling the border states.

Lincoln was also very aware of the importance of controlling the Mississippi River as it gave farmers in the Midwest access to foreign markets. When orders were issued to General John A. McClernand for his Mississippi River expedition "to clear the Mississippi river and open navigation to New Orleans,"[7] Lincoln endorsed the orders and wrote, "This order, though marked confidential, may be shown by Gen. McClernand, to Governors, and even others, when, in his discretion, he believes so doing to be indispensable to the progress of the expedition. I add that I feel deep interest in the success of the expedition, and desire it to be pushed forward with all possible dispatch, consistently with the other parts of the military service."[8] Lincoln's endorsement shows how he appreciated the importance of controlling the Mississippi River but at the same time not dictating how the military is to manage operations.

Lincoln was also aware of the time/distance factor, knowing that having interior lines gave the Confederates a geographic advantage in moving forces around. In a message to General Carlos Buell in January 1862, Lincoln wrote,

> Your dispatch of yesterday is received, in which you say "I have received your letter and Gen. McClellan's; and will, at once devote all my efforts to your views, and his." In the midst of my many cares, I have not seen, or asked to see, Gen. McClellan's letter to you. For my own views, I have not offered, and do not now offer them as orders; and while I am glad to have them respectfully considered, I would blame you to follow them contrary to your own clear judgment—unless I should put them in the form of orders. As to Gen. McClellan's views, you understand your duty in regard to them better than I do. With this preliminary, I state my general idea of this war to be that we have the greater numbers, and the enemy has the greater facility of concentrating forces upon points of collision; that we must fail, unless we can find some way of making our advantage an over-match for his; and that this can only be done by menacing him with superior forces at different points, at the same time; so that we can safely attack, one, or both, if he makes no change; and if he weakens one to strengthen the other, forbear to attack the strengthened one, but seize, and hold the weakened one, gaining so much.[9]

Again, Lincoln's message shows his understanding of geography and his desire not to force his ideas on his generals.

***

In contrast to Lincoln, Davis had extensive military and administrative experience.[10] Davis was a graduate of the United States Military Academy, commanded a regiment in combat during the Mexican War, and had been a very progressive secretary of war. Consequently, Davis was heavily involved in Confederate military operations including the initial creation of the Confederate Army and to a lesser degree the Confederate Navy. One of Davis's advantages and disadvantages was that he personally knew most of the regular army officers who left the United States Army and joined the Confederate Army. The problem was that he knew them as junior officers. Unfortunately, excellent performance as a junior officer does not always mean the person will be an excellent senior officer.

Davis had five different secretaries of war as well as one interim appointment but only one secretary of navy. The difficulty was that Davis micromanaged the business brought before the secretary of war as this was his area of expertise. In contrast, he was not as interested in naval affairs and let Stephen Mallory, the secretary of navy, manage the department. Davis, as well as Lincoln, appointed generals and issued orders to various commands, and he probably did more of this than Lincoln. However, Davis traveled more than Lincoln, who rarely left the capital, although part of this was to deal with issues in Braxton Bragg's Army of Tennessee.

Davis realized if the Confederacy was to remain viable, it had to control as much territory as possible. Part of his thinking was based on geographically determined natural resources while another reason was to keep the Confederacy intact. Some generals, such as Joseph Johnston and Pierre Beauregard, did not understand Davis's thoughts and justified their retreats as Fabian tactics, where the defending army retreats causing the attacking army to lengthen its supply lines and becomes more vulnerable to counterattack. However, an army that was dependent on material that must be produced in factories and requires specific natural resources cannot afford to use Fabian tactics. During World War II, the Soviet army retreated a great distance from its border, but at the same time, the Soviet Union relocated its factories to safe locations. As previously stated, they were also receiving large amounts of natural resources and war material from their allies. Fabian tactics only work when the defending army is not dependent on natural resources and industry that are located in the territory yielded to the enemy. Unless, of course, they can receive material from an outside source to replace resources that are now under enemy control. Although this is the preferred strategy for guerrilla warfare, it is only viable if the guerrillas have a sanctuary and a reliable source of supplies.

Davis interfered with his generals and went down to the operational command sphere with, all too often, a negative impact since this undercut the authority of his generals. An excellent example of this is when Davis, through his secretary of war, Judah Benjamin, ordered Jackson to withdraw his troops from Romney back to Winchester.[11] The problem was that Jackson's winter campaign to take Bath (modern-day Berkeley Springs, West Virginia) and Romney, although it was successful, was too much for the new units. Jackson's objectives for his campaign were twofold. First, by taking Bath, Jackson could control the railroad on opposite sides of the Potomac, thus cutting the B&O Railroad. This would severely hamper Federal transportation and communications between Washington and Ohio. Second, by taking Bath and Romney, Jackson put more space between Winchester and any Federal advance from the north or west, giving him more time to react. However, many of the troops were not the veterans they would later become, and the winter weather was very brutal. Then, some officers, from units other than the Stonewall brigade, used their political influence to get President Davis to order their withdrawal from Romney. The Federal Army quickly reoccupied Romney, and by the 14th of February, after the Confederate troops had been withdrawn or captured, trains were operating where previously they could not.[12] Davis's interference had cost the Confederacy a valuable strategic and operational geographic advantage.

**

For the Federals, the strategic view of geography was different from the grand strategy view but was still in support of Lincoln's grand strategy. General Winfield Scott expressed his strategic plan in a message to General George B. McClellan, who was then commanding the Ohio Volunteers. Scott's plan had three parts. The first part dealt with how many men would be needed. The second part stated,

"We rely greatly on the sure operation of a complete blockade of the Atlantic and Gulf ports soon to commence. In connection with such blockade we propose a powerful movement down the Mississippi to the ocean, with a cordon of posts at proper points." The third part dealt with the "greatest obstacle in the way of this plan—the great danger now pressing upon us—the impatience of our patriotic and loyal Union friends."[13] Scott's thoughts became known as the Anaconda Plan as its intent was a slow strangulation of the Confederacy.

The navy's strategic plan fit Scott's Anaconda Plan perfectly. It was the navy's responsibility to ensure the blockade of the southern ports was as tight as possible and that as few ships as possible were able to slip through it.[14] The navy's problem was ensuring that an adequate number of ships remained on station to stop blockade runners. Since all of the newer ships in the navy had coal-fired boilers, it was necessary for these ships to be regularly resupplied with quality coal of which the Federals had adequate supplies. Resupply ports were just as geographically dependent. They needed to have deep anchorages, be protected from the weather, have the capacity of developing docking facilities, be close to major Confederate ports where the Federal Navy was operating, and be defensible from land attack. Since there were adequate facilities located along the Gulf coast under Federal control, only the Atlantic coast was an issue. Expeditions were sent to secure Hatteras Inlet and Port Royal. Although the strategic geographic decision had been made, capturing both locations became an operational and tactical issue with new technology influencing how the battles were fought in regard to geography.

Although planning for the Port Royal expedition started first, the Hatteras Inlet expedition left first and achieved its objective on the 29th of August 1861. There were a number of reasons the Union had for gaining control of Hatteras Inlet. The primary reason was that Confederate ships were operating from it and capturing Federal merchant ships, which were using the nearby Gulf Stream to sail north. In one case, the *Winslow* captured 16 merchantmen in a six-week period.[15] The loss of numerous Federal merchant ships caused an uproar among Federal merchants and ship owners. Newspapers supported their efforts by publishing a number of articles complaining about the lack of protection by the navy. A secondary reason was that Hatteras was one of the busiest ports in North Carolina in 1861, and closing access to it would improve the blockade.[16] The initial plan was to sink old ships in the channel to block it. However, the idea was rejected as tidal currents would have swept the ships away or scoured out a new channel. As a result, an expedition was needed, and one was assembled to capture the forts at the mouth of the inlet.

The morning after the fleet arrived at Hatteras, Flag Officer Silas Stringham ordered his ships to begin bombarding Fort Clark, one of the two guarding the inlet. In the past, sailing ships had to anchor when they were bombarding a fort. This made them a stationary target for the gunners in the fort, giving the fort's gunners an excellent target. However, most of Stringham's ships were steam powered and did not need to anchor but could continue to move while bombarding the fort. The one ship, the *Cumberland*, that was not steam powered was towed by the *Wabash*.[17] By having his ships continually move, Stringham negated the advantage the fort's gunners had because they could not correct their aim between shots. Technology had helped mitigate geography. However, geography did have an impact as a strong southerly wind disrupted the landing of the Federal troops and eventually cut them off from the fleet. Fortunately for the Federals, the Confederate defenders abandoned Fort Clark, and the Federal troops occupied it unopposed.

During the night, a storm blew up, and the Federal fleet was forced to move offshore. The next day, the weather improved, and the Federal fleet returned to bombard the other Confederate fort, Fort Hatteras. Stringham used the same tactics as had been used against Fort Clark. The Federal fleet was again successful with the only real damage being done to the *Monticello* when it ran aground the previous day. Although Hatteras Inlet did not become a major resupply base for the Federal Navy, it did open large parts of coastal North Carolina to Federal attack and occupation. Its capture fit the Federal's strategy for both the navy and the army.

Port Royal was captured in November 1861 and was also an easy victory for the Federals. At Port Royal, Flag Officer Samuel Du Pont's plan was for his fleet to continuously move in a circle between the two Confederate forts. However, one of his captains observed that he could anchor his ship and enfilade Fort Walker. As a result, Fort Walker surrendered, and the commander of Fort Beauregard, fearing his escape route would be cut off, abandoned the fort. As a result of this victory, Port Royal became the major naval resupply depot for the South Atlantic Blockading Fleet.

Technology helped make these victories possible for the Federal Navy. If the ships in the Federal fleet had not been steam powered, the Federal ships would have sustained more damage and may not have been able to capture all of the forts. Geography determined the navy's objective, and technology helped it overcome geographic issues that would have previously been major obstacles.

***

When the American Civil War began, saltpeter, because of the increased demand for gunpowder, became a crucial strategic material. As previously stated, the best quality saltpeter came from British-controlled India. There was a real fear within the Federal government that Great Britain would fully enforce its neutrality laws and stop the importation of saltpeter to both the Federals and Confederates. Consequently, Lammot du Pont was sent to Great Britain, with the secret backing of the Federal government, to purchase all of the saltpeter he could. Unfortunately for du Pont, the Trent Affair occurred during this same period. As a result, his shipment of saltpeter was threatened with embargo, but the peaceful resolution of the Trent Affair allowed him to ship his precious cargo to the United States.[18] There were multiple reasons for Lincoln not wanting a war with Great Britain while fighting the Confederacy, with one reason being the loss of access to India's quality saltpeter.

The Confederacy was in the same situation as the Federal government, but it did not have as easy access to imported saltpeter. However, good sources of saltpeter could be found in the limestone caves located in a number of the Southern states. Caves in other parts of the country do not produce saltpeter because soil conditions, temperature, and moisture all must be within a specific range. The needed ranges are found only in limestone caves in the Upper South.[19] More importantly, even with the blockade, ships owned by the Confederate Ordnance Department were able to bring a wide range of weapons and minerals, including saltpeter, into Confederate ports. By the end of the war, about 2,700,000 pounds of saltpeter slipped through the blockade, and another 300,000 pounds were obtained from the caves.[20] The Confederacy also created saltpeter beds, although these beds, due to the time needed for them to produce saltpeter, never reached full production.[21] Still, by the end of the war, there were about 70,000 pounds of gunpowder at the Confederate Powder Works.[22] Although the Confederate armies suffered from a lack of material during the war compared to the Federal armies, a lack of gunpowder was not one of the items. There were shortages, but many of these were mostly due to the Confederacy's weak railroad system rather than a lack of resources.

***

Salt is a mineral required for human life, and disruption of Confederate production and importation of it became a target of Federal operations at the operational level. The issue for the Confederacy was that before the war, most of the salt that was needed was imported, but the blockade reduced that amount tremendously. Consequently, the Confederacy was forced to find internal sources. The adjutant general of Alabama calculated that the Confederacy, during the war, required 6,000,000 bushels of salt a year or 300,000,000 pounds, an amount less than what it had been consuming prior to the war.[23] Salt was essential for a number of purposes during the war, beyond individual consumption, that we take for granted with modern refrigeration. Salt was used to cure hams, preserve fish, preserve butter, and preserve hides until they could be tanned. In addition, salt was needed for the horses, mules, and other draft animals being used by the Confederate armies. A shortage of it led to weak or sick animals. As an example, General Jeb Stuart reported to General Robert E. Lee in late 1862 that his horses had a disease that was causing their hoofs to slough, and he partially attributed this to the lack of salt.[24]

There were two main methods of obtaining salt: boiling down water from saline artesian wells or seawater, or mining rock salt. Although salt was available in all of the Confederate states, there were five locations where salt could be economically obtained: on the Great Kanawha River three miles north of Charleston, Virginia (now West Virginia); the Goose Creek Salt Works around Manchester, Kentucky; wells in Clarke, Washington, and Mobile counties in Alabama; wells in north Louisiana; and the wells around Saltville, Virginia.[25] Access to the wells in Kentucky and those around Charleston were lost early in the war and thus contributed little to the Confederacy as a whole. However, the salt wells located near Saltville, Virginia, in the upper Shenandoah Valley, could provide enough salt to supply the entire Confederacy.[26]

Saltville was a town so small that it did not have its own listing in the 1860 census, but population alone does not make a location geographically important. Prior to the Civil War, Saltville was connected to the rest of the country by railroad, which enabled it to sell its salt throughout the country. During the war, this railroad connection became crucial. But an inadequate number of laborers and the deteriorating condition of the railroads meant it became difficult, if not impossible, to effectively transport the salt throughout the Confederacy. Subsequently, other sources were found in various locations in the Confederacy, including acquiring salt from the ocean. The production and distribution of salt was so crucial that many of the men working in the production of salt were exempt from the draft, and the distribution of salt became an item of contention.[27]

Due to its importance, Saltville and other salt-producing sites became targets for Federal raids. Although only limited references can be found in the collected works of Abraham Lincoln, there are numerous references to salt in both the army and navy *Official Records*. Many of the references in the navy's records deal with raids conducted to destroy salt-making operations along the Atlantic and Gulf coasts. One example of the navy's efforts was a raid conducted by Lieutenant Commander John E. Hart of the USS *Albatross*.[28] Rear Admiral David Farragut gave Hart orders in November 1862 to destroy the salt works along the coast between Pensacola and St. Andrews Bay. For the raid, Hart had the *Albatross*, *Bohio*, and *Wanderer* under his command. Hart did not discover any saltworks until he reached St. Andrews Bay. He spent almost two weeks there destroying saltworks, burning boats and houses, and killing horses, mules, and cattle. During this time, his men destroyed salt pans that had an estimated capacity of 32,900 gallons of salt water. In his report, Hart stated, "The shores or waterfront of this bay are immense, and it would give one vessel and her armed boats constant activity, for salt is so much needed by the people of the Confederate States that they will run almost any risk to make it."[29] As noted by Hart, even with continual raiding by the navy, the saltworks were so vital to the Confederacy and lucrative to the producers that saltworks continued to be rebuilt despite being continually raided and destroyed.

The U.S. Army also did its part in destroying Confederate saltworks with its biggest target being the saltworks at Saltville. In 1864, the Saltville salt mines produced 200,000,000 pounds of salt, but the Virginia and Tennessee Railroad was not capable of transporting all of it.[30] The Federal Army was well aware of Saltville and its importance. Two raids were conducted against it in the summer and autumn of 1863, but both were unsuccessful. When General Grant took command, he recognized the importance of the natural resources and communications network in the upper valley. Consequently, he sent a message in February 1864 to General John Schofield asking for his opinion on advancing a column in the spring up the Holston

Valley to get behind General James Longstreet. Grant added, "This enterprise would be hazardous, but would pay well if successful. The destruction of the important bridges between Bristol and Saltville and of salt-works there would compensate for great risks."[31] As part of Grant's bigger effort, a larger Federal force attacked Saltville in October 1864, but it was defeated without causing any damage to the saltworks. The next attempt to destroy the saltworks was in December 1864. By that time, the defending Confederate forces had been reduced because most of the units had been redeployed to other areas where manpower was needed. This attempt by General George Stoneman defeated the defending Confederate forces and inflicted major damage to the saltworks. However, the works were too extensive for the Federal forces to entirely destroy during the short time they were there, and the saltworks were quickly put back in operation although, initially, at a reduced output. In the end, the Confederacy could not develop the needed infrastructure to harvest the salt, the transportation system to distribute it, or the ability to defend it against Federal attempts to destroy the salt.

Although there was enough salt production within the Confederacy from Saltville and the mines in Louisiana and Alabama, in addition to the saltwater distillation efforts along the seacoast, there were three main difficulties limiting distribution. The first was that the Confederate railroad system could not haul all of the salt being produced, and much of the salt that was distilled along the coast could not be easily transported to where it was needed. The second reason was that Federal raids along the coast and against the various salt mines disrupted production. The third reason was that states' rights interfered with a rational "nationwide" distribution system, as individual state governments wanted to make sure that their own citizens were adequately supplied first. Salt is but one example of a crucial mineral that the lack of and the Confederacy's inability to transport it and/or centrally control its distribution helped doom the Confederate cause. It was a mineral that influenced command decisions at the strategic and operational levels.

***

General William T. Sherman's famous March to the Sea was especially geographically dependent. Sherman had to wait until Grant was satisfied that John Hood's army, which was moving north, could be contained by the available forces and that Sherman's campaign would have an excellent chance of success. Then he had to wait until the autumn rains had stopped.[32] He had to wait until the rains stopped as there were no good all-weather roads on which his wagons could move. Sherman was well aware that his wagons and artillery would get bogged down on wet dirt roads. Consequently, he was willing to wait until November to start his campaign. Waiting was also advantageous for Sherman because by the time he started his march, crops had been harvested and were in storage. This contributed to limiting the amount of work his men needed to do to feed themselves and their animals. In his memoirs, Sherman emphasized the necessity of foraging as "no army could have carried along sufficient food and fodder for a march of three hundred miles; so that foraging in some shape was necessary."[33] However, to successfully forage, Sherman had to disperse his army and keep it continually moving. Like Lee at Gettysburg, if Sherman had been forced to concentrate his army, he would have begun to run out of food for the men and forage for the animals. Sherman was only able to make his March to the Sea because there was no significant Confederate forces between him and Savannah. Sherman understood geography and was able to skillfully plan and execute his campaign because of his knowledge.

***

It was not just the eastern, coastal, and western theaters in which geography played an important role, as the same was true for the trans-Mississippi theater. In the trans-Mississippi theater, most of the fighting took place in northern Arkansas and southern Missouri. Most of this area was sparsely populated making it difficult for an army to obtain food for its men or forage for its animals. However, the more populated western part of Missouri near Kansas City was a rich agricultural area and could easily provide both food and forage. This changed after the raid on Lawrence, Kansas, by William Quantrill in the summer of 1862. As a result of that raid, General Thomas Ewing, Jr., issued General Order Number 11. That order depopulated counties in western Missouri because it was thought that these people aided the Confederate raiders. Even though the order was counterproductive since it increased Confederate sympathy in that area, it did have the effect of making it difficult for Confederate units to find food for their men in those counties. The challenge of finding food and forage in southern Missouri and northern Arkansas is illustrated by General Stirling Price's statement about his retreat from Missouri in 1864: "I determined not to risk the crossing of the Arkansas river between Forth [sic] Smith and Little Rock, on which route I could not procure subsistence, forage or grass in anything like sufficient quantity."[34] Geography influences how many people will settle in an area and how rich the farmland is. This in turn influenced armies throughout history as to where it was possible to campaign.

***

During the American Civil War, 223,535 Federal Soldiers were discharged for physical disabilities while 199,720 died from various diseases. In contrast, 110,070 Soldiers were killed or mortally wounded.[35] Most of the men who died from a disease died from "camp diseases" such as measles, mumps, diarrhea, dysentery, and typhoid, as well as malnutrition. Often, the effect of these diseases impacted a number of campaigns and battles. New regiments had to go through a period of "conditioning" during which a large percentage of the unit would become ineffective when they were exposed to a number of communicable diseases such as measles and mumps. If they survived, they became immune to most of them.

At least two diseases, malaria and yellow fever, were geographically limited to the range of the *Anopheles* and *Aedes* mosquitoes, respectively. Most commanders were aware of these diseases and knew that exposure to them could cause death. The threat and effect of these two diseases influenced both the strategic and operational levels. Because of these diseases, General Winfield Scott warned about campaigning below Memphis before the frosts.[36] During the 1862 Peninsula Campaign, General Robert E. Lee and President Jefferson Davis asked for reinforcements from South Carolina, for, as President Davis stated, "General Lee is in the field. Needs reinforcements. Can you give them? Decisive operations are pending here in this section, and the climate already restrains operations on the coast."[37] Federal commanders along the southern coast were equally aware of the consequences of these diseases. General Horatio Wright informed his commander, General David Hunter, in June 1862, "Hearing from Washington that there is no probability of our receiving re-enforcements, and it being all important to provide for the health of the command in the sickly season approaching, I have determined to abandon James Island [near Charleston, South Carolina], in order that the troops may be placed where, in so far as practicable in this climate, they may be out of the way of malarious influences, and where the picket duty will not be so exhausting on our men as at present."[38]

The impact of these geographically dependent diseases was also felt in the western theater. During the "siege" of Corinth in 1862, disease was a factor in General G. Beauregard's decision to retreat and General Henry Halleck's decision not to pursue. General Beauregard explained to Jefferson Davis, in response to a question of "the circumstances and purposes of the retreat," that "our force was reduced by sickness and other causes to about 45,000 effective men of all arms, exclusive of cavalry."[39] On the Federal side, General Halleck informed Secretary of War Edwin Stanton, "Since the evacuation of Corinth and pursuit of the enemy south our army has been comparatively in good condition. The question now arises, can it be kept so during the summer? Or, in other words, can we carry on any summer campaign without having a large portion of our men on the sick list? If we follow the enemy into the swamps of Mississippi there can be no doubt that our army will be disabled by disease."[40]

The first attacks on Vicksburg by General Thomas Williams and Admiral David Farragut, in the summer of 1862, also suffered from the effect of diseases. By the time Williams abandoned his efforts against Vicksburg in July 1862, only 800 men out of the 3,200 he brought to Vicksburg were fit for duty, with up to ten men dying a day. Flag Officer Charles H. Davis's gunboat flotilla was in a similar situation. Hiram Beauchamp, assistant surgeon on the *Benton*, informed Davis that 40 percent of men on board the gunboats were on the sick list and he expected the number to increase.[41] Camp diseases and geographically dependent diseases adversely affected battles, campaigns, and thus, the war. Their impact needs to be taken into account when analyzing any battle or campaign.

***

Another geographic factor that impacted the results of a number of battles, and thus, the war, was acoustic shadows. Acoustic shadows exist where due to geographic conditions, sounds cannot be heard in some locations but will be heard in others even if these locations are much farther away. Although this may seem counterintuitive, it does happen. Charles D. Ross lists seven occurrences during the Civil War in his book *Civil War Acoustic Shadows*. Out of those seven, five impacted the results of the battle. Those five are Seven Pines, Iuka, Perryville, Chancellorsville, and Five Forks. In all five cases, the battlefield was heavily wooded, the generals could not see all of their units, and at least one of the opposing commanders was not able to hear the sounds of a battle occurring a few miles from him. In some circumstances, the weather conditions accentuated the impact. In the case of Seven Pines, General Joseph Johnston, because he could not hear the fighting taking place on the Confederate right flank, delayed the attack on the Federal right flank until it was too late. If Johnston had attacked earlier before General Edwin Sumner's troops had crossed the Chickahominy River, the Federal left would have probably been broken, and Johnston would have gained an important victory. At Perryville, General Braxton Bragg attacked the left flank of General Don Buell's army. The acoustic shadow was such that no one at Buell's headquarters, including General Alexander McCook, commander of the corps under attack, realized the Confederates were attacking. McCook found out about the battle after he rode back from army headquarters to his corps. Consequently, McCook's corps fought most of the battle with only limited support from adjacent units. Since Buell greatly outnumbered Bragg, had he known about the battle before late afternoon, there would have been a strong possibility he could have inflicted a severe defeat on Bragg. The next day when Buell planned for a simultaneous three-corps attack, Bragg had retreated. In the other three cases, acoustic shadows had similar impact on the battles where one side became disadvantaged due to the fact that their commanders could not hear the sounds of the battle. Acoustic shadows still exist today. Although technology has reduced their impact, they still need to be understood, for it is possible that they can influence the outcome of a battle.

***

Just because a general, or any officer, had an excellent understanding of geography did not mean they were strong leaders or successful. General George McClellan is a perfect example of this. McClellan's knowledge and understanding of geography was probably better than most Civil War generals. McClellan's duties as an engineering officer in the Mexican War and his work on the Illinois Central Railroad and the Ohio and Mississippi Railroad gave him a superior knowledge and understanding of geography. His decision to approach Richmond from the east using the York and James Rivers as supply routes, with the idea of laying siege to Richmond, was an excellent one. The reason is that it was a far better route than going overland from Washington because the Federal Army could avoid crossing a number of rivers that the Confederate Army could easily defend. McClellan's decision, although his campaign was not successful, was reinforced years later by General Grant when he was forced to besiege Richmond from the east.

***

The examples discussed in this chapter are just a few of the numerous incidences from the Civil War in which geography had an impact. Every reader of this book can most likely think of an example, and if all were listed, this chapter would be much, much longer. Geography influences each level of command and was viewed by each level of command differently. Its impact was ignored by commanders to their detriment and needs to be understood by anyone studying a battle or campaign.

12

Geography, Technology, and the American Civil War

Without the Industrial Revolution and the associated advances in technology, the Federal government would in all likelihood have been unsuccessful in stopping the secession of the Confederacy.

There were a number of technological advances that influenced how all levels of command viewed geography during the Civil War and changed how war was waged. The five technological advances that had the greatest influence on geography were the steam engine, machine tools, interchangeable parts, the telegraph, and rifling. The steam engine, machine tools, and interchangeable parts impacted all four levels of command. These were technological advances most people would not consider when discussing the technologies that changed warfare, but their impact was tremendous. In contrast, the telegraph affected only two levels of command—strategic and operational—as it allowed high-level commanders to communicate with their subordinates almost instantaneously. The use of rifled muskets and cannon influenced only the operational and tactical levels of command, although both indirectly affected grand strategy and strategy. Still, the importance of these two technological advances on how the war was fought cannot be underestimated. There were a number of other technological advances, such as repeating rifles, aerial balloons, and breech-loading artillery, that transformed the battlefield but did not change how commanders viewed geography.

The steam engine influenced the three highest levels of command through railroads and steamships. As previously discussed, steam power changed naval warfare during the Civil War. This was especially true when ironclad ships were introduced. No longer did naval commanders have to give primary consideration to tides and river currents when conducting operations. Although they still had to contend with them, as long as their engines produced enough power to compensate for the force created by tides and currents, they knew that they could overcome it and successfully steam against it. It would have been a very different naval war without steam-powered ships. It is highly unlikely the Federals would have been as successful in the Mississippi River Valley without steam-powered naval support. Neither General McClellan's Peninsula Campaign nor General Grant's siege of Petersburg could have occurred without naval support.

Along with ships, the steam-powered railroad allowed large numbers of troops to be rapidly transported across the country, down the coast, and up rivers. One of the most famous railroad movements of the war was when General James Longstreet's corps was transferred by rail, in the summer of 1863, from Virginia to Tennessee in time for them to participate in the Battle of Chickamauga. Shortly after that, in response to the Confederate victory at Chickamauga, the Federals transported over 20,000 men, more than 1,000 miles from the Army of the Potomac to Tennessee in less than two weeks. Neither of the movements could have occurred in that relatively short period without the use of the steam-powered railroad.

Even though the transportation of troops during the Civil War by railroad receives the most attention, the most common use of the railroad was to transport supplies. The load animal-drawn wagons could carry was much more limited than what could be carried by a single railroad car. Grant was fully aware of the advantages a railroad had over wagons when it came to transporting supplies. The importance he placed on using railroads can be seen by the military railroad he had constructed that ran behind the Federal lines at Petersburg and connected to his supply base at City Point. Railroads were so important to the war that the Federals created the United States Military Railroads (USMRR) under the command of Daniel C. McCallum. The USMRR worked closely with the army and either built or repaired railroad lines as needed. Without the efforts of the men in the USMRR, the Federals' war effort would have been severely hampered. Railroads helped negate most of the influence geography had on wagons.

Without the railroad, Sherman's Atlanta campaign would not have occurred, and if it had, it would have probably ended in failure. Sherman acknowledged this dependency:

> To have delivered regularly that amount [1,600 tons of supplies] of food and forage by ordinary wagons would have required thirty-six thousand eight hundred wagons of six mules each, allowing each wagon to have hauled two tons twenty miles each day, a simple impossibility in roads such as then existed in that region [northern Georgia] of country. Therefore, I reiterated that the Atlanta campaign was an impossibility without these railroads; and only then, because we had the men and means to maintain and defend them, in addition to what were necessary to overcome the enemy.[1]

The railroads' ability to overcome many of the time and distance obstacles created by geography became a key factor during the Civil War, and its importance did not decrease with time.

There were only a few occasions during the war in which a major army was any distance from a friendly operating railroad or a navigable river. The few times this happened were Confederate General Henry H. Sibley's New Mexico campaign, Federal General Ulysses S. Grant's Vicksburg campaign, Confederate General Robert E. Lee's Gettysburg Campaign, Confederate General Sterling Price's Missouri campaign, Federal General William T. Sherman's March to the Sea, and Confederate

General John B. Hood's Tennessee campaign. The four Confederate campaigns were unsuccessful, while the two Federal campaigns were triumphant.

The lack of adequate logistic support was a major reason behind the failure of the four Confederate campaigns. During Sibley's 1862 New Mexico campaign, finding an adequate source of food for his men became a major and debilitating issue. Although there were a number of issues that led to his defeat, including the Federal Army, in his report on his operations in New Mexico, Sibley stated,

> In concluding this report, already extended beyond my anticipations, it is proper that I should express the conviction, determined by some experience, that, except for its political geographical position, the Territory of New Mexico is not worth a quarter of the blood and treasure expended in its conquest. As a field of military operations it possesses not a single element, except in the multiplicity of its defensible positions. The indispensable element, food cannot be relied upon.[2]

Without having access to a railroad or a navigable river, Sibley could not provide his men with the logistic support they needed—geography triumphed. General Hood faced a similar problem during his 1864 Tennessee campaign. Transportation of logistic support was a major issue for Hood. He informed the Confederate Secretary of War, James A. Seddon, shortly after his army arrived at Nashville, "Middle Tennessee, although much injured by the enemy, will furnish an abundance of commissary stores, but ordnance and certain quartermaster's stores will have to come from the rear, and therefore it is very important that the railroad should be repaired at once from Cherokee to Decatur."[3] Hood was too optimistic about Middle Tennessee providing food for his men and horses because it was December and neither crops nor forage would have been in the fields. Plus, the Federal Army had been in the area for a couple of years, and any surplus food would have been taken by them. Sam Watkins, who was at Nashville under Hood's command, stated in his memoirs that the Confederate soldiers had "sunken cheeks and famine-glistening eyes."[4] Although overwhelming Federal superiority in numbers was the main reason for the Confederate defeat at Nashville, that it was winter and that both the men and horses in the Confederate Army were poorly fed and clothed had a bearing on their defeat.

Although there were a number of reasons Lee advocated for the Army of Northern Virginia to move into Pennsylvania, one major reason was that Virginia could no longer provide sufficient food and forage for the army. There were two principle reasons for this. First, northern Virginia had been devastated by the war. British Lieutenant Colonel Arthur Fremantle noted in his diary,

> The country [northern Virginia] is really magnificent, but as it has supported two large armies for two years, it is now completely cleaned out. It is almost uncultivated, and no animals are grazing where there used to be hundreds. All fences have been destroyed, and numberless farms burnt, the chimneys alone left standing. It is difficult to depict and impossible to exaggerate the sufferings which this part of Virginia has undergone.[5]

Second, Virginia, had experienced a serious drought in 1862. Consequently, little had been harvested that autumn. Then the spring of 1863 had been too wet, and thus farmers had not been able to plant much wheat, grass, or feed grain. As a result, food for the men was hard to find, and the horses and mules had to be widely dispersed to obtain enough forage. If the Army of Northern Virginia did not move north into rich farmland that had not suffered from either the war or the weather, it would slowly become weaker as the men and animals would not have received enough nutrition.[6]

There were a number of geographic reasons for the invasion route Lee chose. First, he had to cross the Potomac River upriver from the fall line at Washington as the Federal Navy could not get warships above it. Downriver from the fall line was out of the question as any crossing there would be quickly cut off from Virginia by the Federal Navy. Second, the Shenandoah Valley becomes the Cumberland Valley once the valley crosses the Potomac River. Both valleys are protected by a range of mountains to their east with easily defendable passes. Therefore, the Confederate Army could use the good road network, to include the all-weather macadamized roads, in both valleys while using a minimum force to protect its right flank from the Army of the Potomac. The Cumberland Valley was also as rich in agriculture as the Shenandoah Valley and would provide easy foraging for the troops and plenty of forage for the horses and mules. In addition, any movement by Confederate forces into the Cumberland Valley posed a threat that could not be ignored by the Federals and would quickly draw Federal troops into Pennsylvania.

Once the Army of Northern Virginia moved into Pennsylvania, the long logistic distance between its base and their location played an important role during Lee's 1863 Gettysburg Campaign. The base for the army was Winchester. All of their ordnance supplies had to be transported by wagon from the railroad depot at Staunton to Winchester and then on to the army. The supply trains also had to be protected since they were moving through enemy territory. This, of course, created another demand for troops who were needed to fight, not guard wagons.

Securing food for the men and forage for the animals was not an issue since the Confederate Army was moving through a rich agricultural area. However, to obtain enough food and forage, the army had to be dispersed. But if it was dispersed, it would be subject to being defeated in detail by the Federal Army. Once Lee received definite information that the Army of the Potomac was moving against him, he had to bring his army together. The problem was that once the army was concentrated, it would quickly deplete all of the food and forage in its immediate area. In contrast, the Federal Army was being kept well supplied by railroad. Lee's challenge was that he could not keep his army concentrated for any length of time without running the risk of starving his men and horses.

The amount of small-arms ammunition and artillery projectiles the Army of Northern Virginia used during the three-day battle was tremendous. Lee no longer had enough ammunition and projectiles to sustain another multiday battle. Then the presence of the Army of the Potomac limited the ability of Confederate quartermaster officers to seek food for the men and forage for the animals. Both of these were major reasons for Lee ordering the retreat. During the retreat, many of the foraging parties were attacked by Federal cavalry, and the Confederate Army was forced to send out larger units or not send out foraging parties at all. Lee stated in his report to General S. Cooper, adjutant and inspector general, "Owing to the strength of the enemy's position, and the reduction in our ammunition, a renewal of the engagement could not be hazarded, and the difficulty of procuring supplies rendered it impossible to continue longer where we were [Gettysburg]."[7]

Lee's problems did not end with the retreat because the Potomac River, due to flooding, became a tremendous obstacle, and his pontoon bridge had been partially destroyed. Lee stated, "The Potomac was found to be so much swollen by the rains that had fallen incessantly since our entrance into Maryland as to be unfordable. Our communications with the south side were thus interrupted, and it was difficult to procure either ammunition or subsistence, the latter being enhanced by the high waters impeding the working of the neighboring mills."[8] Geography along with the Army of the Potomac were the main factors in limiting Lee's options.

However, Lee was not aware that the Federal Army was also having difficulties. First, it too had been involved in the three days of fighting at Gettysburg and had suffered a tremendous number of casualties including many officers. In addition, the Federal Army was following in the footsteps of the Confederate Army, and that army had already taken as much of the food and forage in its line of march as possible. The rain also made it impossible for the supply trains to keep up with the faster-moving cavalry and infantry. Many of the men were completely worn out, and many of the horses were broken down.[9] Although Abraham Lincoln was disappointed that George Meade had not crushed Lee's army, he did not understand all of the obstacles Meade was facing. However, Lincoln was probably more disappointed in Meade's statement saying he had driven the enemy out of Federal territory because Meade did not understand that in Lincoln's view, the entire country was Federal territory. The two men had very different geographic views of the war.

Price's 1864 Missouri campaign also had problems with forage and food. His problems came from two issues. First, the areas he was moving through had been either devastated by the war or were sparsely populated. To fight against the superior Federal forces, his army had to stay concentrated and be continually on the move. The challenge with staying concentrated was that any available food and forage were quickly consumed by the first units, and following units were left with little or nothing. His need to keep his army in continuous movement did not allow his quartermasters to spend the time needed to obtain food and forage from more-distant farms. Although Price barely mentions issues with food and forage, some of his subordinate commanders were more vocal. Colonel Colton Green, one of Price's brigade commanders, stated,

> The brigade was not again engaged with the enemy, but endured the severest privations and sufferings during the march through Indian Territory to Boggy Depot, which place we reached on the 18th of November. For twenty-five days we were without forage. For

twenty-three days we subsisted on beef without salt, frequently issued in insufficient quantities, and for three days were without food at all. The loss in animals was very heavy, and many wagons were abandoned in consequence.[10]

Although the Federal Army had a lot to do with Price's defeat, the lack of proper logistic support was the final breaking point for his army's demoralization. Price did not adequately take into account the geography of the terrain in which he would be campaigning.

Grant's first attempt to seize Vicksburg was an overland campaign from the north and on the eastern side of the Mississippi River. However, his plans were thwarted when Confederate cavalry destroyed his supply base at Holly Springs and damaged the railroad line between Jackson, Tennessee, and Columbus, Kentucky. Grant stated in his memoirs, "This cut me off from all communications with the north for more than a week, and it was more than two weeks before rations or forage could be issued from stores obtained in the regular way. This demonstrated the impossibility of maintaining so long a line of road over which to draw supplies for an army moving in an enemy's country."[11] The cutting of his supply lines forced Grant to gather food and forage from the surrounding countryside. In doing so, Grant discovered that his army "could have subsisted off the country for two months instead of two weeks."[12]

Due to the logistic lessons Grant learned from his first attempt to take Vicksburg, he deliberately cut his own supply lines during his 1863 campaign and was successful. Grant succeeded for several reasons. First, his army was without a supply line only from 4 May to 18 May (two weeks) and the only major engagement he had to fight was Champion Hill, a one-day battle. Second, Grant knew his men could easily live off the land, so his supply wagons carried only hard bread, coffee, and salt in addition to ammunition. To ensure he had enough wagons for the ammunition, Grant ordered that horses, mules, and anything capable of carrying ammunition, which included carriages and wagons used to carry bales of cotton, were impressed for the army. Then, when the army reached the Mississippi River near Vicksburg, Grant's "first anxiety was to secure a base of supplies on the Yazoo River above Vicksburg."[13] Once Grant had accomplished his goal, he did not worry about his logistic supply line being interdicted by the Confederates, as all of his supplies came by boat down the Mississippi River and the Federal Navy had complete control of the river.[14]

Sherman's March to the Sea was equally successful. His campaign lasted from the 15th of November 1864 to the 13th of December when Fort McAllister was secured and Sherman made contact with the Federal fleet. Prior to the beginning of the campaign, Sherman reduced the number of artillery pieces and wagons in his army. He also instructed that each Soldier have 40 rounds of ammunition on his person, that there was an extra 300 rounds per man in the trains, along with 200 artillery projectiles for each of his artillery pieces. The army also carried enough rations for 20 days, along with a cattle herd and five days' worth of forage. Sherman was not concerned about food and forage as he knew his army would be moving through territory no other army had marched through. Sherman kept his army well dispersed so that all units could easily obtain an adequate supply of food and forage. Still, when Sherman reached the coast, his first concern was making contact with the Federal Navy and securing a safe supply line through them.[15]

Keeping an army widely dispersed but keeping each column within supporting distance of the others was a common formation for armies living off the land. During the Napoleonic Wars, many of the armies lived off the land and were forced to disperse for each column to have enough land that had not already been stripped clean by preceding units. Napoleon was a master of this, and his armies would advance in separate but supporting columns when they invaded another country, but only if enough food and fodder was available for the men and horses. By doing this, an army could move faster since the number of supply wagons accompanying the army would be dramatically reduced. However, when foraging was not feasible, the number of supply wagons had to be increased, or the army had to stay near a navigable river where barges could be used to supply it.

***

The importance of steam-powered ships during the Civil War cannot be overstated. Steam power decreased (but did not eliminate) naval officers' concerns with winds, tides, and currents. Steam power allowed ships to go against a current even with an unfavorable wind. Without steam power, the Federal campaign on the inland waterways would have been very difficult. Although it was easy for any ship to go downriver, it would have been almost impossible for a ship, solely powered by the wind, to travel up the Mississippi. In fact, it is very doubtful if the Federal fleet could have conducted upriver attacks on Forts Henry and Donelson. Nor would the navy have been able to support the 1864 Red River campaign without steam-powered ships. On the open ocean, steam power allowed the Federal Navy to maintain a close blockade of the Southern ports. Steam power also allowed Federal ships to go up the coastal rivers with warships and troopships. It would have been a far different naval war without steam power, one in which it is very likely that the secession of the Confederacy would have succeeded.

Although steam power was essential to Federal victory during the war, neither side could have successfully waged war without an adequate supply of horses and mules. These animals were essential to all of the armies, and a shortage of these animals or weak and inferior animals reduced the effectiveness of their artillery and cavalry besides potentially immobilizing their supply wagons. However, both sides had to avoid buying or impressing too many horses and mules within their own territory. If they did, farmers would not be able to plant or harvest their crops. In enemy territory, it was an advantage to take as many animals as possible since doing so would hurt the enemy's economy.

Not all horses and mules met the requirements of the military. All of the animals were inspected prior to being accepted, and unless an army was desperate, standards were high. In addition to other requirements, cavalry horses had to be between 15 (60 inches) and 16 (64 inches) hands high[16] and they were to be at least five years old but not older than nine. Artillery horses had to be larger than cavalry horses. Their requirements were that they be at least 15½ hands high, be from six to ten years old, weigh at least 1,050 pounds, and be a dark color.[17] These standards meant that for a horse to be used by the cavalry or artillery during the Civil War, it had to be born before the war started.

Mules had to meet different criteria than horses as they could be shorter, 14 hands high, and younger, not less than four and not more than nine years old. Still, both sides used horses and mules that did not meet these requirements, normally due to the fact that they desperately needed the animals or to keep them away from the enemy. An advantage mules had over horses was that they could survive on less and poorer quality food.[18] Federal quartermaster regulations stated that mules would receive the same amount of hay as horses and oxen, 14 pounds, but would receive only 9 pounds of grain compared to 12 pounds of corn, oats, or barley.[19] However, a normal mule team for a wagon was six, while for horses, it was four, and pulling wagons was the most frequent use of mules. The employment of mules by the U.S. Army continued well past the Civil War and past the deactivation of the last cavalry unit, as the last two operational mule units were not deactivated until 1956.[20] Today, mules and other pack animals continue serving armies in areas of the world where the terrain is difficult and weather makes flying challenging. Technology has yet to fully replace the "lowly" mule.

Except at the beginning of the war, the Confederate armies had difficulties meeting the continuous demand for horses and mules.[21] The challenge for the Confederate armies began when they lost control of the Upper South—Kentucky and Tennessee. These two states, along with the Shenandoah Valley and southwestern Virginia, were primary breeding grounds for horses and mules. The Lower South normally bought their horses and mules from these areas because the people in the Lower South only selectively bred a few horses for saddle or racing purposes. Although there were a large number of horses available from Texas, they were either too small or they could not be transported across the Mississippi River. The Confederate Army's policy was that cavalrymen had to furnish their own mounts. So once a man was dismounted, he was often forced to go home, which may be a long distance away. The result would be that his services would be lost to the army until he returned. In some cases, dismounted cavalrymen were transferred to infantry units, while infantrymen who could provide a horse were transferred to the cavalry. The government furnished the horses and mules needed by the artillery and wagons. Initially, they obtained the needed animals from Virginia and North Carolina.

By 1863, the Army of Northern Virginia's lack of horses and mules, along with an inadequate supply of forage, had begun to impact operations. On the 7th of February, General Lee wrote a long message to General Stonewall Jackson concerning the condition of the army's horses. In the message, Lee discussed the deficit of forage being provided to the army and the need to relocate horses where fodder could be found. Lee concluded his message with the comment, "The artillery officers must attend closely to their horses, seeing that they have every possible attention and comfort, and if nothing better can be done, turned out during the day, that they may browse on the stubble, twigs, &c. Life at least can be preserved with other forage that can be procured."[22]

About a week later, General Lee wrote President Jefferson Davis explaining why he could not make an attack on the Army of the Potomac: "The rivers and streams are all swollen beyond fording; we have no bridges, and the roads are in a liquid state, and nearly impracticable. In addition, our horses and mules are in that reduced state that the labor and exposure incident to an attack would result in their destruction."[23] The issue did not disappear when spring and new grass arrived as the demand was so great that by April of 1863, Lee wrote to General William N. Pendleton, his chief of artillery, "The destruction of horses in the army is so great that I fear it will be impossible to supply our wants."[24] The lack of forage for his army's horses was directly impacting the operations of the Army of Northern Virginia.

Lee's movement into Pennsylvania that summer gave his army access to a new source of horses. However, the respite was only temporary. In August, after the Battle of Gettysburg, Lee was again forced to inform Davis that his army was unable to attack the Federal Army due to issues with his army's horses.

> Nothing prevents my advancing now but the fear of killing our artillery horses. They are much reduced, and the hot weather and scarce forage keeps them so. The cavalry also suffer, and I fear to set them at work. Some days we get a pound of corn per horse and some days more; some none. Our limit is 5 pounds per day per horse. [Federal regulations, as stated in chapter 1, required that horses receive 14 pounds of hay and 12 pounds of corn, oats, or barley per day.] You can judge of our prospects. General Fitz. Lee is getting north of the Rappahannock, below Fredericksburg, about 1,000 pounds per day, which is a considerable relief on that wing. Everything is being done by me that can be to recruit the horses. I have been obliged to diminish the number of guns in the artillery, and fear I shall have to lose more.[25]

The lack of horses and mules along with a lack of forage never got any better, and Lee's cavalry became weaker and lost its previous superiority over Federal cavalry. Understanding Lee's need for horses helps explain one reason Lee thought highly of John Mosby, as he was able to capture horses from the Federal Army and send them south for use by Confederate units. Even so, General Pendleton wrote to Colonel A.H. Cole, inspector general for transportation, in February 1865: "The question of our horse supply is hardly second to that of supplying men for the army, or food for the men, and it is of great importance that all measures be adopted, both for keeping up the stock in the Confederacy, and for having strong teams in sufficient number for our artillery and transportation by the opening of our spring campaign."[26] Cole had just written, about a week earlier, to General Alexander Lawton, Confederate quartermaster general, that he estimated the Confederate armies would need 6,000 horses and 4,000 mules, but only about 5,000 could be obtained east of the Mississippi River.[27]

Jefferson Davis wrote after the war that in early March 1865, he and General Lee had a long conference. At the conference, Lee informed Davis "that the evacuation of Petersburg was but a matter of time."[28] When Davis questioned Lee on whether it would be better to withdraw at once, Lee replied "that his artillery and draught horses were too weak for the roads as they were then, and that he would have to wait until they became firmer."[29] The Army of Northern Virginia was so short of healthy horses and mules that by the time Lee was forced to retreat from Petersburg, he had to leave behind all of his heavy artillery along with ten pieces of light artillery and some small mortars.[30] Later, at Amelia Court House, General William N. Pendleton, Lee's chief of artillery, found it necessary to destroy 95 caissons.[31] Along with the loss of artillery pieces, the Confederate cavalry was a shadow of its former self. The lack of an adequate number of horses, along with an inadequate supply of forage for these animals, directly impacted the Army of Northern Virginia's operations.

Although the Federals were better supplied with horses and mules and could obtain an adequate amount of fodder to feed them, they too faced shortages. Supplying horses and mules was one of Lincoln's numerous concerns. Lincoln was concerned enough about the supply of horses and mules that in November 1862, he issued an executive order. His order prohibited the export of horses and mules from the United States with the exception of any state or territory bounded by the Pacific Ocean.[32] Lincoln was also reported to have said, when he learned Mosby had captured Brigadier General Edwin Stoughton (along with a number of horses), that "he did not so much mind the loss of a brigadier general, for he could make another in five minutes; but those horses cost $125 apiece!"[33] Lincoln was also worried, when Grant took command, that Grant would be like his predecessors and make demands Lincoln could not fulfill and then blame any defeat on Lincoln. However, Lincoln was to be pleasantly surprised, for when Grant asked him about the approximately 15,000 dismounted cavalrymen near Harpers Ferry who could not be mounted due to the lack of horses, Grant only asked for permission to put them in the infantry.[34]

One reason neither side seldom conducted extensive winter operations, except in the Deep South, was that they would have to carry enough feed for their horses and mules. For a campaign lasting more than a week, the number of wagons needed to haul the necessary forage would have been more than either army, especially Confederate armies, could provide. Sherman's March to the Sea was one of the exceptions. His advantage was that he was moving through the Deep South in an area that had not previously been visited by a Federal army and where the winter weather was mild enough that forage could easily be found. Geography and the impact it had on food supplies were always considered by a good commander.

***

During the Civil War, the Federal Army used three methods for transmitting messages operationally—the telegraph, signal flags/torches, and courier—but only the telegraph was used at the strategic level. Although the army's signal corps is considered to have its origin in 1860, its communications ability was limited to signal flags and torches. A civilian organization, the United States Military Telegraph, was created in which only supervisory personnel were commissioned officers who reported directly to the secretary of war.[35] There were issues concerning both means of communications with signal flags and torches being more impacted by geography than the telegraph. However, the telegraph was limited to locations in which there were telegraph lines. Another issue was that the members of the U.S. Military Telegraph did not come under the command of the military officers they were supporting. Obviously, this caused many difficulties. Still, by 1864, telegraph units in the Army of the Potomac were equipped with mobile stations housed in wagons that used batteries for power. This enabled telegraph lines to be run from the brigade to higher commands for every change in position or, when the army was on the march, for a halt at night. All of this was accomplished without orders having to be given.[36] Couriers were also impacted by geographic conditions with the main one being the weather. Rain and muddy roads would slow them down, and they could get lost or, worse, captured. Consequently, the telegraph was used more at higher levels, while couriers were used at lower levels of command.

Although the telegraph, signal flags, and signal torches affected the operational level of command, the biggest impact was using the telegraph at the strategic level. Without the telegraph, it would have made Grant's ability to control all of the Federal armies much more difficult, if not impossible. This was because there would have been a tremendous time lag between when Grant would send a message and when it would be received. Without the telegraph, many messages would arrive too late, as events would have occurred that would make the message outdated. The importance of the telegraph to the strategic level of command cannot be overestimated. General Sherman stated in his memoirs, "The value of the magnetic telegraph in war cannot be exaggerated, as was illustrated by the perfect concert of action between the armies in Virginia and Georgia during 1864. Hardly a day intervened when General Grant did not know the exact state of facts with me, more than fifteen hundred miles away as the wires ran."[37] Lincoln also made extensive use of the telegraph and was a frequent visitor to the secretary of war's telegraph office. Lincoln used the telegraph to keep informed of events around the country and to keep in contact with his generals. Excellent telegraph communications was one of the key components of the Federal victory.

In contrast, Confederate efforts to fully utilize their telegraph system did not achieve the same results. The Confederacy had the same technology and background in communications as the Federals and used the telegraph, signal flags, and torches along with couriers. However, their use of them was much more limited due to their limited resources in both material and manpower. For the Confederacy, its available technology could not overcome the geographic distances, lack of natural resources, and industrial capability that its army, navy, and industry had to deal with.

***

The advent of machine tools and interchangeable parts allowed both sides, especially the Federals, to supply the large armies needed to fight the war. The introduction of steam-powered machines also helped because it allowed factories to be located away from a source of water that had been the only viable source of power for the machines. Without weapons with interchangeable parts made by machine tools, it would have been impossible for either side to supply the large number of rifles their armies needed in the time required. This same principle applies to all the other pieces of equipment the armies required—wagons, uniforms, tents, and railroads, to name a few. Steam power was essential to the success of the Federals. As previously stated, steam-powered ships allowed the Federal Navy to travel up rivers and maintain a close blockade on Southern ports. If the South had seceded 20 years earlier, it probably would have gained its independence. Without the technology available in 1860, it would have been very difficult for the Federals to subdue the Confederacy.

Technology made tremendous advances between 1840 and 1860. Beyond being able to supply large armies and build a large navy, these technological advances mitigated the advantage the vast distances in the South gave to the Confederacy. While steam-powered ships were common in 1840, high-pressure steam engines had not yet been perfected, and the river steamboat had not reached its full potential. Both sides would have used steam-powered riverboats, but they would not have been as numerous or as powerful. The seagoing navy was a completely different matter. The problem was that paddles did not work very well in the ocean and were exposed to enemy fire. The solution was a below-water propeller, but it was not introduced until the 1840s.[38] It would have been very difficult for the Federal Navy to maintain a close blockade with just sailing ships, and naval attacks on forts would have been very different. It would also have been true that it would be more difficult for blockade runners, but they had the advantage of waiting until conditions were right.

Railroads also existed in 1840, and in the United States, there were 2,800 miles of track; by 1860, there were over 30,000 miles—a vast increase.[39] Sherman's Atlanta campaign was only made possible by the fact that his forces were supplied by railroad. The problem was that with 1840 technology, it would have been impossible to keep his army supplied, and the Deep South would have remained a secure haven. The technology of 1860 was one of the main reasons the Federals won the war, for it mitigated the geographic advantages of the Confederacy. It was a war with technology that neither side had previously experienced.

***

Much has been written about the influence rifled muskets and cannons had on the Civil War. The main impact of these weapons was at the operational and tactical levels of command. During the Mexican War, there were only a few units armed with rifled muskets, as the majority of the men were armed with smoothbore muskets. In Grant's memoirs, he stated that during the Mexican War, "at a distance of a few hundred yards a man might fire at you all day without your finding it out."[40] However, during the Civil War, many men were killed at 400 yards or more by bullets fired from rifled muskets. This new technology changed how officers and their men viewed terrain. Although loading a rifled musket was best accomplished when a man was standing up, all the men realized that if they could be seen, they could be killed.

The new technology made the artillery used during the Civil War far superior to what had previously been used. Mobile artillery became lighter, and siege guns became larger. Both, due to rifling, had an exponential increase in their ranges and ability to penetrate masonry. Confederate Fort Pulaski was forced to surrender when Federal rifled siege artillery created breeches in its walls at ranges unimaginable when the fort was constructed. The bombardment of Fort Pulaski was not the only example of long-range destruction. Federal artillery was able to bombard Charleston, South Carolina, at distances previously thought inconceivable. This bombardment created such destruction that period photographs of Charleston make it look like a bombed-out city from World War II, as shown in Photograph 12-1. This bombardment was accomplished by Parrott rifled guns, varying in size from a 30-pounder to a 400-pounder, firing exploding shells. One 30-pounder, with a range of 6,700 yards, fired 4,594 shells in 69 days before it burst. Out of those 4,594 shells, 4,253 reached the city.[41] This firing continued day and night, and in the end, Charleston was a ruined city. The ranges these guns were capable of achieving and the destruction they produced was something no one had ever experienced before.

**

All of the technical advances during the mid–1800s were dependent on access to minerals such as iron, coal, salt, potassium nitrate (saltpeter), sulfur, as well as gold and silver. A country also needed the necessary industrial and population base to make the required equipment. The Federals were geographically well supplied with all of the necessary minerals, and the few minerals it did not have, it could easily import. Plus, the Federals possessed a large industrial base and had a large enough population to supply men for the army and the factories. With its open ports, people from Europe were able to migrate to the Northern states and supply additional manpower for the army and factories. This was a luxury the Confederacy did not have.

In contrast, the South did not have the necessary minerals, was unable to import enough of them, had lost the sites to Federal control, or the sites were under continual threat. In addition, the Confederacy's industrial base was extremely limited, especially after New Orleans was lost, and there were not enough men to supply the needs of the army and the factories without using slaves. Slaves were used in the factories, although in a very limited way, throughout the war. Confederate armies also used slaves in supporting roles, and only at the very end of the war did

Photograph 12-1: Ruins of Charleston, South Carolina, as viewed from the Circular Church in April 1865. During World War II, other cities would experience similar destruction (Library of Congress).

they begin to use slaves in organized fighting units, but it was too late to make any difference. Another limiting factor was that when the Federal Army threatened a location close to an armory or factory—for example, Richmond—the men at the factories would be required to stop work and man the defenses. Colonel (later Brigadier General) Josiah Gorgas, chief of Confederate ordnance, summarized the Ordnance Department's issues with what their workmen were being subjected to:

> A further purchase of at least 50,000 [small arms] will be necessary for the coming year unless the operations of the armories can be placed on a permanent footing by declaring all skilled mechanics engaged on them absolutely exempt from military duty, attaching them permanently to the Ordnance Department, and encouraging in every way the growth of this class of workmen. I cannot lay too much stress on the necessity for legislative action on this point in order to give assurance to the workmen.[42]

The Confederacy was short of available men, excluding the use of slaves, and could not fulfill all of the manpower requirements the war forced on it.

Jefferson Davis fully realized the problems the Confederacy had in this area. He stated after the war that at the beginning of the war, "among ourselves were few who realized how totally deficient the Southern states were in all which was necessary to the active operations of an army."[43] Davis emphasized the importance of the logistic efforts facing the Confederacy when he dedicated two chapters to this in his two-volume postwar book *The Rise and Fall of the Confederate Government.* As Davis wrote, "If our people had not gone to war without counting the cost, they were nevertheless involved in it without means of providing for its necessities."[44]

Even with all of these issues, the Confederacy made a gallant effort to overcome both of these deficits by importing material through the blockade, using fast ships to slip through the blockade, transferring machines from the Harpers Ferry armory to other armories deeper in the South, and by expanding manufacturing capacity. Blockade runners were essential to the survival of the Confederacy. Between 1 November 1863 and 8 December 1864, a large amount of military equipment was shipped into Wilmington, North Carolina, and Charleston, South Carolina. During those months, 69,000 rifles, 43 cannons, 1,507,000 pounds of lead, 1,933,000 pounds of saltpeter, 545,000 pairs of boots and shoes, as well as many other supplies for the military were processed through those two harbors. Although the Federal blockade was having an impact, it was not tight enough to keep vital supplies from reaching the Confederacy. The Confederacy also worked at increasing its industrial base in regard to military equipment. By the end of the war, the industrial base of the Confederacy, in the territory it still controlled, had increased. The best example is the construction by the Confederate Ordnance Department of a modern, for the time, gunpowder factory in Augusta, Georgia. In the end, the efforts were too late as the Confederacy lost more territory, harbors were captured, and Federal raids destroyed material. The Confederacy could not overcome its geographic disadvantages.

***

Geography had a major impact on the Civil War and directly contributed to the Federal victory. Technology lessened the impact of geography, and the Federals' superior ability to produce the needed technology gave them a decisive advantage. Both sides were very aware of geographically dependent resources and fought to control them or to deny the other side from controlling them. Without the Industrial Revolution and the associated advances in technology, the Federal government would probably not have been successful in stopping the secession of the Confederacy. In that case, geography would have worked against the Federals.

13

Geography and the Future

Technology may mitigate the impact of geography, but it will never eliminate it.

The Battle of Cedar Creek did not end the fighting in the Valley. Although Jubal Early was able to assemble a small force in the upper Valley after most of his units were sent back to Richmond, his force was effectively destroyed during the Battle of Waynesboro. There were also the partisan forces, especially John Mosby's. Still, the Battle of Cedar Creek ended large-scale fighting in the Valley. The Confederates were never again strong enough to contest Federal control of Winchester and the lower Valley. Nathaniel Banks and Stonewall Jackson were both correct, as Winchester was the key to the Valley and the Valley was the key to Virginia. Philip Sheridan agreed with Banks when he informed Charles Dana that the key to the Valley was Opequon Creek, just outside of Winchester, as it was more a deep canyon than a stream. From Opequon Creek, Sheridan felt he could construct fortifications that would guard the approaches to the Potomac River.[1] The Confederates' permanent loss of control of Winchester and the Valley gave the initiative in Virginia to the Federals for the rest of the war. Robert E. Lee was forced to react to maneuvers by the Federal armies and, except for the attack on Fort Stedman, was forced to watch the slow strangulation of his army.

***

Geography has and always will influence military operations at all levels. In future wars, there will be other strange attractors in the chaos of war, such as Winchester, that by themselves will be considered unimportant. Winchester became a strange attractor during the war due to its geographic location and the geography around it that made it a rich farming community. The struggle for Winchester was long and bloody. Both sides needed to control Winchester to be successful in the Virginia theater. Its geographic location made it an ideal launching point for Confederate campaigns and raids into the North, while its rich farmland allowed a military force to become self-sufficient in food for the men and forage for the animals. For the Confederacy, the incursions into the North from Winchester had a much greater political impact than militarily—something Ulysses S. Grant learned the hard way. For the Federal government, control of Winchester was vital if they were to stop Confederate incursions. Control of Winchester was vital to both sides, militarily and politically.

No country or military force will ever be able to eliminate geography's influence. Even though technology will mitigate the impact of geography, it will never eliminate it as technology will change the geographic features that will be important. The geographic feature that was considered important a hundred years ago may become unimportant in the future. The converse is also true in that the geographic feature that was considered unimportant, or not even known, may become crucial in the future. Since it is impossible to predict the future, it is also futile to predict what geographic features will be important in the future. Who would have predicted in 1860 that small countries in the Middle East would be so important to the world's economy in the 20th century because of the amount of oil they control?

A location's population density should not be a prime consideration when considering the geographic importance of a site. Winchester and Saltville are two prime examples of this. Both were relatively small towns with Saltville being so small that it did not have its own listing in the 1860 census. Today, many of the major oil fields are not situated in densely populated areas. A large population does not necessarily mean that a site is geographically important.

Another issue that must be considered when leaders contemplate becoming involved in a conflict is its length. In a short conflict, access to natural resources is very seldom important, but in a long conflict, access becomes crucial. During World Wars I and II, Germany became starved for natural resources while the Allies did not. In contrast, during the short wars between Israel and various Muslim countries, topography, not geography, was most important. These wars were short enough that Israel, which lacks large quantities of natural resources within its boundaries, did not have to worry about running out of resources needed to fight the wars.

Consideration must also be given to man-made topographic features such as canals, tunnels, and bridges. The Suez and Panama Canals are locations transcending topography. The Suez Canal has been the scene of fighting, and the Panama Canal was heavily defended during World War II. The tunnel underneath the English Channel and other major tunnels throughout the world are crucial bottlenecks that are potential targets for an enemy. Bridges are also choke points with the Chesapeake Bay Bridge Tunnel, for example, going across the mouth of the Chesapeake Bay being a prime location to block the bay to shipping. Currently, the Chinese are building artificial islands in the South China Sea to further their disputed claim to that area. Who knows what impact these new topographic/geographic features will have? Our ability to change topography has many unintended consequences economically, militarily, and politically.

One geographic area that is becoming more important every year is the geography of outer space. Society has become dependent on satellites orbiting earth in a geosynchronous or stationary orbit—a geographic phenomenon. These satellites provide worldwide communications and global positioning (GPS) information. They are also positioned by many militaries to continually provide photographs and other information on areas of the world of interest to them. Unfortunately, our dependence on them has allowed us to lose the ability to fully function without them. Just consider what happens when people lose their GPS signal. As with any technology, it is a double-edged sword.

There are other dangers in outer space. Solar flares are a current danger to our society and to astronauts we send to outer space. Then there is the danger of a large asteroid or comet impacting our planet. Who knows, assuming we do achieve intergalactic travel, what geographically dependent items will be discovered during these travels? Whatever happens in regard to outer space, its geographic effects must always be taken into consideration and, if disregarded, will likely have a tremendous negative impact.

All that being said, our society is still reliant on geographically dependent items such as oil and minerals (iron and magnesium being two examples). In addition, food—most of which can only be grown or raised in limited geographic areas—and fresh water are geographically dependent. As our climate changes—and it will change even without our assistance—these two items will become more crucial to the world's society as a whole. What geographic aspects will affect our future remains to be seen, but geography will continue to influence our lives. Then there is global warming, which is cyclical even without human involvement. Global warming and cooling have happened before and will happen again. The impact of either event will have negative consequences for some areas of the world, while having positive ramifications for others. Those who disregard geography and the implication it will have on their plans are frequently surprised to their regret. What geographic aspects will influence our future remains to be seen, but geography will continue to have an impact on our lives.

***

Leaders need to understand their nation's geographic strengths and weaknesses as well as those of their opponents, in addition to being aware of how each level of command views geography. Any strength can be a weakness. In the case of Great Britain, one of its geographic strengths is that it is an island. Yet, being an island means that it can easily be isolated by a nation with a stronger navy and, today, air force. For the United States, a geographic strength is that we are a great distance from our potential enemies. But that means that we must be able to transport our military a great distance to fight those enemies. Today, no country is geographically independent and each has certain geographic strengths and weaknesses. What those strengths and weaknesses are depend on who the enemy is and the potential length of any conflict. Leaders must be aware of all of this if they expect to be successful in any conflict.

Each of the levels of command will view geography differently. What may be unimportant at the grand strategy level may be a critical feature at the operational and/or tactical levels. Although leaders at the highest level need to be aware of the geographic view of commanders at lower levels, they need to keep their attention focused on their own level. Too much emphasis from a higher level on a lower level will all too frequently result in an implosion. Still, higher level leaders must not let events at lower levels have too much influence on their decisions as happened during the previously discussed events that started the French and Indian/Seven Years' War. On the other hand, not having knowledge of the geographic impact of their decisions will have on lower levels of command will lead to unrealistic expectations of what lower level commanders can achieve. It is a delicate balancing act, one only good leaders can achieve.

Appendix A: Macadamized Roads

Macadamized roads were the superhighways of the 19th century.

Macadamized roads were dry, smooth, all-weather roads. Traveling on them was faster and safer than on a dirt, loose gravel, or planked road. They were a successful method of alleviating the limitations geography placed on road travel. Any community and region that had them experienced increased commerce as they decreased the time required to travel from one location to another. The military also found the roads to be very useful as they helped speed up travel and lessen the strain placed on horses and mules pulling heavy loads. Macadamized roads were the superhighways of the time.

During the Civil War, macadamized roads could be found in most states, and armies from both sides used them whenever they could. Macadamized roads were important as they gave a significant speed and time advantage to the side making use of them. They also allowed wheeled vehicles to move when other roads were impassable. One example from the Civil War is General Stonewall Jackson's use of the macadamized Valley Turnpike during his 1862 Valley campaign. By using it, his troops were able to outmarch Federal units who were marching on dirt roads. Then, during the Chancellorsville Campaign, General Robert E. Lee was able to quickly move units from Fredericksburg to Chancellorsville on two excellent roads—one macadamized and the other planked.[1] In contrast, dirt roads could quickly become impassable due to heavy use and wet weather. General William Rosecrans reported in February 1862, "The roads are now very bad; almost impossible to move wagons except on macadamized roads."[2] General Ambrose Burnside's infamous January 1863 Mud March is another example of how dirt roads could slow down and even stall an army's movement. Burnside's offensive plans quickly fell apart when an unseasonable period of mild temperatures turned all the dirt roads around Fredericksburg, Virginia, into muddy quagmires, making any movement, especially by artillery and wagons, all but impossible. If the macadamized road located on the south side of the Rappahannock River had been on the northern side, Burnside would have had an advantage over General Lee, and his maneuver may have succeeded. Macadamized roads gave a distinct advantage to the side that controlled them.

There were problems when a military unit used a macadamized road. First, cavalry could not make a silent approach on it. The reason was that their horses' iron horseshoes would make a distinctive metallic ring on the road.[3] Colonel William Duffield stated in an 1862 report about an attack by Brigadier General Nathan Bedford Forrest's cavalry, "The noise of so many hoofs at full speed upon the macadamized roads was so great that the alarm was given before the head of the column reached our pickets, about 1 mile distant, so that our men were formed and ready to receive them, although they came at full speed."[4] However, as macadamized roads were not as common as dirt roads, this was not a significant issue during the war. An additional issue for horses was without horseshoes, they could not use a macadamized road because the hard surface would damage their unprotected hoofs. But again, this was seldom an issue. A bigger problem was that for infantry units, macadamized roads made the soldiers' shoes wear out faster. For Federal units, this was not a major problem as they were well supplied. But for the poorly supplied Confederate units, with men who did not have shoes, it would have been a difficult situation. This could have forced some Confederate units to march parallel to a macadamized road, thus causing those units to move at a much slower pace.

Even with these issues, commanders preferred to stay near a macadamized road if they could not be located close to a railroad. Brigadier General William W. Loring informed General Jackson in January 1862, "In brief, the advantages of the enemy are in having the base of their operations at the railroad with nearly three times our force, while the position of this command is indefensible, and over 40 miles from its source of supply, with none of the roads macadamized, and which must necessarily become impassable in a short time with ordinary freight."[5] This opinion is reinforced by General William T. Sherman's message to Major General James McPherson in April 1864: "The macadamized road to Whitesburg [Tennessee] certainly is a strong point in its favor."[6] Macadamized roads were important and influenced commanders' decisions.

**

Stone roads had existed for centuries, and the quality stone Roman roads were well known in the 18th century. However, paved stone roads were only found in major cities during the late 1700s because they were very expensive to build. In the countryside, roads were planked, dirt, or loose gravel of which many were not well maintained. Consequently, wagons moved slowly, and even "high-speed" postal carriages were slow. The roads were dangerous, too, and high-speed carriages overturned all too often on dirt and gravel roads. On dirt roads, ruts and potholes were the culprits. On gravel roads, the problem was that the gravel was shoveled onto the road in a manner such that the center of the road would be significantly higher than its sides. The theory was that the gravel would eventually be forced from the center to the sides. However, this did not occur, and thus, carriages traveled on gravel roads at an angle. So when the angle got too great or when going around a turn, the carriages would become top heavy and overturn.[7]

There were other issues with planked, dirt, and loose gravel roads. Plank roads did not hold up very well to heavy traffic while dirt roads all too often became impassable during the wet season or after a heavy rain. Although gravel roads were considered to be better, they also had problems. First, stones of any type and size were used. If rounded rocks were used, they would never "bond" and would continually slide off each other. Stone size also mattered, for if the stones are wider than the width of the wheels passing over them, "the wheels of the carriages will keep them in constant motion. This, prevented their consolidation; because, when a wheel rests only on one part of a stone, the other part rises."[8] Consequently, wheeled vehicles either pushed their way through the stones or were forced to rise over each individual stone.[9] This would make for a very bumpy ride and more importantly, work the horses harder. Additionally, water penetrated the road and kept the subsurface wet. Then, when the weather became cold, the water froze and caused the road to buckle. Also, the gravel and stone would not be cleaned of dirt before it was thrown on the road, and this dirt would also retain water, adding to the buckling. Traveling by carriage on such roads would not have been a pleasant experience.

John McAdam, for whom macadamized roads are named, became interested in the quality of the roads in Great Britain when he was appointed "a Magistrate and Commissioner of the roads in Scotland."[10] While in that position, he noticed how inadequate the roads were and realized there were two main reasons for this. First, the roads were not constructed based on scientific principles. Second, the people who had been selected to inspect the roads and manage the money paid for tolls were not qualified.[11] Consequently, McAdam became a strong advocate for better roads and developed an improved system for constructing gravel roads. In 1811, McAdam made a presentation to a committee of the House of Commons. At the meeting, he informed the committee that British roads were in bad condition due to poor construction. He recommended that based on scientific principles, the gravel on roads should be ten inches in depth and that the size of the stones should not exceed one inch.[12] McAdam stressed to the committee that the current specification for the size of the stones was very vague and resulted in stones being used that were too large. McAdam stated, "The size of the stone used on a road must be in due proportion to the space occupied by a wheel of ordinary dimensions on a smooth level surface, this point of contact will be found to be, longitudinally about an inch, and every piece of stone put into a road, which exceeds an inch in any of its dimensions is mischievous."[13]

In January 1816, McAdam was given a district near Bristol to use as an experiment for his new system.[14] His experiment was a success, and in 1819, he testified before a committee explaining his new system and the success it had been.[15] His testimony was supported by a number of witnesses. Although initially there was significant resistance to his system, its success could not be denied, and his method of constructing and managing roads spread throughout Great Britain. His method was adopted in the United States and became the basis for the specifications used to construct all-weather gravel toll roads in this country.

McAdam's system was very straightforward. Once the route of the road had been determined, the natural surface was to be disturbed as little as possible. But there needed to be a three-inch difference in height from the center of the road to each side. This was so that water would drain off the road. Ditches were dug on each side of the road, so the stone in the road would be three to four inches above the level of the water in the ditch. Stone was broken so that no piece was more than six ounces in weight. The broken stone was cleaned of all dirt, and then clean, broken stone was scattered on the road two to three inches in depth at a time with the total final depth being ten inches. Once the stone had been scattered, it was raked smooth. No large stones or other material was to be laid between the stone and the earth. Once the road had been laid, a person watched the road and raked in any tracks made by passing vehicles until the road had been united into one mass. Over time, the wheels from the passing vehicles would compress the stones so that they formed a solid mass and acted as one piece of stone. Once this had occurred, the surface would be smooth, water would drain off the road, and stones would not be displaced by passing vehicles. The road would not require any repairs until it had been worn down. Once it needed repairs, the surface of the road needed to be loosened and additional broken stone added. The surface had to be loosened so that the new stone would bond with the older stone. Repairs were best made when the weather was not dry.[16]

McAdam's road-building method was not the only successful smooth, all-weather road, as Thomas Telford had constructed a similar road, the Holyhead road.[17] The major difference between the two methods was that McAdam insisted that all of the stones be the same size as he believed "it is well known to every skiful [sic] and observant road-maker, that if strata of stone of various sizes be placed as a road, the largest stones will constantly work up by the shaking and pressure of traffic, and that the only mode of keeping the stones of a road from motion, is to use materials of a uniform size from the bottom."[18] In contrast, Telford built his roads with large stones on the bottom and smaller stones on top.[19] Both methods were successful and tremendously reduced the cost of maintaining a road. However, McAdam's method was substantially cheaper and became the dominant system in Great Britain. McAdam was also a prolific writer and wrote extensively about road construction. In 1824, he published the seventh edition of his *Remarks on the Present System of Road Making*. Both of these factors allowed his name to be associated with smooth, all-weather gravel roads.

As with any system, as experience was gained constructing the roads, it was realized that variations were necessary due to different types of soil. Two of the changes were that larger stones were used as the base and adding a binding agent to the upper level became the norm. Both practices were ones McAdam advocated against. Still, constructing a macadamized road was expensive and required more expertise and work than a dirt road. Austin Fletcher calculated that during 1906 in Massachusetts, the cost of 21.74 miles of macadamized road using local stone with a center depth of 6 inches, a side depth of 4 inches, and a width of 15 feet was $3,696 per mile, which is approximately $100,000 in 2015.[20] Due to the expense involved in building and maintaining a macadamized road, tolls were charged to anyone using it. However, since a macadamized road was a smooth, all-weather road, people were willing to pay the toll. Macadamized roads could be profitable once the initial construction costs were paid. John Williams estimated, based on his experience with macadamized roads near Cincinnati, that in 1838, $4.59 in tolls was collected for every dollar's worth of wear put on the road.[21]

In the United States, by the end of the 1800s, most macadamized roads were between 12 and 16 feet wide with shoulders between 3 and 5 feet in width on both sides of the road. If the road was less than 12 feet wide, it would not be possible for two wagons/vehicles to pass without getting on the shoulder. If this happened, the edge of the road, along with the shoulder, would probably be damaged. During the 19th century, it was believed that gravel had to be 12 inches deep after compacting. By the 20th century, it had been found that macadamized roads did not need to be that thick, and a uniform thickness of six inches in depth or six inches at the crown and four inches at the edges became the norm.[22] Construction of a macadamized road had to be continuous with no stage getting too far ahead of the following phase. This was important, for if one stage got too far in front of the next, damage might be done to the leading stage and work would need to be redone.

The first stage in constructing a macadamized road was preparation of the site. This consisted of removing the dirt to the desired depth and making the grade of the road as level as possible. In most cases, a complete level grade was not possible. In the United States, by the 20th century, the generally accepted maximum grade was 5 percent or a vertical rise of 5 feet in 100 feet of horizontal distance.[23] If the grade did not exceed 5 percent, horses could trot up the grade with little difficulty.[24] However, it was not always possible to follow this rule when the road went through mountains. Beyond horses having difficulty in traversing a steeper grade, there was the issue of being able to maintain such a steep road since rain as well as wear and tear would cause the road to wash away, making it expensive to maintain. Once the future road had been graded, the subgrade was then established. The material used in the subgrade was specified and "should be composed of porous material free from clay or loam, firm, and sufficiently strong to sustain any load likely to come upon the road at any time of the year."[25]

Drainage on both sides of the road was necessary, and there were a number of different methods to achieve this. The key was to make sure the drains were adequate enough to keep water away from the dirt subsurface, while simultaneously supporting the outer edges of the road. One method was to fill a narrow trench with broken stone and gravel, ensuring that there were trenches cut perpendicular to the main drainage trench, which would allow water to flow away from the road.

The type of gravel used in macadamized roads varied tremendously. Most companies preferred to use local stone since it was cheaper than hauling stone over great distances. Hardness and toughness were the two key qualities desired in the stone.[26] If local stone did not have these qualities, a decision had to be made on whether it was more economical to use inferior local stone and pay for more road maintenance or to haul in better quality stone. Although it is unknown what type of stone was used on the Valley Turnpike, in all probability local stone was used as there was, and is, plenty of it, as anyone who has traveled through the Valley can attest. By the 20th century, tables had been developed comparing the qualities of various types of stone, but this information was most likely not available when the Valley Turnpike was built.

Once the subgrade and drainage ditches had been prepared and gravel had been sized, the next step was to pack the dirt, or subgrade, so that it was "hard, smooth, and carefully crowned."[27] Crowning meant that the center of the road was higher than the sides so water would drain off the road into the gutters, leaving the road dry. The subgrade was to be crowned at the same angle as the main surface so that gravel would not be wasted, assuming a uniform thickness of the gravel was desired. If the gravel was to be thicker in the center due to the crown, then crowning the subgrade was not necessary. The purpose for compacting the subgrade was that if the dirt was not hard, the gravel would be pressed into it and be wasted. Smoothness of the subgrade made it easier to maintain a uniform thickness of the gravel when it was laid.

The next step was laying the lower course of gravel. This level normally consisted of stones from 1¼ to 2½ inches in diameter. These stones were to be spread onto the subgrade by a shovel or an automatic spreading wagon. The stones were not to be dumped from a wagon directly onto the subgrade since this would usually result in an uneven road. The reason for this was when the gravel was dumped, the stones would separate into different sizes with the smaller stones being in the middle. Then, when spread, the different sizes of stones would not be evenly distributed. However, the thickness of the spread had to be less than six inches. The rationale was that if the layer was six inches or more in depth, it could not be compacted easily. Consequently, if either course of gravel was to be six inches or more in depth, it would be necessary to have a number of spreadings for each course. Once a level had been laid, water was put on it to assist in the rolling. However, only a limited amount of water was used to prevent the dirt subsurface from becoming wet. The rolling and compacting would begin on the outer edges, and once they were properly compacted, the roller would be gradually moved toward the crown. The gravel was considered to be properly compacted when a crawling motion or wave was no longer seen in front of the roller.[28]

Once the lower course of gravel had been laid and compacted, the upper course could be laid. These stones were to be between ½ and 1¼ inches in diameter. They would be spread and compacted in the same manner as the lower course. Spreading and compacting the upper course would quickly follow the compacting of the lower course. If it was not, the horses and wagons being used in the construction would most likely damage the unfinished road as they traveled on it.[29]

After the upper course has been compacted, the binder was spread over it. The binder consisted of stone dust and fragments of stone that did not exceed ½ inch in diameter. Once the binder had been spread, a watering cart was used to flush the binder down into the voids. Normally, not more than one inch of binder was needed. However, enough binder was needed to fill the voids and cover the upper course of stone. Once the binder had been applied, the road would be wet down and then rolled until water puddled on its surface.[30]

After every section of the road was completed, it was put into use as soon as possible and preparations began for maintaining the road. Over a period, the road would need resurfacing. This meant a new upper course and binder would need to be applied. The road should never get to the point where the lower course was exposed. In addition, the drains alongside of the road and any culverts needed to be kept clean so water would easily flow through them. If properly maintained, a macadamized road would last for decades.

The advent of the automobile signaled the end of the macadamized road. Previously, slow-moving wagons with metal strips around their wheels slowly ground the stones into powder, which replaced the binding powder that had been blown or washed away. Faster moving automobiles and trucks with their narrower rubber tires created a dust that was lifted far above the road and would be blown away by the wind. The fast-moving rubber tires would also pull small stones out of the roadbed. Because of this, new bindings had to be found. The new bindings were coal tar and oils, which eventually led to the asphalt roads we know today.[31]

***

The Valley Turnpike got its start on the 3rd of March 1834 when the Valley Turnpike Company was incorporated by an act of the Virginia Assembly. The act authorized the company to build a turnpike from Winchester to Harrisonburg, a distance of about 68 miles. Money was raised to fund the construction of the road by selling subscriptions of $25 each. Once enough subscriptions had been sold to finance three-fifths of the estimated cost of the turnpike, $250,000, the Virginia Board of Public Works was authorized to buy the rest of the shares. Before that road was finished, the Virginia Assembly passed an act incorporating the Harrisonburg and Staunton Turnpike Company on the 30th of March 1837. This turnpike would be 25 miles long. The two roads eventually connected, and the two companies appear to have merged. The turnpike between Harrisonburg and Staunton was estimated to cost $100,000. As with the Winchester to Harrisonburg Turnpike, shares of $25 were sold, and once three-fifths of the money had been raised, the Virginia Board of Public Works was authorized to purchase the remaining shares. Like many projects, the final cost was more than what was estimated, and the final total expenditure for both

Photograph A1–1: The Valley Turnpike, U.S. Route 11, prior to being covered with asphalt (photograph taken in the 1930s, courtesy David Lee Ingram).

turnpikes was $425,000. However, the turnpikes were earning money before they were completed, for as fast as a five-mile stretch was finished, a toll gate was erected and tolls collected. When both turnpikes were completed in 1841, although bridges had not been built across all of the streams, there were 18 full toll gates, one every five miles, and one fractional gate at Staunton.[32] (Photographs of the Valley Turnpike, taken in the 1930s just prior to it being covered with asphalt, can be seen in Photographs A1–1 and A1–2.)

The Virginia Board of Public Works, which had oversight of all major Virginia turnpikes, was created in 1816. Shortly after the board's creation, the Virginia Assembly enacted a statute for the general regulation of turnpikes. The statute was very detailed on how turnpikes were to be built and what rights a turnpike company had in taking land as well as gravel and lumber. The statute also set toll rates and detailed how frequently toll booths could be built. Two requirements were that turnpikes were to be 60 feet wide and not have any grades exceeding 3½ degrees. However, the Valley Turnpike must have received an exception for both of these rules, as parts of the turnpike were less than 60 feet wide and had slopes that exceeded 3½ degrees. The challenge was the turnpike owners wanted to save money, but users and the Virginia Assembly wanted a straight, flat, wide, smooth road.[33]

Photograph A1-2: The Valley Turnpike, U.S. Route 11, prior to being covered with asphalt (photograph taken in the 1930s, courtesy David Lee Ingram).

    The Valley Turnpike was one of the superhighways of its time, and it became the major north-south artery in the Valley. It sped up travel and was used extensively by both sides during the war. By the end of the war, the Valley Turnpike was most certainly in a state of disrepair due to the heavy usage it experienced, and it is doubtful that little, if any, maintenance was conducted on it during the war. Still, even in a state of disrepair, this macadamized road was a better road than the dirt roads in the valley.

Appendix B: Major Battles for Winchester

Table starts on next page.

Appendix B: Major Battles for Winchester 199

Name of Battle	Location	Date	CSA Leader	USA Leader	Approximate Number Engaged and Casualties	Objectives	Results	Comments
First Kernstown	In Frederick County south of Winchester and in the vicinity of the Valley Turnpike	23 March 1862	Gen. Stonewall Jackson	Col. Nathan Kimball	Number Engaged CSA—3,600–3,800 USA—8,500–9,000 Casualties CSA—718 USA—590	Jackson attacked the Federal forces at Kernstown believing he outnumbered them with the objective of preventing Federal forces in the Valley from reinforcing George McClellan's army in the peninsula.	Jackson was defeated, but Abraham Lincoln was concerned enough about the potential threat to Washington that he kept units to defend Washington. As a result, these units were not sent to reinforce McClellan.	Considered to be the opening battle of Jackson's Valley campaign.
First Battle of Winchester	Just south of Winchester in the vicinity of the Valley Turnpike	25 May 1862	Gen. Stonewall Jackson	Gen. Nathaniel Banks	Number Engaged CSA—16,000 USA—6,500 Casualties CSA—400 USA—2,019	Jackson attacked the Federal forces at Winchester with the objective of keeping Federal units in the Valley rather than reinforcing McClellan.	Jackson was victorious but was not able to retain Winchester very long due to the threat of being cut off by Federal units in the upper Valley.	Part of Jackson's Valley campaign. It was a major victory for the Confederacy as it kept a large number of Federal units in the Valley.

Name of Battle	Location	Date	CSA Leader	USA Leader	Approximate Number Engaged and Casualties	Objectives	Results	Comments
Second Battle of Winchester	Just south, west, and north of Winchester	13–15 June 1863	Gen. Richard Ewell	Gen. Robert Milroy	Number Engaged CSA—12,500 USA—7,000 Casualties CSA—269 USA—4,443	Ewell attacked the Federal forces at Winchester for the purpose of clearing the Valley of Federal forces so that the Army of Northern Virginia could advance into Pennsylvania.	Ewell was victorious and all but destroyed Milroy's division.	A victory that gave the Confederacy the hope Ewell would be another Stonewall Jackson.
Second Kernstown	In Frederick County, south of Winchester and in the vicinity of the Valley Turnpike	24 July 1864	Gen. Jubal Early	Gen. George Crook	Number Engaged CSA—13,000 USA—10,000 Casualties CSA—600 USA—1,200	Early attacked Crook for the purpose of regaining control of the lower Valley.	Early was victorious and forced Crook to retreat.	A victory that allowed Early to reoccupy Winchester and send his cavalry to burn Chambersburg.
Third Battle of Winchester or the Battle of Opequon	Just east, north, and within Winchester	19 September 1864	Gen. Jubal Early	Gen. Philip Sheridan	Number Engaged CSA—15,200 USA—39,236 Casualties CSA—3,611 USA—5,018	Sheridan attacked Early, after Richard Anderson's force left to join Robert E. Lee at Petersburg, for the purpose of gaining control of the lower Valley.	Sheridan was victorious and inflicted a major defeat on Early's army.	A victory that gave the Federals control of the lower Valley, control that it would retain for the rest of the war.

Major Battles for Winchester

Name of Battle	Location	Date	CSA Leader	USA Leader	Approximate Number Engaged and Casualties	Objectives	Results	Comments
Battle of Cedar Creek	At the very southern part of Frederick County and in the vicinity of the Valley Turnpike	19 October 1864	Gen. Jubal Early	Gen. Horatio Wright, then Gen. Philip Sheridan	Number Engaged CSA—15,265 USA—31,944 Casualties CSA—2,910 USA—5,665	Early attacked the Federal camp at Cedar Creek with the purpose of driving the Federal army out of the Valley.	Although Early was initially victorious, at the end of the day, he was forced to retreat.	A victory that sealed Federal control of the lower Valley.

The number engaged and casualties in this table comes from the U.S. Department of the Interior's Study of Civil War Sites in the Shenandoah Valley of Virginia.

Appendix C: Confederate Invasions and Raids of the North

Table starts on next page.

Location	Year	Month(s)	Name of Raid	Confederate Leader	Size/Composition[1]	Objective	Results	Comments
New Mexico	1862	February–April	New Mexico campaign—Not a raid but an invasion, as its goal was to conquer territory.	Brigadier General Henry Hopkins Sibley	A force of over 1,750 men consisting of cavalry, and later dismounted cavalry, with some artillery.	Invade the northern New Mexico Territory in an attempt to gain control of the Southwest, including the gold fields of Colorado and the ports of California.	Battle of Glorieta Pass and the loss of the Confederate wagon train forced the Confederates to retreat.	Lack of logistics was the main reason for defeat.
Maryland	1862	September	Antietam campaign	General Robert E. Lee	Army of Northern Virginia, approximately 62,000 men.	Protect northern Virginia, gain supplies and gain recruits from Maryland.	Incursion achieved some of its goals but gave Abraham Lincoln the opportunity to announce his Emancipation Proclamation. If the incursion had been successful, there is the possibility that Maryland may have seceded.	Incursion was too short for any major logistic issues to arise.
Ohio	1862	August–September	Jenkins's raid	Brigadier General Albert Jenkins	A force of about 500 cavalry.	Destroy the Baltimore and Ohio Railroad and capture needed supplies.	Jenkins's raid revealed Federal weaknesses in the Kanawha Valley caused by the transfer of 5,000 troops to eastern Virginia prior to the Second Battle of Bull Run, but he did not destroy the railroad. However, he did cross into Ohio and captured Racine, Ohio.	A short raid with a small group of men.

Location	Year	Month(s)	Name of Raid	Confederate Leader	Size/Composition[1]	Objective	Results	Comments
Pennsylvania	1862	October	J.E.B. Stuart's Chambersburg raid	Major General J.E.B. Stuart	A force of about 1,800 cavalry and artillery.	Destroy the railroad bridge over the Conococheague Creek, bring back horses and capture government officials who might be exchanged for captured Confederate leaders or sympathizers, and gather information of the position, force, and probable intention of the Federal Army.	Partially successful but did not destroy the Conococheague Creek bridge.	Captured a number of horses needed by the Confederate Army.
Indiana and Ohio	1863	June–July	Morgan's raid	Brigadier General John Hunt Morgan	A force of about 2,000 men consisting of cavalry with some artillery.	Divert the attention of the Federal Army, stir up pro-Southern sentiments in the North, and bring the war to the North.	Morgan was captured, and most of his men were either captured or killed.	Blocked by the Ohio River and Federal gunboats.
Kansas	1863	August	Quantrill's raid/Lawrence massacre	William Quantrill	A force of about 150 to 300 men, all cavalry.	Retaliation for similar Federal raids in Missouri.	Raid was successful but resulted in Federal brigadier general Thomas Ewing, Jr.'s General Order No. 11, causing the eviction of thousands of Missourians in four counties from their homes near the Kansas border.	Too short of a raid to have any worries about logistics. In addition, the force split up after the raid.

Confederate Invasions and Raids of the North

Location	Year	Month(s)	Name of Raid	Confederate Leader	Size/Composition[1]	Objective	Results	Comments
West Virginia	1863	April–May	Jones-Imboden raid	Brigadier Generals William E. Jones and John D. Imboden	Two separate commands with a total of about 7,000 men, all cavalry.	Disrupt traffic on the Baltimore and Ohio Railroad and reassert Confederate authority in western Virginia in an effort to derail the growing statehood movement.	Militarily, the raid was successful but not politically, as the new state was created.	A short raid where logistics did not become an issue.
Pennsylvania	1863	June–July	Gettysburg campaign	General Robert E. Lee	Army of Northern Virginia, approximately 72,000 men.	Protect Northern Virginia, move the war into the North, and relieve pressure on Vicksburg.	Kept the Federal Army out of northern Virginia but did not relieve the pressure on Vicksburg.	A very long logistic trail.
Maryland and the District of Columbia	1864	July	Early's Washington raid	Lieutenant General Jubal Early	Second Corp, Army of Northern Virginia, approximately 10,000 men.	Push Federal Army out of the Valley, threaten Washington, free Confederate prisoners at Point Lookout, and relieve pressure on Lee at Petersburg.	Short-term success but caused Grant to take the threat from the Valley seriously.	Raid was too short for logistics to be an issue.
Pennsylvania	1864	July–August	McCausland's and Johnson's raid	Brigadier Generals John McCausland and Bradley Johnson	A force of about 2,800 cavalry and artillery.	Burn the town of Chambersburg, PA, unless a ransom was paid. Town was burned.	Accomplished mission but took very heavy losses returning to Virginia.	Losses suffered would hamper Confederate cavalry in the Valley during future operations.

Location	Year	Month(s)	Name of Raid	Confederate Leader	Size/Composition[1]	Objective	Results	Comments
Missouri	1864	September–November	Price's Missouri expedition	Major General Sterling Price	A force of cavalry and artillery. Started out with about 12,000 men, but only 8,000 were armed. Added about 5,000 recruits in Missouri.	Divert the attention of the Federal Army and possibly gain control of Missouri for the Confederacy.	Had some successes but was ultimately driven back into Arkansas.	Problems with logistics. (On list as, except for guerrillas, the Federals controlled Missouri.)
Vermont	1864	October	St. Albans raid	Lieutenant Bennett Young	A force of 12–25 men, all cavalry.	Rob banks to help fund future raids and to force the Federal Army to divert troops to defend the U.S.-Canadian border.	Raid was successful but forced Canada to stop any further raids from its territory.	Too short of a raid to have any worries about logistics.

Arizona Territory, California, Colorado, Dakota, Idaho Territory, Maine, Massachusetts, Minnesota, Montana, Nebraska, Nevada, Oregon, and Utah

The list of states and territories shown also had military actions in them during the war. Many of these actions were draft riots, scouts, and expeditions, or actions were against Indians. A complete list of all recorded actions can be found in *When and Where We Met Each Other.*

Chapter Notes

Introduction

1. *Study of Civil War Sites in the Shenandoah Valley of Virginia*, U.S. Department of the Interior, National Park Service, Interagency Resources Division, 1992, 1.

2. Dabney W. Watts, Chairman of the Winchester-Frederick County Centennial Commission 1960, *Civil War Battles in Winchester and Frederick County, Virginia 1861–1865*, Carr Publishing Co., Boyce, VA, 1960, back cover. It needs to be noted that many of these occupations and evacuations were conducted by small cavalry forces with some happening the same day. Still, each change presented danger and problems for Winchester's occupants.

3. *Weekly Philadelphia Times*, June 2, 1877.

4. *War of the Rebellion: A Compilation of the Official Records of the Union and Confederate Armies* (henceforth cited as *ORA*), Government Printing Office, Washington, D.C., 1881–1901, Series I, Volume XII, Part I, 546.

5. James I. Robertson, Jr., *Stonewall Jackson*, Macmillan, New York, 1997, 527.

6. Don E. Fehrenbacher and Virginia Fehrenbacher, editors, *Recollected Words of Abraham Lincoln*, Stanford University Press, Stanford, 1996, 167.

7. Barbara W. Tuchman, *The Guns of August*, Macmillan, New York, 1962, 17–18.

8. Audie Murphy, *To Hell and Back*, Bantam Books, New York, 1983, 82.

9. Carl Von Clausewitz, edited and translated by Michael Howard and Peter Paret, *On War*, Princeton University Press, Princeton, 1984, 89.

10. Carl Von Clausewitz, edited and translated by Michael Howard and Peter Paret, *On War*, Princeton University Press, Princeton, 1984, 87.

11. John I. Alger, *Definitions and Doctrine of the Military Art*, Avery Publishing Group, Wayne, NJ, 1985, 8–11.

12. Today, there are known deposits of coal and iron in the south, but during the Civil War these deposits were either not known or not worked.

Chapter 1

1. Bruce Catton, *The Army of the Potomac: A Stillness at Appomattox*, Doubleday, Garden City, NY, 1953, 272–273.

2. The information in this paragraph on the pre–Civil War history of Winchester came from Frederic Morton's *The Story of Winchester in Virginia*, Shenandoah Publishing House, Strasburg, VA, 1925, 40–42, 65–83, 88–90.

3. Much of the information in this paragraph comes from Frederic Morton's *The Story of Winchester in Virginia*, Shenandoah Publishing House, Strasburg, VA, 1925, 40–41.

4. Data concerning the population, agriculture, and manufacturing in Winchester and Frederick County comes from Joseph C. Kennedy, Superintendent of Census, *Population of the United States in 1860; Compiled from the Original Returns of the Eighth Census*, under the Direction of the Secretary of the Interior, Government Printing Office, Washington, D.C., 1864, 500–520.

5. *ORA*, Series I, Volume XLIII, Part II, 272–273.

6. *ORA*, Series I, Volume XLIII, Part I, 815.

7. Regimental commanders Colonel William H. Ball's report of the battle states that his regiment, the 122nd Ohio Volunteer Infantry, was posted late on the 14th in the principal fortification, which would have been Fort Milroy. *ORA*, Series I, Volume XXVII, Part II, 67–68.

8. James J. Hartley, edited by Garber A. Davidson, *The Civil War Letters of the Late 1st Lieutenant James J. Hartley, 122nd Ohio Infantry Regiment*, McFarland, Jefferson, NC, 1998, 41–42.

9. George Blotcher, Diary, Handley Library Archives, MMF-Civil War Diaries/Letters, Blotcher, George; 1556 THL.

10. *ORA*, Series I, Volume XLIII, Part I, 43.

11. The number of men involved in the battles came from the U.S. Department of Interior's *Study of Civil War Sites in the Shenandoah Valley of Virginia*, although in some cases were rounded up or down.

12. *ORA*, Series I, Volume XXVII, Part I, 178.

13. George B. McClellan, *McClellan's Own Story*, Charles L. Webster, New York, 1887, 192.

14. There is an excellent description of the Valley and its main roads in Jubal Early's *A Memoir of the Last Year of the War for Independence in the Confederate States of America*, Charles W. Button, Lynchburg, VA, 1867, 35–39.

15. *ORA*, Series I, Volume XII, Part I, 706.

16. *ORA*, Series I, Volume XLIII, Part I, 41.

17. *ORA*, Series I, Volume XLIII, Part I, 41.
18. Richard R. Duncan, editor, *Alexander Neil and the Last Shenandoah Valley Campaign*, White Mane, Shippensburg, PA, 1996, 39.
19. Martin F. Schmitt, editor, *General George Crook, His Autobiography*, University of Oklahoma Press, Norman, 1960, 121.
20. Martin F. Schmitt, editor, *General George Crook, His Autobiography*, University of Oklahoma Press, Norman, 1960, 121.
21. The Battle of Droop Mountain has been credited with being the battle that took place at the highest elevation, 3597 feet, during the Civil War.
22. There is a summary of the fighting that took place around Beverly in Stan Cohen's *The Civil War in West Virginia*, Pictorial Histories, Charleston, WV, 1995, 72.
23. U.S. Department of Interior's *Study of Civil War Sites in the Shenandoah Valley of Virginia*, Interagency Resources Division, 31.
24. The weight of an ambulance during the Civil War came from *The Medical and Surgical History of the War of the Rebellion*, Government Printing Office, Washington, D.C., 1883, 946, and the weight of a six-mule wagon came from an e-mail message from Luther D. Hanson, United States Army Quartermaster Museum, dated 21 January 2015.
25. Joseph Roberts, *The Hand Book of Artillery*, 5th edition, D. Van Nostrand, New York, reprint of the 1863 edition, 175.
26. Colonel Theodore S. Case, *The Quartermaster's Guide*, P.M. Pinokard, Saint Louis, 1865, 42.
27. *ORA*, Series I, Volume XXIII, Part II, 601.
28. *ORA*, Series I, Volume XLIII, Part II, 174–175. This topic is discussed in more detail in Chapter 11. Obviously, Sherman's March to the Sea is an exception, but Sherman took a large quantity of supplies with him, and his army lived off the land. In addition, he did not have to fight any major battles during his march, and the first thing he did when he got to the coast was to open a supply line through the Navy.
29. *Report of the President and Directors to the Stockholders of the South Side R.R. Co.*, Office South Side Rail Road Company, Petersburg, November 25, 1865, and Frank Helvestine, "The Development of a Great Railroad," *Norfolk and Western Magazine*, July 1923, 76.
30. Joseph E. Johnston, *Narrative of Military Operations*, D. Appleton, New York, 1874, 31–32.
31. Joseph E. Johnston, *Narrative of Military Operations*, D. Appleton, New York, 1874, 31–32.
32. Joseph E. Johnston, *Narrative of Military Operations*, D. Appleton, New York, 1874, 31.
33. *ORA*, Series I, Volume XLIII, Part I, 41.
34. J. Stoddard Johnston, "Sketches of Operations of General John C. Breckinridge," *Southern Historical Society Papers*, Richmond, Volume 7, No. 2, 1879, 320.
35. Captain Charles M. Blackford, "The Campaign and Battle of Lynchburg," *Southern Historical Society Papers*, Richmond, Volume 30, 1902, 279–280.
36. J. Stoddard Johnston, "Sketches of Operations of General John C. Breckinridge," *Southern Historical Society Papers*, Richmond, Volume 7, No. 3–Conclusion, 1879, 386.
37. There is an excellent study on salt in the Confederacy in Ella Lonn's *Salt as a Factor in the Confederacy*, University of Alabama Press, Tuscaloosa, 1965.

Chapter 2

1. It should be noted that the streams shown on Maps 2-1 to 2-4 are not accurately placed. These small streams, which were not significant obstacles, are more accurately placed on Map 2-5.
2. *ORA*, Series I, Volume XII, Part I, 164.
3. R.L. Dabney, *Life and Campaigns of General T.J. (Stonewall) Jackson*, Sprinkle Publications, Harrisonburg, VA, 1977, 311.
4. *ORA*, Series I, Volume XII, Part I, 380.
5. *ORA*, Series I, Volume XII, Part I, 380–381.
6. Peter Cozzens, *Shenandoah 1862: Stonewall Jackson's Valley Campaign*, University of North Carolina Press, Chapel Hill, 2008, 151–153.
7. Peter Cozzens, *Shenandoah 1862: Stonewall Jackson's Valley Campaign*, The University of North Carolina Press, Chapel Hill, NC, 2008, 159–160.
8. *ORA*, Series I, Volume XII, Part I, 385–386.
9. *ORA*, Series I, Volume XII, Part I, 352–353.
10. *ORA*, Series I, Volume XII, Part I, 361–365.
11. *ORA*, Series I, Volume XII, Part I, 381.
12. *ORA*, Series I, Volume XII, Part I, 339.
13. *ORA*, Series I, Volume XII, Part I, 381.
14. *ORA*, Series I, Volume XII, Part I, 408. Unfortunately, General Garnett did not write a report probably due to the fact that Jackson had him under arrest.
15. Maj. Frank B. Jones, Diary, Handley Library Archives, 424 WFCHS, Box 1.
16. *ORA*, Series I, Volume XII, Part I, 366–367.
17. *ORA*, Series I, Volume XII, Part I, 369.
18. Michael D. Wallick, *Dr. Christian Schwartz with the 67th Ohio Volunteers*, self-published, 2018, 54–56.
19. William S. Young, "Fighting Them Over, What Our Veterans Have to Say About Their Old Campaigns, Shenandoah Valley, Criticising [sic] Gen. Capehart's Article on That Campaign," *The National Tribune*, April 18, 1889, p. 4, Library of Congress.
20. *ORA*, Series I, Volume XII, Part I, 341.
21. *ORA*, Series I, Volume XII, Part I, 378.
22. Nathan Kimball, "Fighting Jackson at Kernstown," *Battles and Leaders of the Civil War*, Castle, Secaucus, 308.
23. *ORA*, Series I, Volume XII, Part I, 383–384.
24. *Collected Works of Abraham Lincoln*, University of Michigan, Digital Library Production Services, 2001, Ann Arbor, accessed 6 May 2015, Volume 5, 184–185.
25. Stephen W. Sears, *George B. McClellan: The Young Napoleon*, Ticknor & Fields, New York, 1988, 175.

26. Mary Anna Jackson, *Life and Letter of General Thomas J. Jackson*, Sprinkle Publications, Harrisonburg, VA, 1995, 248–249.

Chapter 3

1. George B. McClellan, *McClellan's Own Story*, Charles L. Webster, New York, 1887, 345.
2. James M. McPherson, *Embattled Rebel: Jefferson Davis as Commander in Chief*, Penguin, New York, 2014, 81.
3. George B. McClellan, *McClellan's Own Story*, Charles L. Webster, New York, 1887, 344.
4. Clifford Dowdey and Louis H. Manarin, editors, *The Wartime Papers of R.E. Lee*, Virginia Civil War Commission, Little, Brown, Boston, 1961, 127.
5. *ORA*, Series I, Volume XII, Part III, 893.
6. Henry Kyd Douglas, *I Rode with Stonewall*, University of North Carolina Press, Chapel Hill, 1968, 65.
7. Henry Kyd Douglas, *I Rode with Stonewall*, University of North Carolina Press, Chapel Hill, 1968, 65.
8. Jed Hotchkiss comments about the rain and hail in his journal. Archie P. McDonald, editor, *Make Me a Map of the Valley: The Civil War Journal of Stonewall Jackson's Topographer*, Southern Methodist University Press, Dallas, 1973, 48.
9. *ORA*, Series I, Volume XII, Part I, 704.
10. *ORA*, Series I, Volume XII, Part I, 574.
11. *ORA*, Series I, Volume XII, Part I, 574.
12. *ORA*, Series I, Volume XII, Part I, 794.
13. *ORA*, Series I, Volume XII, Part I, 606.
14. Howard McHenry, *Recollections of a Maryland Confederate Soldier and Staff Officer Under Johnston, Jackson and Lee*, Morningside, Dayton, 1975, 109–110.
15. *ORA*, Series I, Volume XII, Part I, 617.
16. *ORA*, Series I, Volume XII, Part I, 737.
17. *ORA*, Series I, Volume XII, Part I, 706.
18. *ORA*, Series I, Volume XII, Part III, 235.
19. *ORA*, Series I, Volume XII, Part III, 276.
20. *ORA*, Series I, Volume XII, Part III, 276.
21. *ORA*, Series I, Volume XII, Part III, 425.
22. *ORA*, Series I, Volume XII, Part III, 425.
23. Douglas Southall Freeman, *Lee's Lieutenants*, Volume 1, Charles Scribner's Sons, New York, 1970, 482.
24. Archie P. McDonald, editor, *Make Me a Map of the Valley: The Civil War Journal of Stonewall Jackson's Topographer*, Southern Methodist University Press, Dallas, 1973, 10.
25. *ORA*, Series I, Volume XIX, Part I, 139.

Chapter 4

1. *ORA*, Series I, Volume XXVII, Part II, 192.
2. *ORA*, Series I, Volume XXVII, Part II, 158.
3. *ORA*, Series I, Volume XXVII, Part II, 159.
4. *ORA*, Series I, Volume XXVII, Part II, 49.
5. *ORA*, Series I, Volume XXVII, Part II, 50. Milroy later told the Board of Inquiry, "The language used in my telegram expressive of my confidence in my ability to hold Winchester was used with reference to any contingency which would probably happen. I did not mean that I could hold it against such an army as that which I knew to be at the disposal of General Lee, and it was no part of my duty to watch the movements of that army." *ORA*, Series I, Volume XXVII, Part II, 51. Milroy was overconfident in his ability to defend Winchester, as can be seen in other messages, and he was trying to justify his actions to the board.
6. *ORA*, Series I, Volume XXVII, Part II, 50.
7. *ORA*, Series I, Volume XXVII, Part II, 197. A factor that probably influenced Lincoln's decision was that General Schenck was a friend and had endorsed him for president. Schenck was also a former congressman. In addition, Lincoln was a man who believed little could be gained by continuing to persecute people who had already been indirectly punished. Another factor was that the Federal victory at Gettysburg overshadowed the defeat at Winchester.
8. *ORA*, Series I, Volume XXVII, Part II, 177–178.
9. *ORA*, Series I, Volume XXVII, Part II, 178–179.
10. *ORA*, Series I, Volume XXVII, Part II, 157–158.
11. *ORA*, Series I, Volume XXVII, Part II, 41.
12. *ORA*, Series I, Volume XXVII, Part II, 92.
13. *ORA*, Series I, Volume XXVII, Part II, 43.
14. *ORA*, Series I, Volume XXVII, Part II, 178. Milroy later told his Board of Inquiry, "I supposed that with my fortifications I was able to stand some two or three times my own forces." *ORA*, Series I, Volume XXVII, Part II, 93.
15. *ORA*, Series I, Volume XXVII, Part II, 178.
16. *ORA*, Series I, Volume XXVII, Part II, 161.
17. *ORA*, Series I, Volume XXVII, Part II, 161.
18. *ORA*, Series I, Volume XXVII, Part II, 107.
19. *ORA*, Series I, Volume XXVII, Part II, 147.
20. *ORA*, Series I, Volume XXVII, Part II, 132.
21. *ORA*, Series I, Volume XXVII, Part II, 99-100.
22. *ORA*, Series I, Volume XXVII, Part II, 146.
23. A full explanation of Lee's reasons for moving into Pennsylvania can be found in Douglas Southall Freeman's *R.E. Lee*, Volume III, Charles Scribner's Sons, New York, 1963, 18–28.
24. *ORA*, Series I, Volume XXVII, Part II, 461.
25. *ORA*, Series I, Volume XXVII, Part II, 462.
26. *ORA*, Series I, Volume XXVII, Part II, 146.
27. *ORA*, Series I, Volume XXVII, Part II, 478.
28. Terry L. Jones, editor, *Civil War Memoirs of Captain William J. Seymour*, Louisiana State University, Baton Rouge, 1991, 62.
29. *ORA*, Series I, Volume XXVII, Part II, 463.
30. J. Warren Keifer, *Slavery and Four Years of War: A Political History of Slavery in the United States, Together with a Narrative of the Campaigns and Battles of the Civil War in Which the Author Took Part*, Volume II, G.P. Putnam and Sons, New York, 1900, 13.

31. Terry L. Jones, editor, *Civil War Memoirs of Captain William J. Seymour,* Louisiana State University, Baton Rouge, 1991, 61–62.
32. *ORA*, Series I, Volume XXVII, Part II, 64.
33. *ORA*, Series I, Volume XXVII, Part II, 85.
34. *ORA*, Series I, Volume XXVII, Part II, 500.
35. *ORA*, Series I, Volume XXVII, Part II, 501.
36. *ORA*, Series I, Volume XXVII, Part II, 119.
37. J. Warren Keifer, *Slavery and Four Years of War: A Political History of Slavery in the United States, Together with a Narrative of the Campaigns and Battles of the Civil War in Which the Author Took Part,* Volume II, G.P. Putnam and Sons, New York, 1900, 15–16.
38. *ORA*, Series I, Volume XXVII, Part II, 441, and *ORA*, Series I, Volume XXVII, Part II, 502.
39. J. Warren Keifer, *Slavery and Four Years of War: A Political History of Slavery in the United States, Together with a Narrative of the Campaigns and Battles of the Civil War in Which the Author Took Part,* Volume II, G.P. Putnam and Sons, New York, 1900, 16.
40. *ORA*, Series I, Volume XXVII, Part III, 502.
41. *ORA*, Series I, Volume XXVII, Part III, 967.

Chapter 5

1. *ORA*, Series I, Volume XXXVII, Part I, 346.
2. The movements of Early's force can be found in his autobiography, *A Memoir of the Last Year of the War for Independence in the Confederate States of America,* Charles W. Button, Lynchburg, VA, 1867, 63–64.
3. *ORA*, Series I, Volume XXXVII, Part I, 269.
4. *ORA*, Series I, Volume XXXVII, Part I, 295, 327.
5. Martin F. Schmitt, editor, *General George Crook, His Autobiography,* University of Oklahoma Press, Norman, 1960, 123.
6. Jubal A. Early, *A Memoir of the Last Year of the War for Independence,* Charles W. Button, Lynchburg, VA, 1867, 64.
7. Archie P. McDonald, editor, *Make Me a Map of the Valley: The Civil War Journal of Stonewall Jackson's Topographer,* Southern Methodist University Press, Dallas, 1973, 217.
8. *ORA*, Series I, Volume XXXVII, Part I, 292.
9. I. Gordon Bradwell, "When General Mulligan Was Killed," *Confederate Veteran,* Volume XXXV, No. 1, January 1927, 14.
10. Armistead L. Long, "General Early's Valley Campaign," *Southern Historical Society Papers,* Volume 3, 117.
11. Richard R. Duncan, editor, *Alexander Neil and the Last Shenandoah Valley Campaign,* White Mane, Shippensburg, PA, 1996, 54.
12. Richard R. Duncan, editor, *Alexander Neil and the Last Shenandoah Valley Campaign,* White Mane, Shippensburg, PA, 1996, 55.
13. Richard R. Duncan, editor, *Alexander Neil and the Last Shenandoah Valley Campaign,* White Mane, Shippensburg, PA, 1996, 55.
14. *ORA*, Series I, Volume XXXVII, Part I, 347.

Chapter 6

1. *ORA*, Series I, Volume XLIII, Part I, 755.
2. U.S. Grant, *Personal Memoirs of U.S. Grant,* Volume II, Charles L. Webster, New York, 1886, 562.
3. U.S. Grant, *Personal Memoirs of U.S. Grant,* Volume II, Charles L. Webster, New York, 1886, 556.
4. U.S. Grant, *Personal Memoirs of U.S. Grant,* Volume II, Charles L. Webster, New York, 1886, 556.
5. U.S. Grant, *Personal Memoirs of U.S. Grant,* Volume II, Charles L. Webster, New York, 1886, 558.
6. *ORA*, Series I, Volume XLIII, Part I, 57.
7. *ORA*, Series I, Volume XLIII, Part I, 57–58.
8. *ORA*, Series I, Volume XLIII, Part I, 719 and 721.
9. *ORA*, Series I, Volume XLIII, Part I, 83–84.
10. Philip H. Sheridan, *Personal Memoirs of P.H. Sheridan,* Volume I, Charles L. Webster, New York, 1888, 499–500.
11. *ORA*, Series I, Volume XXXVI, Part I, 30.
12. For anyone interested in reading an excellent, even-handed study of Jefferson Davis' presidency I would recommend James McPherson's *Embattled Rebel: Jefferson Davis as Commander in Chief.*
13. Jubal A. Early, *A Memoir of the Last Year of the War for Independence in the Confederate States of America,* Charles W. Button, Lynchburg, VA, 1867, 40.
14. Jubal A. Early, *A Memoir of the Last Year of the War for Independence in the Confederate States of America,* Charles W. Button, Lynchburg, VA, 1867, 50.
15. *ORA*, Series I, Volume XXXVII, Part I, 769–770.
16. *ORA*, Series I, Volume XXXVII, Part II, 596.
17. *ORA*, Series I, Volume XXXVII, Part II, 599.
18. *ORA*, Series I, Volume XXXVII, Part II, 595.
19. *ORA*, Series I, Volume LXIII, Part I, 43.
20. *ORA*, Series I, Volume XLIII, Part I, 916–917.
21. *ORA*, Series I, Volume XLIII, Part I, 816.
22. Philip H. Sheridan, *Personal Memoirs of P.H. Sheridan,* Volume I, Charles L. Webster, New York, 1888, 487.
23. Philip H. Sheridan, *Personal Memoirs of P.H. Sheridan,* Volume I, Charles L. Webster, New York, 1888, 488. The philosophy of war that Sheridan learned during the Civil War was applied during the Indian Wars with similar results as the destruction he ordered in the Valley.
24. Jubal A. Early, *A Memoir of the Last Year of the War for Independence in the Confederate States of America,* Charles W. Button, Lynchburg, VA, 1867, 81.
25. Jubal A. Early, *A Memoir of the Last Year of the War for Independence in the Confederate States of America,* Charles W. Button, Lynchburg, VA, 1867, 81.

26. Jubal A. Early, *A Memoir of the Last Year of the War for Independence in the Confederate States of America*, Charles W. Button, Lynchburg, VA, 1867, 81.
27. *ORA*, Series I, Volume XLIII, Part II, 69.
28. Philip H. Sheridan, *Personal Memoirs of P.H. Sheridan*, Volume I, Charles L. Webster, New York, 1888, 476.
29. *ORA*, Series I, Volume XLIII, Part I, 856–857.
30. *ORA*, Series I, Volume XLIII, Part I, 841.
31. *ORA*, Series I, Volume LXIII, Part I, 775
32. *ORA*, Series I, Volume XLIII, Part I, 1006.
33. Jubal A. Early, *A Memoir of the Last Year of the War for Independence in the Confederate States of America*, Charles W. Button, Lynchburg, VA, 1867, 80.
34. Jubal A. Early, *A Memoir of the Last Year of the War for Independence in the Confederate States of America*, Charles W. Button, Lynchburg, VA, 1867, 58 and 79.
35. Philip H. Sheridan, *Personal Memoirs of P.H. Sheridan*, Volume I, Charles L. Webster, New York, 1888, 497–499.
36. The Berryville Canyon from the time of the Civil War no longer exists as it has been leveled and a highway, VA Route 7, goes through it.
37. James E. Taylor, *With Sheridan up the Shenandoah Valley in 1864*, Morningside, Dayton, 1989, 378.
38. *ORA*, Series I, Volume XLIII, Part II, 103.
39. *ORA*, Series I, Volume XLIII, Part II, 102–103.
40. *ORA*, Series I, Volume XLIII, Part II, 102.
41. Philip H. Sheridan, *Personal Memoirs of P.H. Sheridan*, Volume II, Charles L. Webster, New York, 1888, 17.
42. Philip H. Sheridan, *Personal Memoirs of P.H. Sheridan*, Volume II, Charles L. Webster, New York, 1888, 26.
43. *ORA*, Series I, Volume XLIII, Part I, 361.
44. Jubal A. Early, *A Memoir of the Last Year of the War for Independence in the Confederate States of America*, Charles W. Button, Lynchburg, VA, 1867, 87–88.
45. *ORA*, Series I, Volume XLIII, Part I, 168–170.
46. *ORA*, Series I, Volume XLIII, Part I, 271–272.
47. *ORA*, Series I, Volume XLIII, Part I, 317–318.
48. *ORA*, Series I, Volume XLIII, Part I, 361.
49. *ORA*, Series I, Volume XLIII, Part I, 362.
50. *ORA*, Series I, Volume XLIII, Part I, 162–163.
51. *ORA*, Series I, Volume XLIII, Part I, 443–446.
52. Henry A. Du Pont, *The Campaign of 1864 in the Valley of Virginia and the Expedition to Lynchburg*, National Americana Society, New York, 1925, 117. This is in conflict to Sheridan's autobiography, but since his autobiography is self-serving, as most are, I decided to go with Du Pont's statement as he was with Sheridan when Upton was making his attack and was there when the messenger arrived.
53. Lemuel Abijah Abbott, *Personal Recollections and Civil War Diary, 1864*, Free Press Printing Company, Burlington, VT, 1908, 150–166.
54. *ORA*, Series I, Volume XLIII, Part II, 102–103.
55. *ORA*, Series I, Volume XLIII, Part I, 554. E
56. The number of men in Ramseur's division comes from *ORA*, Series I, Volume XLIII, Part I, 1011. The number of men in Wright's and Emory's corps comes from *ORA*, Series I, Volume XLIII, Part I, 61.
57. *ORA*, Series I, Volume XLIII, Part I, 47.
58. *ORA*, Series I, Volume XLIII, Part I, 361.
59. *ORA*, Series I, Volume XLIII, Part I, 47.
60. *ORA*, Series I, Volume XLIII, Part I, 362.
61. *ORA*, Series I, Volume XLIII, Part I, 150.
62. *ORA*, Series I, Volume XLIII, Part I, 402.
63. *ORA*, Series I, Volume XLIII, Part I, 427.
64. *ORA*, Series I, Volume XLIII, Part I, 443.
65. *ORA*, Series I, Volume XLIII, Part II, 202.
66. *ORA*, Series I, Volume XLIII, Part II, 308.
67. *ORA*, Series I, Volume XLIII, Part I, 561.
68. *ORA*, Series I, Volume XLIII, Part I, 562.
69. Henry Kyd Douglas, *I Rode with Stonewall*, University of North Carolina Press, Chapel Hill, 1984, 316–317, and Jeffry D. Wert, *From Winchester to Cedar Creek*, Stackpole, Mechanicsburg, PA, 1997, 184, 193–194, and 216–217.
70. *ORA*, Series I, Volume XLIII, Part I, 560.
71. *ORA*, Series I, Volume XLIII, Part II, 919.
72. *ORA*, Series I, Volume XLIII, Part I, 50.
73. *ORA*, Series I, Volume XLIII, Part II, 174.
74. *ORA*, Series I, Volume XLIII, Part II, 487.
75. *ORA*, Series I, Volume XLIII, Part II, 487.
76. *ORA*, Series I, Volume XLIII, Part II, 487.
77. *ORA*, Series I, Volume XLIII, Part II, 210.
78. The Union high command knew Winchester was indefensible unless manned by a very large garrison as noted in a message from General Halleck to General Grant in October 1864. The message can be found in *ORA*, Series I, Series XLIII, Part II, 272–273.

Chapter 7

1. E.A. Paul, "The Battle of Cedar Creek," *The New York Times*, October 27, 1964.
2. *ORA*, Series I, Volume XLIII, Part I, 50.
3. *ORA*, Series I, Volume XLIII, Part I, 50.
4. *ORA*, Series I, Volume XLIII, Part I, 559.
5. *ORA*, Series I, Volume XLIII, Part I, 51.
6. *ORA*, Series I, Volume XLIII, Part I, 432.
7. *ORA*, Series I, Volume XLIII, Part I, 51–52.
8. *ORA*, Series I, Volume XLIII, Part I, 52.
9. *ORA*, Series I, Volume XLIII, Part I, 365.
10. Henry A. Du Pont, *The Campaign of 1864 in the Valley of Virginia and the Expedition to Lynchburg*, National Americana Society, New York, 1925, 152.
11. Henry A. Du Pont, *The Campaign of 1864 in the Valley of Virginia and the Expedition to*

Lynchburg, National Americana Society, New York, 1925, 152.
  12. *ORA*, Series I, Volume XLIII, Part I, 158.
  13. *ORA*, Series I, Volume XLIII, Part I, 158.
  14. General John B. Gordon, *Reminiscences of the Civil War*, Charles Scribner's Sons, New York, 1904, 334.
  15. It is well worth the hike to Signal Knob for the view and to fully understand why it was used as a signal point during the war.
  16. Terry L. Jones, editor, *Civil War Memoirs of Captain William J. Seymour*, Louisiana State University, Baton Rouge, 1991, 148.
  17. E.A. Paul, "The Battle of Cedar Creek," *The New York Times*, October 27, 1964.
  18. Henry A. Du Pont, *The Campaign of 1864 in the Valley of Virginia and the Expedition to Lynchburg*, National Americana Society, New York, 1925, 156. Henry Du Pont later received a Medal of Honor for his actions during the battle.
  19. Henry A. Du Pont, *The Campaign of 1864 in the Valley of Virginia and the Expedition to Lynchburg*, National Americana Society, New York, 1925, 156.
  20. Jubal A. Early, *A Memoir of the Last Year of the War for Independence*, Charles W. Button, Lynchburg, VA, 1867, 106.
  21. *ORA*, Series I, Volume XLIII, Part I, 365.
  22. Jubal A. Early, *A Memoir of the Last Year of the War for Independence*, Charles W. Button, Lynchburg, VA, 1867, 104.
  23. Jubal A. Early, *A Memoir of the Last Year of the War for Independence*, Charles W. Button, Lynchburg, VA, 1867, 107.
  24. D. Augustus Dicket, *History of Kershaw's Brigade*, Elbert H. Aull, Newberry, SC, 1899, 449.
  25. D. Augustus Dicket, *History of Kershaw's Brigade*, Elbert H. Aull, Newberry, SC, 1899, 450.
  26. I. Gordon Bradwell, "Battle of Cedar Creek, VA," *Confederate Veteran*, Volume XXVII, No. 11, November 1919, 412.
  27. Scott C. Patchan, *The Last Battle of Winchester*, Savas Beatie, El Dorado Hills, CA, 2013, 482. *ORA*, Series I, Volume XLIII, Part I, 61. *ORA*, Series I, Volume XLIII, Part I, 974.
  28. Jubal A. Early, *A Memoir of the Last Year of the War for Independence*, Charles W. Button, Lynchburg, VA, 1867, 109.
  29. *ORA*, Series I, Volume XLIII, Part I, 562.
  30. *ORA*, Series I, Volume XLIII, Part I, 53.
  31. Augustus Hamlin, "Who Recaptured the Guns at Cedar Creek October 19, 1864?" *Papers of the Military Historical Society of Massachusetts: The Shenandoah Campaigns of 1862 and 1864 and the Appomattox Campaign 1865*, Volume VI, 1907, 208.
  32. There is some confusion about the actual cause of the blockage with one source (Augustus Hamlin, "Who Recaptured the Guns at Cedar Creek October 19, 1864?" *Papers of the Military Historical Society of Massachusetts: The Shenandoah Campaigns of 1862 and 1864 and the Appomattox Campaign 1865*, Volume VI, 1907, 208) stating that the bridge was blocked by two wagons with each of the wagons having a wheel over opposite sides of the bridge and only enough room for a horse to pass between them. Another source (Benjamin W. Crowninshield, "Cedar Creek," *Papers of the Military Historical Society of Massachusetts: The Shenandoah Campaigns of 1862 and 1864 and the Appomattox Campaign 1865*, Volume V, 1907, 175) states that a plank or two were broken and a wagon had overturned. There were two bridges involved, one in Strasburg and another just south of Strasburg. The one just south of Strasburg was the initial cause of the blockage which then led to a blockage occurring on the bridge in Strasburg. Consequently, the confusion from the two sources is just a matter of which bridge they saw.

Chapter 8

  1. James L. Robertson, Jr., *Stonewall Jackson*, Macmillan, New York, 1997, 347.
  2. *ORA*, Series I, Volume XIX, Part I, 139.
  3. *ORA*, Series I, Volume XIX, Part I, 720.
  4. *ORA*, Series I, Volume XIX, Part I, 720.
  5. *ORA*, Series I, Volume XIX, Part I, 720.
  6. *ORA*, Series I, Volume XXI, Part I, 34.
  7. *ORA*, Series I, Volume XXI, Part I, 860.
  8. *ORA*, Series I, Volume XXI, Part I, 875.
  9. *ORA*, Series I, Volume XXVII, Part I, 101.
  10. *ORA*, Series I, Volume XXVII, Part I, 102.
  11. *ORA*, Series I, Volume XXVII, Part I, 102.
  12. U.S. Grant, *Personal Memoirs of U.S. Grant*, Charles L. Webster, New York, 1886, 316.

Chapter 9

  1. A detailed discussion of the fate of the Norse in Greenland can be found in Jared Diamond's *Collapse*, Penguin, New York, 2006, 178–276.
  2. All of the information in this paragraph about cod is taken from Mark Kurlansky's book *Cod*, Walker, New York, 1997.
  3. Cod can be found in other oceans, but most of the fighting for the right to fish for cod has occurred in the North Atlantic.
  4. Jared Diamond, *Guns, Germs, and Steel*, Vintage, London, 1998, 406–408.
  5. A detailed discussion of Roman mines can be found in Oliver Davies' *Roman Mines in Europe*, Clarendon Press, Oxford, 1935.
  6. A detailed discussion of Venetian ship building can be found in Frederic Chapin Lane's *Venetian Ships and Shipbuilders of the Renaissance*, Johns Hopkins Press, Baltimore, 1934.
  7. A detailed discussion of the impact the need to secure reliable sources of naval stores can be found in P.K. Crimmin's article "Searching for British Naval Stores: Sources and Strategy c. 1802–1860," *The Great Circle*, Volume 18, No. 2, 1996, 113–124.
  8. A detailed discussion of gunpowder can be found in Edward B. McCaul, Jr.'s *The Mechanical*

Fuze and the Advance of Artillery in the Civil War, McFarland, Jefferson, NC, 2010, and Jack Kelly's *Gunpowder*, Basic Books, New York, 2004.

9. A detailed discussion of the United States vulnerability to its lack of strategic minerals can be found in Kent Hughes Butts' *Strategic Minerals in the New World Order*, Strategic Studies Institute, U.S. Army War College, Carlisle Barracks, PA, 1993.

10. The information in this paragraph came from Lino Camprubi's "Resource Geopolitics: Cold War Technologies, Global Fertilizers, and the Fate of Western Sahara," *Technology and Culture*, Volume 56, No. 3, July 2015, 676–703, and from the United States' State Department website, http://www.state.gov/, accessed 14 September 2015.

11. A detailed discussion of the impact the amount of food and water a galley could carry and the number of rowers it could hold can be found in John F. Guilmartin, Jr.'s *Galleons and Galleys*, Cassell, London, 2002.

12. An excellent example of geography influencing the development of a technology can be found in Lawrence V. Mott's *The Development of the Rudder: A Technological Tale*, Texas A&M University Press, College Station, 1997.

Chapter 10

1. The information about Sun Tzu's writings comes from Sun Tzu, edited by James Clavell, *The Art of War*, Delacorte Press, New York, 1983.

2. The information about Niccolò Machiavelli's writings comes from Niccolò Machiavelli, *The Art of War*, a revised edition of the Ellis Farneworth translation, Da Capo Press, New York, 1965.

3. The information about Niccolò Machiavelli's writings comes from Niccolò Machiavelli, *The Art of War*, a revised edition of the Ellis Farneworth translation, Da Capo Press, New York, 1965, p. 204.

4. Baron De Jomini, translated by Capt. G.H. Mendell and Lieutenant W.P. Craighill, *The Art of War*, Greenwood Press, Westport, CT, copy of 1862 edition, 45.

5. Baron De Jomini, translated by Capt. G.H. Mendell and Lieutenant W.P. Craighill, *The Art of War*, Greenwood Press, Westport, CT, copy of 1862 edition, 80.

6. Baron De Jomini, translated by Capt. G.H. Mendell and Lieutenant W.P. Craighill, *The Art of War*, Greenwood Press, Westport, CT, copy of 1862 edition, 130.

7. Baron De Jomini, translated by Capt. G.H. Mendell and Lieutenant W.P. Craighill, *The Art of War*, Greenwood Press, Westport, CT, copy of 1862 edition, 244.

8. Eugene J. Palka and Francis A. Galgano, *Military Geography from Peace to War*, McGraw Hill, Boston, 2005, 1.

9. Daniel J. Hughes, editor, translated by Harry Bell and Daniel J. Hughes, *Moltke: On the Art of War*, Presidio Press, Novato, CA, 1993, 93.

10. Douglas Porch, *Wars of Empire*, Smithsonian History of Warfare, 2000, p. 115.

11. For more information on Macadamized Roads see Appendix 1.

12. C.E. Wood's book *Mud: A Military History* goes into detail about the impact mud has had on military operations.

13. J.F.C. Fuller, *Machine Warfare*, Hutchinson, London, 1941, 183.

14. John Connor, "Climate, Environment, and Australian Frontier Wars: New South Wales, 1788–1841," *The Journal of Military History*, Volume 81, No. 4, October 2017, 985–1006.

15. Carl H. Fritsche, interview of Carl H. Fritsche on 27 December 2000 by Edward B. McCaul, Jr.

16. Information in this paragraph concerning fuel supplies in World War II came from Roland G. Ruppenthal, *United States Army in World War II, The European Theater of Operations, Logistical Support of the Armies*, Volume I, Center of Military History, United States Army, Washington, D.C., 1989, 504–510.

17. Information about the British plans to bomb the Baku oilfields came from Patrick R. Osborn's "Operation Unthinkable," *MHQ: The Quarterly Journal of Military History*, Volume 12, No. 2, Winter 2000, 26–31.

18. T.H. Vail Motter, *United States Army in World War II, The Middle East Theater, The Persian Corridor and Aid to Russia*, Center for Military History, United States Army, Washington, D.C., 1985, 284.

19. David M. Glantz and Jonathan M. House, *When Titans Clashed: How the Red Army Stopped Hitler*, University Press of Kansas, Lawrence, 1995, 150.

20. There is an excellent discussion of the logistic/geographic issues confronting the Axis forces in Martin Van Creveld's *Supplying War*, Cambridge University Press, New York, 1977.

21. Emperor Wilhelm II's interest in a large navy was heavily influenced by his reading of Alfred Thayer Mahan's *The Influence of Sea Power upon History* and, thus, Mahan could be blamed for Britain's entry into European alliances before World War I and, therefore, the blame for the massive loss of life during World War I.

22. The economy and industrial base of the United States was the largest in the world with Imperial Germany being second.

23. Martin Gilbert, *The First World War: A Complete History*, Henry Holt, New York, 1994, 256.

24. There is an extended discussion about the start of the Seven Years' War in Daniel Baugh's *The Global Seven Years War 1754–1763*, Routledge Taylor & Francis Group, New York, 2011, 57–66.

Chapter 11

1. Noah Andre Trudeau, *Southern Storm*, HarperCollins, New York, 2008, 100.

2. *Collected Works of Abraham Lincoln*, Volume 5, University of Michigan, Digital Library Production Services, Ann Arbor, 2001, 388–389.

3. Horace Porter, *Campaigning with Grant*, Blue and Grey Press, Secaucus, 1984, 408.

4. General John B. Gordon, *Reminiscences of the Civil War*, Charles Scribner's Sons, New York, 1904, 393. Even though parts of General Gordon's reminiscences have been shown to be incorrect, as he modified events to emphasize fraternity between Federal and Confederate soldiers, I believe that this part of his reminiscences is correct.

5. A good summary of Lincoln's issues with Fremont can be found in Doris Kearns Goodwin's *Team of Rivals*, Simon & Schuster, New York, 2005, 388–396.

6. *Collected Works of Abraham Lincoln*, University of Michigan, Digital Library Production Services, 2001, Ann Arbor, Volume 4, 533, accessed 6 May 2015.

7. *Collected Works of Abraham Lincoln*, University of Michigan, Digital Library Production Services, 2001, Ann Arbor, Volume 4, 469, accessed 6 May 2015.

8. *Collected Works of Abraham Lincoln*, University of Michigan, Digital Library Production Services, 2001, Ann Arbor, Volume 4, 469, accessed 6 May 2015.

9. *Collected Works of Abraham Lincoln*, University of Michigan, Digital Library Production Services, 2001, Ann Arbor, Volume 5, 99, accessed 6 May 2015.

10. James M. McPherson's *Embattled Rebel: Jefferson Davis as Commander in Chief*, Penguin, New York, 2014, is an excellent and balanced analysis of Davis as the commander in chief of the Confederacy.

11. There is an excellent description of the campaign in James I. Robertson Jr.'s *Stonewall Jackson: The Man, The Soldier, The Legend*, Macmillan, New York, 1997, 298–322.

12. Festus P. Summers, *The Baltimore and Ohio in the Civil War*, G.P. Putnam's Sons, New York, 1939, 113–114.

13. *ORA*, Series I, Volume 51, Part I, 369–370.

14. Legally, the "blockade" was a port closure of the ports in the Confederacy. This was due to Secretary of the Navy Gideon Welles' insistence it be considered a port closure as a blockade would have given belligerent status to the Confederacy. The difference is that a port closure act implied the ports were still part of the Union. E.B. Potter and Chester W. Nimitz, editors, *Sea Power: A Naval History*, Prentice Hall, Englewood Cliffs, NJ, 1960, 250.

15. John G. Barrett, *The Civil War in North Carolina*, University of North Carolina Press, Chapel Hill, 1963, 35.

16. John G. Barrett, *The Civil War in North Carolina*, University of North Carolina Press, Chapel Hill, 1963, 33.

17. The USS *Cumberland* was later rammed and sunk by the CSS *Virginia* at Newport News in March 1862.

18. The information about Lammot du Pont's mission came from Gerard Colby's *Du Pont Dynasty*, L. Stuart, Secaucus, 1984, 67–71.

19. Robert C. Whisonant, *Arming the Confederacy*, Springer International, New York, 2015, 51.

20. George W. Rains, "History of the Confederate Powder Works," An Address Delivered by Invitation before the Confederate Survivors' Association, at its Fourth Annual Meeting, on Memorial Day, April 26th, 1882, *The Newburgh Daily News Print*, Newburgh, New York.

21. Although the topic of his book is Confederate artillery, there is an interesting discussion of the Confederate effort to manufacture gunpowder in Jennings Cropper Wise's *The Long Arm of Lee*, Volume I, University of Nebraska Press, Lincoln, 1991, 42–47.

22. George W. Rains, "History of the Confederate Powder Works," An Address Delivered by Invitation before the Confederate Survivors' Association, at its Fourth Annual Meeting, on Memorial Day, April 26th, 1882, *The Newburgh Daily News Print*, Newburgh, NY.

23. Ella Lonn, *Salt as a Factor in the Confederacy*, University of Alabama Press, Tuscaloosa, 1965, 1–2.

24. *ORA*, Series I, Volume XIX, Part 2, 709.

25. Ella Lonn, *Salt as a Factor in the Confederacy*, University of Alabama Press, Tuscaloosa, 1965, 19–20.

26. Ella Lonn, *Salt as a Factor in the Confederacy*, University of Alabama Press, Tuscaloosa, 1965, 25–28.

27. Ella Lonn's book, *Salt as a Factor in the Confederacy*, University of Alabama Press, Tuscaloosa, 1965, is an excellent source on how crucial salt was to the Confederacy.

28. Lieutenant Commander Hart's report can be found in the *ORA*, Series I, Volume 19, 373–376, 378. The report of Acting Master George W. Browne, commander of the *Bohio*, can be found in the *Official Records of the Union and Confederate Navies in the War of the Rebellion*, Government Printing Office, Washington, D.C., Series I, Volume 19, 377–378. Henceforth cited as *ORN*.

29. *ORN*, Series I, Volume 19, 376.

30. Robert C. Whisonant, *Arming the Confederacy*, Springer International, New York, 2015, 101.

31. *ORA*, Series I, Volume XXXII, Part 2, 402.

32. There is an excellent discussion of Sherman's planning for his campaign in Noah Andre Trudeau's *Southern Storm*, HarperCollins, New York, 2008, 33–58.

33. William T. Sherman, *Memoirs of General William T. Sherman*, Volume Two, Two Volumes Complete in One, Indiana University Press, Bloomington, 1957, 183.

34. "The Missouri Campaign of 1864-Report of General Stirling Price," *Southern Historical Society Papers*, Richmond, Volume 7, 1879, 228.

35. Paul E. Steiner, *Disease in the Civil War*, Charles C. Thomas, Springfield, IL, 1968, 8.

36. *ORA*, Series I, Volume LI, Part I, 370.

37. *ORA*, Series I, Volume XIV, 534.

38. *ORA*, Series I, Volume XIV, 47.

39. *ORA*, Series I, Volume X, Part I, 775.

40. *ORA*, Series I, Volume XVI, Part II, 62.
41. *ORN*, Series I, Volume 23, 239–241.

Chapter 12

1. William T. Sherman, *Memoirs of General William T. Sherman*, Volume II, Indiana University Press, Bloomington, 1957, 399.
2. *ORA*, Series I, Volume IX, 511–512.
3. *ORA*, Series I, Volume XLV, Part I, 658.
4. Sam R. Watkins, *Co. Aytch*, Morningside, Dayton, 1992, 224.
5. Walter Lord, editor, *The Fremantle Diary*, Capricorn Books, New York, 1954, 178.
6. An excellent listing of all of the items brought back to Virginia can be found in Kent Masterson Brown's *Retreat from Gettysburg*, University of North Carolina Press, Chapel Hill, 2005.
7. *ORA*, Series I, Volume XXVII, Part II, 309.
8. *ORA*, Series I, Volume XXVII, Part II, 309.
9. Kent Masterson Brown's *Retreat from Gettysburg*, University of North Carolina Press, Chapel Hill, 2005, 254. E
10. *ORA*, Series I, Volume XLI, Part I, 692.
11. U.S. Grant, *Personal Memoirs of U.S. Grant*, Volume I, Charles L. Webster, New York, 1886, 433.
12. U.S. Grant, *Personal Memoirs of U.S. Grant*, Volume I, Charles L. Webster, New York, 1886, 435.
13. U.S. Grant, *Personal Memoirs of U.S. Grant*, Volume I, Charles L. Webster, New York, 1886, 527.
14. A more complete discussion of Grant's issues with supplies and his solutions can be found in the *Personal Memoirs of U.S. Grant*, Volume I, Charles L. Webster, New York, 1886, 488–530.
15. A more complete discussion of Sherman's issues with his march to the sea can be found in the *Memoirs of General William T. Sherman*, Indiana University Press, Bloomington, 1957.
16. The height of a horse is determined by measuring the distance from the ground to the highest point on its withers, with the withers being the ridge between its shoulder bones.
17. Colonel Theodore S. Case, *The Quartermaster's Guide*, P.M. Pinckard, Saint Louis, 1865, 262.
18. Emmett M. Essin, *Shavetails & Bell Sharps: The History of the U.S. Army Mule*, University of Nebraska Press, Lincoln, 1997, 4. Essin's book is an excellent book detailing the history of the Army's use of mules.
19. Colonel Theodore S. Case, *The Quartermaster's Guide*, P.M. Pinckard, Saint Louis, 1865, 42.
20. Emmett M. Essin, *Shavetails & Bell Sharps: The History of the U.S. Army Mule*, University of Nebraska Press, Lincoln, 1997, 1.
21. An excellent article on the impact horses had on the Army of Northern Virginia is Charles W. Ramsdell's "General Robert E. Lee's Horse Supply, 1862–1865," *The American Historical Review*, Volume 35, No. 4, July 1930, 756–777.
22. *ORA*, Series I, Volume LX, Part II, 678–679.
23. *ORA*, Series I, Volume XXV, Part II, 627.
24. *ORA* Series I, Volume XXV, Part II, 749.
25. *ORA*, Series I, Volume XXIX, Part II, 665.
26. *ORA*, Series I, Volume XLVI, Part II, 1208–1209.
27. *ORA*, Series I, Volume XLVI, Part II, 1190.
28. Jefferson Davis, *The Rise and Fall of The Confederate Government*, Volume I, Garrett and Massie, Richmond, Memorial Edition, 550.
29. Jefferson Davis, *The Rise and Fall of The Confederate Government*, Volume I, Garrett and Massie, Richmond, Memorial Edition, 550–551.
30. Chris M. Calkins, *The Appomattox Campaign: March 29–April 9, 1865*, Schroeder Publications, Lynchburg, VA, 2015, 59.
31. Chris M. Calkins, *The Appomattox Campaign: March 29–April 9, 1865*, Schroeder Publications, Lynchburg, VA, 2015, 85.
32. *Collected Works of Abraham Lincoln*, Volume 6.
33. G.G. Benedict, *Vermont in the Civil War*, Volume II, The Free Press Association, Burlington, VT, 1888, 429. Lincoln's has been quoted differently in a number of books about Stoughton's capture, but the idea that he was more worried about the loss of the horses rather than the general remains the same.
34. Bruce Catton, *Grant Takes Command*, Little, Brown, Boston 1969, 177.
35. While the Signal Corps did try to gain control over the military's use of the telegraph, it was unsuccessful. A book discussing the history of the Signal Corps is *Getting the Message Through* by Rebecca Raines.
36. U.S. Grant, *Personal Memoirs of U.S. Grant*, Volume II, Charles L. Webster, New York, 1886, 205–207.
37. William T. Sherman, *Memoirs of General William T. Sherman*, Volume II, Indiana University Press, Bloomington, 1957, 398.
38. Martin Van Creveld, *Technology and War*, The Free Press, New York, 1991, 200.
39. Gary Cross and Rick Szostak, *Technology and American Society: A History*, 2nd edition, Pearson Prentice Hall, Upper Saddle River, NJ, 2005, 99.
40. U.S. Grant, *Personal Memoirs of U.S. Grant*, Volume I, Charles L. Webster & Company, New York, 1886, 95.
41. *ORA*, Series I, Volume XXVIII, Part I, 31–32.
42. *ORA*, Series IV, Volume III, 733.
43. Jefferson Davis, *The Rise and Fall of The Confederate Government*, Volume II, Garrett and Massie, Richmond, Memorial Edition, 272–273.
44. Jefferson Davis, *The Rise and Fall of The Confederate Government*, Volume I, Garrett and Massie, Richmond, Memorial Edition, 274.

Chapter 13

1. *ORA*, Series I, Volume XLIII, Part II, 487.
1. *ORA*, Series I, Volume XXV, Part I, 196.
2. *ORA*, Series I, Volume XXIII, Part I, 48.
3. Austin B. Fletcher, *Macadam Roads*, U.S.

Department of Agriculture, Washington, D.C., 1908, 21.

4. *ORA*, Series I, Volume XVI, Part I, 801–802.

5. *ORA*, Series I, Volume V, 1055.

6. *ORA*, Series I, Volume XXXII, Part III, 276.

7. John L. McAdam, *Remarks on the Present System of Road Making*, Longman, Hurst, Rees, Orme, Brown, and Green, Paternoster Row, London, 1824, 86.

8. John l. McAdam, *Memorial on the Subject of Turnpike Roads* (1817?), 5.

9. Anyone who has pushed a full wheel barrel or ridden a bike on an unpacked gravel road has experienced and can appreciate this effect and how much extra work it creates.

10. John L. McAdam, *Memorial on the Subject of Turnpike Roads* (1817?), 1.

11. John L. McAdam, *Memorial on the Subject of Turnpike Roads* (1817?), 3.

12. John L. McAdam, *Remarks on the Present System of Road Making*, J.M. Gutch, Bristol, England, 1816, 31–32.

13. John L. McAdam, *Remarks on the Present System of Road Making*, J.M. Gutch, Bristol, England, 1816, 32.

14. John L. McAdam, *Remarks on the Present System of Road Making*, Longman, Hurst, Rees, Orme, Brown, and Green, Paternoster Row, London, 1824, 223.

15. All of the testimony and the report of the committee can be found in John L. McAdam's *Remarks on the Present System of Road Making*, Longman, Hurst, Rees, Orme, Brown, and Green, Paternoster Row, London, 1824.

16. The information in this paragraph came from T.C.'s *Road-Making on Mr. McAdam's System*, Bristol, 1819 (probably Thomas Codrington), 1–2.

17. Thomas Telford became known for his construction of bridges, canals, and buildings as those are the structures on which he concentrated.

18. John L. McAdam, *Remarks on the Present System of Road Making*, Longman, Hurst, Rees, Orme, Brown, and Green, Paternoster Row, London, 1824, 47.

19. John L. McAdam, *Remarks on the Present System of Road Making*, Longman, Hurst, Rees, Orme, Brown, and Green, Paternoster Row, London, 1824, 189.

20. Austin B. Fletcher, *Macadam Roads*, U.S. Department of Agriculture, Washington, D.C., 1908, 22.

21. John S. Williams, *Improved McAdamized Roads*, R.P. Brooks, Cincinnati, 1838, preface.

22. Austin B. Fletcher, *Macadam Roads*, U.S. Department of Agriculture, Washington, D.C., 1908, 5–6.

23. Austin B. Fletcher, *Macadam Roads*, U.S. Department of Agriculture, Washington, D.C., 1908, 12.

24. Austin B. Fletcher, *Macadam Roads*, U.S. Department of Agriculture, Washington, D.C., 1908, 12.

25. Austin B. Fletcher, *Macadam Roads*, U.S. Department of Agriculture, Washington, D.C., 1908, 6.

26. Austin B. Fletcher, *Macadam Roads*, U.S. Department of Agriculture, Washington, D.C., 1908, 6.

27. Austin B. Fletcher, *Macadam Roads*, U.S. Department of Agriculture, Washington, D.C., 1908, 16.

28. The information in this paragraph comes from Austin B. Fletcher's *Macadam Roads*, U.S. Department of Agriculture, Washington, D.C, 1908.

29. Austin B. Fletcher, *Macadam Roads*, U.S. Department of Agriculture, Washington, D.C., 1908, 20–21.

30. Austin B. Fletcher, *Macadam Roads*, U.S. Department of Agriculture, Washington, D.C., 1908, 18–21.

31. The information in this paragraph about Macadamized Roads comes from Austin B. Fletcher's *Macadam Roads*, U.S. Department of Agriculture, Washington, D.C., 1908.

32. Most of the information in this paragraph came from John W. Wayland's *The Valley Turnpike Winchester to Staunton*, Volume IV, Winchester-Frederick County Historical Society, Winchester, VA, 1967.

33. Most of the information in this paragraph came from Warren R. Hofstra's and Karl Raitz's *The Great Valley Road of Virginia*, University of Virginia Press, Charlottesville, 2010.

Appendix B

1. The reason this data has been included is to show the relative strength of each incursion. The exact strength for each incursion varies depending upon the source of the data. The data for the size and composition for each incursion came from *The War of the Rebellion: A Compilation of the Official Records of the Union and Confederate Armies* with the exception of Quantrill's and McCausland/Johnson's raids. The lower figure of 150 for Quantrill's raid comes from O.S. Barton's *Three Years with Quantrill* while the higher number comes from Union reports in the *Official Records*. The size of the force for McCausland's and Johnson's raid comes from Fritz Haselberger's *Confederate Retaliation: McCausland's 1864 Raid*.

Bibliography

Primary Sources

Battles for Winchester

Abbott, Major Lemuel Abijah, *Personal Recollections and Civil War Diary, 1864*, Free Press Printing Co., Burlington, VT, 1908.

Atlas to Accompany the Official Records of the Union and Confederate Armies, compiled by Capt. Calvin D. Cowles, Government Printing Office, Washington, D.C., 1891–1895.

Blotcher, George, Diary, Stewart Bell, Jr., Archives Room, Handley Regional Library, Winchester, VA, MMF-Civil War Diaries/Letters, Blotcher, George; 1556 THL. The entire diary can be found at the York Country Heritage Trust.

Bradwell, I. Gordon, "Battle of Cedar Creek, VA," *Confederate Veteran*, Volume XXVII, No. 11, November 1919, 411–412.

Bradwell, I. Gordon, "When General Mulligan Was Killed," *Confederate Veteran*, Volume XXXV, No. 1, January 1927, 14–15.

Bradwell, I. Gordon, "With Early in the Valley," *Confederate Veteran*, Volume XXII, No. 11, November 1914, 504–505.

Carter, Thomas Henry, *A Gunner in Lee's Army*, edited by Graham T. Dozier, University of North Carolina Press, Chapel Hill, 2014.

Colt, Margaretta Barton, *Defend the Valley*, Oxford University Press, New York, 1999.

Cooke, John Esten, *The Life of Stonewall Jackson*, Charles B. Richardson, New York, 1863.

Craig, Thomas H., "Fighting Them Over, What Our Veterans Have to Say About Their Old Campaigns, Shield's Division, A Delayed Report of the 84th PA. at Kernstown," *The National Tribune*, November 21, 1889, p. 3, Library of Congress.

Crowninshield, Benjamin W., "Cedar Creek," *Papers of the Military Historical Society of Massachusetts: The Shenandoah Campaigns of 1862 and 1864 and the Appomattox Campaign 1865*, Volume V, 1907, 154–181.

DeForest, John William, "Sheridan at Winchester," *The Civil War Reader*, edited by Richard B. Harwell, Konecky & Konecky, New York, 1958, 300–320.

Dicket, D. Augustus, *History of Kershaw's Brigade*, Elbert H. Aull, Newberry, SC, 1899.

Douglas, Henry Kyd, *I Rode with Stonewall*, University of North Carolina Press, Chapel Hill, 1968.

Dowdey, Clifford, and Louis H. Manarin, editors, *The Wartime Papers of R.E. Lee*, Virginia Civil War Commission, Little, Brown, Boston, 1961.

Du Pont, Henry A., *The Campaign of 1864 in the Valley of Virginia and the Expedition to Lynchburg*, National Americana Society, New York, 1925.

Early, Jubal Anderson, *Autobiographical Sketch and Narrative of the War Between the States*, Smithmark, New York, 1994.

Early, Jubal A., *A Memoir of the Last Year of the War for Independence*, Charles W. Button, Lynchburg, VA, 1867.

Early, Jubal A., "Winchester, Fisher's Hill, and Cedar Creek," *Battles and Leaders of the Civil War*, Volume IV, Castle, Secaucus, 522–530.

Gilmore, Colonel Harry, *Four Years in the Saddle*, Harper & Brothers, New York, 1866.

Gordon, General John B., *Reminiscences of the Civil War*, Charles Scribner's Sons, New York, 1904.

Graham, Dozier, *A Gunner in Lee's Army: The Civil War Letters of Thomas Henry Carter*, University of North Carolina Press, Chapel Hill, 2014.

Grant, U.S., *Personal Memoirs of U.S. Grant*, Vol. I & II, Charles L. Webster, New York, 1886.

Hamlin, Augustus, "Who Recaptured the Guns at Cedar Creek October 19, 1864?" *Papers of the Military Historical Society of Massachusetts: The Shenandoah Campaigns of 1862 and 1864 and the Appomattox Campaign 1865*, Volume VI, 1907, 183–208.

Hartley, James J., edited by Garber A. Davidson, *The Civil War Letters of the Late 1st Lieutenant James J. Hartley, 122nd Ohio Infantry Regiment*, McFarland, Jefferson, NC, 1998.

Hotchkiss, Jed, *Virginia, Confederate Military History*, Volume III, Confederate Publishing Company, Atlanta, 1899.

Howard, McHenry, *Recollections of a Maryland Confederate Soldier and Staff Officer Under Johnston, Jackson and Lee*, Morningside, Dayton, 1975.

Jackson, Mary Anna, *Life and Letter of General Thomas J. Jackson*, Sprinkle Publications, Harrisonburg, VA, 1995.

Jones, Maj. Frank B., Diary, Stewart Bell, Jr., Archives Room, Handley Regional Library, Winchester, VA., 424 WFCHS, Box 1.

Jones, Terry L., editor, *Civil War Memoirs of Captain William J. Seymour*, Louisiana State University, Baton Rouge, 1991.

Keifer, J. Warren, *Slavery and Four Years of War: A Political History of Slavery in the United States, Together with a Narrative of the Campaigns and Battles of the Civil War in Which the Author Took Part*, Volume II, G.P. Putnam and Sons, New York, 1900.

Kimball, Nathan, "Fighting Jackson at Kernstown," *Battles and Leaders of the Civil War*, Volume II, Castle, Secaucus, 302–313.

Long, Armistead L., "General Early's Valley Campaign," *Southern Historical Society Papers*, Volume 3, 177.

McDonald, Archie P., editor, *Make Me a Map of the Valley: The Civil War Journal of Stonewall Jackson's Topographer*, Southern Methodist University Press, Dallas, 1973.

Merritt, General Wesley, "Sheridan in the Shenandoah Valley," *Battles and Leaders of the Civil War*, Volume IV, Castle, Secaucus, 500–521.

Paul, E.A., "The Battle of Cedar Creek," *The New York Times*, October 27, 1964.

Rhodes, Robert Hunt, editor, *All for the Union: The Civil War Diary and Letters of Elisha Hunt Rhodes*, Orion Books, New York, 1985.

Schmitt, Martin F., editor, *General George Crook, His Autobiography*, University of Oklahoma Press, Norman, 1960.

Sheridan, P.H., *Personal Memoirs of P. H. Sheridan*, 2 vols., Charles L. Webster, New York, 1888.

Stevens, Hazard, "The Battle of Cedar Creek," *Papers of the Military Historical Society of Massachusetts: The Shenandoah Campaigns of 1862 and 1864 and the Appomattox Campaign 1865*, Volume VI, 1907, 83–181.

Taylor, James E., *With Sheridan up the Shenandoah Valley in 1864*, Morningside, Dayton, 1989.

Taylor, Richard, *Destruction and Reconstruction: Personal Experiences of the Late War*, D. Appleton, New York, 1879.

Thacker, Victor L., editor, *French Harding Civil War Memoirs*, McClain Printing Company, Parsons, WV, 2000.

Wallick, Michael D., *Dr. Christian Schwartz with the 67th Ohio Volunteers*, self-published, 2018.

The War of the Rebellion: A Compilation of the Official Records of the Union and Confederate Armies, Government Printing Office, Washington, D.C., 1881–1901.

Whittier, Charles J., Correspondence, Stewart Bell, Jr., Archives Room, Handley Regional Library, Winchester, VA., MMF-Civil War Diaries/Letters, Whittier, Charles, 855 THL.

Young, William S., "Fighting Them Over, What Our Veterans Have to Say About Their Old Campaigns, Shenandoah Valley, Criticising [sic] Gen. Capehart's Article on That Campaign," *The National Tribune*, April 18, 1889, p. 4, Library of Congress.

Other Primary Sources

Ammen, Daniel, "Du Pont and the Port Royal Expedition," *Battles and Leaders of the Civil War*, Volume I, *The Opening Battles*, Castle, Secaucus, 1982, 671–691.

Bates, David Homer, *Lincoln in the Telegraph Office*, The Century Company, New York, 1907.

Blackford, Captain Charles M., "The Campaign and Battle of Lynchburg," *Southern Historical Papers*, Volume 30, Richmond, 1902, 279–332.

Boteler, Colonel Alexander R., "Stonewall Jackson's Discontent," *Weekly Philadelphia Times*, Volume 1, No. 14, June 2, 1877, 1.

Case, Colonel Theodore S., *The Quartermaster's Guide*, P.M. Pinckard, St. Louis, 1865.

Collected Works of Abraham Lincoln, University of Michigan, Digital Library Production Services, 2001, Ann Arbor, accessed 6 May 2015.

Davis, Jefferson, *The Rise and Fall of The Confederate Government*, two volumes, Garrett and Massie, Richmond, Memorial Edition.

Fehrenbacher, Don E., and Virginia Fehrenbacher, editors, *Recollected Words of Abraham Lincoln*, Stanford University Press, Stanford, 1996.

Freeman, Douglas Southall, editor, *Lee's Dispatches*, G.P. Putnam's Sons, New York, 1957.

Hawkins, Rush C., "Early Coast Operations in North Carolina," *Battles and Leaders of the Civil War*, Volume I, *The Opening Battles*, Castle, Secaucus, 1982, 632–659.

Johnston, Colonel J. Stoddard, "Sketches of Operations of General John C. Breckinridge, No. 2," *Southern Historical Society Papers*, Volume 7, Richmond, 1879, 317–323.

Johnston, Colonel J. Stoddard, "Sketches of Operations of General John C. Breckinridge, No. 3–Conclusion," *Southern Historical Society Papers*, Volume 7, Richmond, 1879, 385–392.

Johnston, Joseph E., *Narrative of Military Operations*, D. Appleton, New York, 1874.

Kennedy, Joseph C., Superintendent of Census, *Population of the United States in 1860; Compiled from the Original Returns of the Eighth Census*, under the Direction of the Secretary of the Interior, Government Printing Office, Washington, D.C., 1864.

Lord, Walter, editor, *The Fremantle Diary*, Capricorn Books, New York, 1954.

McClellan, George B., *McClellan's Own Story*, Charles L. Webster, New York, 1887.

The Medical and Surgical History of the War of the Rebellion, Government Printing Office, Washington, D.C., 1883.

Miers, Earl Schenck, editor, *Lincoln Day by Day: A Chronology 1809–1865*, Volume III: *1861–1865*, Lincoln Sesquicentennial Commission, Washington, D.C., 1960.

Morrison, John G., *Civil War Diary, 1861–1865*, Naval Historical Center Library.

Murphy, Audie, *To Hell and Back*, Bantam, New York, 1983.

Official Records of the Union and Confederate

Navies in the War of the Rebellion, Government Printing Office, Washington, D.C..
Porter, Horace, *Campaigning with Grant*, The Blue and Grey Press, Secaucus, 1984.
Report of the President and Directors to the Stockholders of the South Side R.R. Co., Office South Side Rail Road Company, Petersburg, November 25, 1865.
Scott, Colonel Henry Lee, *Military Dictionary*, Greenwood Press, New York, 1968.
Sherman, William T., *Memoirs of General William T. Sherman*, Two Volumes Complete in One, Indiana University Press, Bloomington, 1957.
Roberts, Joseph, *The Hand-Book of Artillery*, 5th edition, D. Van Nostrand, New York, reprint of the 1863 edition.
Vandiver, Frank E., editor, *The Civil War Diary of General Josiah Gorgas*, University of Alabama Press, Tuscaloosa, 1947.
Watkins, Sam R., *Co. Aytch*, Morningside, Dayton, 1992.

Secondary Sources

Battles for Winchester

Beck, Brandon H., *The Third Battle of Winchester*, H.E. Howard, Lynchburg, VA, 1997.
Beck, Brandon H., *Winchester's Three Battles*, Angle Valley Press, Winchester, VA, 2016.
Carroll, John M., *Custer in the Civil War: His Unfinished Memoirs*, Presidio Press, San Rafael, CA, 1977.
Catton, Bruce, *The Army of the Potomac: A Stillness at Appomattox*, Doubleday, Garden City, NY, 1953.
Coffey, David, *Sheridan's Lieutenants*, Rowman & Littlefield, New York, 2005.
Cozzens, Peter, *Shenandoah 1862: Stonewall Jackson's Valley Campaign*, University of North Carolina Press, Chapel Hill, 2008.
Dabney, R.L., *Life and Campaigns of General T.J. (Stonewall) Jackson*, Sprinkle Publications, Harrisonburg, VA, 1977.
Davis, Daniel T., and Phillip S. Greenwalt, *Bloody Autumn: The Shenandoah Valley Campaign of 1864*, Savas Beatie, El Dorado Hills, CA, 2013.
Delauter, Roger U., Jr., *Winchester in the Civil War*, 2nd edition, H.E. Howard, Lynchburg, VA, 1992.
Duncan, Richard R., *Beleaguered Winchester: A Virginia Community at War, 1861–1865*, Louisiana State University Press, Baton Rouge, 2007.
Duncan, Richard R., editor, *Alexander Neil and the Last Shenandoah Valley Campaign*, White Mane, Shippensburg, PA, 1996.
Ecelbarger, Gary L., *"We are in for it!" The First Battle of Kernstown*, White Mane, Shippensburg, PA, 1997.
Fordney, Chris, "A Town Embattled," *Civil War Times Illustrated*, Volume XXXIV, No. 6, 30–37, 70.
Freeman, Douglas Southall, *Lee's Lieutenants*, Volumes 1 and 3, Charles Scribner's Sons, New York, 1970.
Freeman, Douglas Southall, *R.E. Lee*, Volume III, Charles Scribner's Sons, New York, 1963.
Gallagher, Gary W., editor, *Struggle for the Shenandoah: Essays on the 1864 Valley Campaign*, Kent State University Press, Kent, OH, 1991.
Heatwole, John L., *The Burning: Sheridan's Devastation of the Shenandoah Valley*, Howell Press, Charlottesville, VA, 1998.
Henderson, G.F.R., *Stonewall Jackson and the American Civil War*, Volume I, The Blue Gray Press, Secaucus, 1987.
Kennedy, Frances H., editor, *The Civil War Battlefield Guide*, The Conservation Fund, Houghton Mifflin, Boston, 1990.
Kennon, Lyman W.V., "The Valley Campaign of 1864: A Military Study," *Confederate Veteran*, Volume XXVI, No. 12, December 1918, 517–523.
Lardas, Mark, *Shenandoah 1864, Sheridan's valley campaign*, Osprey, New York, 2014.
Lewis, Thomas A., *The Guns of Cedar Creek*, Dell, New York, 1988.
Mahon, Michael G., *The Shenandoah Valley: 1861–1865 The Destruction of the Granary of the Confederacy*, Stackpole Books, Mechanicsburg, PA, 1999.
Miller, William J., *Mapping for Stonewall: The Civil War Service of Jed Hotchkiss*, Elliott & Clark, Washington, D.C., 1993.
Moore, Albert Burton, *Conscription and Conflict in the Confederacy*, Macmillan, New York, 1924.
Morton, Frederic, *The Story of Winchester in Virginia*, Shenandoah Publishing House, Strasburg, VA, 1925.
Morton, Louis, "Vermonters at Cedar Creek," *Vermont History*, The Proceedings of the Vermont Historical Society, Volume XXXIII, No. 2, April 1965.
Nicolay, John G., and John Hay, *Abraham Lincoln: a History*, Volume Nine, The Century Co., New York,1914.
Nofi, Albert A., "Stonewall in the Shenandoah Valley," *Strategy & Tactics*, March-April, No. 67, 4–13.
Northern Virginia Daily, *Standing Ground: The Civil War in the Shenandoah Valley*, Shenandoah Publishing Company, Strasburg, VA, 1996.
Noyalas, Jonathan A., editor, *"Give the enemy no rest!" Sheridan's 1864 Shenandoah Campaign*, Shenandoah Valley Battlefields Foundation, Winchester Printers, Winchester, VA, 2007.
Noyalas, Jonathan A., *The Battle of Cedar Creek: Victory from the Jaws of Defeat*, History Press, Charleston, SC, 2009.
Noyalas, Jonathan A., *"My Will Is Absolute Law": A Biography of Union General Robert H. Milroy*, McFarland, Jefferson, NC, 2006.
Patchan, Scott C., *The Last Battle of Winchester*, Savas Beatie, El Dorado Hills, CA, 2013.
Patchan, Scott C., "Opequon Creek," *Blue & Gray*, Volume XXVII, Issue 2.
Patchan, Scott C., *Shenandoah Summer: The 1864*

Valley Campaign, University of Nebraska Press, Lincoln, 2007.
Pfanz, Donald C., *Richard S. Ewell: A Soldier's Life*, University of North Carolina Press, Chapel Hill, 1009.
Phillips, Edward H., *The Shenandoah Valley in 1864: An Episode in the History of Warfare*, The Military College of South Carolina, Charleston, SC, 1965.
Pond, George E., *The Shenandoah Valley in 1864*, The Blue & Gray Press, New York, 1959.
Robertson, James I., Jr., *Stonewall Jackson*, Macmillan, New York, 1997.
Prowell, George R., *History of the Eighty-Seventh Regiment, Pennsylvania Volunteers*, Press of the York Daily, York, PA, 1903.
Stackpole, Edward J., *Sheridan in the Shenandoah: Jubal Early's Nemesis*, Bonanza Books, New York, 1961.
Summers, Festus P., *The Baltimore and Ohio in the Civil War*, G.P. Putnam's Sons, New York, 1939.
U.S. Department of the Interior, National Park Service, Interagency Resources Division, *Study of Civil War Sites in the Shenandoah Valley of Virginia*, Pursuant to Public Law 101-628, September 1992.
Watts, Dabney W., Chairman of the Winchester-Frederick County Centennial Commission 1960, *Civil War Battles in Winchester and Frederick County, Virginia 1861-1865*, Carr Publishing, Boyce, VA, 1960.
Wert, Jeffery D., *From Winchester to Cedar Creek*, Stackpole Books, Mechanicsburg, PA, 1997.
Whitehorne, Joseph W.A., *The Battle of Cedar Creek*, Center of Military History, United States Army, Washington, D.C., 1992.
Wise, Jennings Cropper, *The Long Arm of Lee*, Volume 2: *Chancellorsville to Appomattox*, University of Nebraska Press, Lincoln, 1991.

Impact of Geography

Blij, Harm de, *Why Geography Matters*, Oxford University Press, New York, 2005.
Butts, Kent Hughes, *Strategic Minerals in the New World Order*, Strategic Studies Institute, U.S. Army War College, Carlisle Barracks, PA, 1993.
Caldwell, Douglas R., Judy Ehlen, and Russell S. Harmon, editors, *Studies in Military Geography and Geology*, Kluwer Academic, Boston, 2004.
Collins, John M., *Military Geography for Professionals and the Public*, Brassey's, Washington, D.C., 1988.
Caldwell, Douglas R., Judy Ehlen, Russell S. Harmon, *Studies in Military Geography and Geology*, Kluwer Academic, Boston, 2004.
Collins, John M., *Military Geography for Professionals and the Public*, National Defense University Press, Washington, D.C., 1998.
Connor, John, "Climate, Environment, and Australian Frontier Wars: New South Wales, 1788-1841," *The Journal of Military History*, Vol. 81, No. 4, October 2017, Society for Military History, 985-1006.
Cressy, David, *Saltpeter: The Mother of Gunpowder*, Oxford University Press, Oxford, 2013.
Davies, Oliver, *Roman Mines in Europe*, Clarendon Press, Oxford, 1935.
Diamond, Jared, *Collapse*, Penguin, New York, 2006.
Diamond, Jared, *Guns, Germs, and Steel*, Vintage, London, 1998.
Goff, Richard D., *Confederate Supply*, Duke University Press, Durham, 1969.
Grabau, Warren E., *Ninety-Eight Days: A Geographer's View of the Vicksburg Campaign*, University of Tennessee Press, Knoxville, 2000.
Guilmartin, John F., Jr., *Galleons and Galleys*, Cassell, London, 2002.
Hurt, R. Douglas, *Agriculture and the Confederacy*, University of North Carolina Press, Chapel Hill, 2015.
Kaplan, Robert D., *The Revenge of Geography*, Random House, New York, 2012.
Keegan, John, *The Price of Admiralty*, Viking Penguin, New York, 1989.
Kelly, Jack, *Gunpowder*, Basic Books, New York, 2004.
Krick, Robert K., *Civil War Weather in Virginia*, University of Alabama Press, Tuscaloosa, 2007.
Kurlansky, Mark, *Cod: A Biography of the Fish that Changed the World*, Walker and Company, New York, 1997.
Lane, Frederic Chapin, *Venetian Ships and Shipbuilders of the Renaissance*, Johns Hopkins Press, Baltimore, 1934.
Lonn, Ella, *Salt as a Factor in the Confederacy*, University of Alabama Press, Tuscaloosa, 1965.
Maguire, T. Miller, *Outlines of Military Geography*, Cambridge University Press, Cambridge, 1899.
McCaul, Edward B., Jr., *The Mechanical Fuze and the Advance of Artillery in the Civil War*, McFarland, Jefferson, NC, 2010.
McPherson, James M., *Battle Cry of Freedom*, Oxford University Press, New York, 1988.
Meier, Kathryn Shively, *Nature's Civil War*, University of North Carolina Press, Chapel Hill, 2013.
Mott, Lawrence V., *The Development of the Rudder: A Technological Tale*, Texas A&M University Press, College Station, 1997.
O'Sullivan, Patrick, and Jesse W. Miller, Jr., *The Geography of Warfare*, St. Martin's Press, New York, 1983.
O'Sulllivan, Patrick Michael, *The Geography of War in the Post Cold War World*, Edwin Mellen Press, Lewiston, NY, 2001.
Palka, Eugene J., and Francis A. Galgano, *Military Geography from Peace to War*, McGraw-Hill, Boston, 2005.
Peltier, Louis C., and G. Etzel Pearcy, *Military Geography*, D. Van Nostrand, New York, 1996.
Pepper, David, and Alan Jenkins, editors, *The Geography of Peace and War*, Basil Blackwell, New York, 1985.

Porch, Douglas, *Wars of Empire*, HarperCollins, New York, 2006, Smithsonian History of Warfare.
Ross, Charles D., *Civil War Acoustic Shadows*, White Mane, Shippensburg, PA, 2001.
Stapleton, Darwin H., "Introducing Clean War," *American Heritage of Invention & Technology*, Volume 14, number 3, Winter 1999, 24–35.
Steiner, Paul E., *Disease in the Civil War*, Charles C. Thomas, Springfield, IL, 1968.
Stephenson, Michael, editor, *Battlegrounds: Geography and the History of Warfare*, National Geographic, Washington, D.C., 2003.
Terrain Factors in the Russian Campaign, CMH Pub 104-5, Center of Military History, United States Army, Washington, D.C., 1986.
Tuchman, Barbara W., *The Guns of August*, Macmillan, New York, 1962.
Whisonant, Robert C., *Arming the Confederacy*, Springer International, New York, 2015.
Winters, Harold A., Gerald E. Galloway Jr., William J. Reynolds, and David W. Rhyne, *Battling the Elements: Weather and Terrain in the Conduct of War*, Johns Hopkins University Press, Baltimore, 1998.
Wise, Jennings Cropper, *The Long Arm of Lee*, Volume I, University of Nebraska Press, Lincoln, 1991.
Wood, C.E., *Mud: A Military History*, Potomac, Washington, D.C., 2006.
Woodward, Rachel, *Military Geographies*, Blackwell, Malden, MA, 2004.

Theory of War

Calusewitz, Carl Von, *On War*, edited by Michael Howard and Peter Paret, Princeton University Press, Princeton, 1976.
Fuller, J.F.C., *Machine Warfare*, Hutchinson & Co., London, 1941.
Halleck, H. Wager, *Elements of Military Art and Science*, D. Appleton, New York, 1859.
Hughes, Daniel J., editor, translated by Harry Bell and Daniel J. Hughes, *Moltke: On the Art of War*, Presido Press, Novato, CA, 1993,
Jomini, Baron De, *The Art of War*, translated by Capt. G.H. Mendell and Lieutenant W.P. Craighill, Greenwood Press, Westport, CT, copy of 1862 edition.
Lanza, Conrad H., *Napoleon and Modern War*, Military Service Publishing Company, Harrisburg, PA, 1949.
Machiavelli, Niccolò, *The Art of War*, a revised edition of the Ellis Farneworth translation, Da Capo Press, New York, 1965.
Mahan, Alfred Thayer, *The Influence of Seapower Upon History*, Hill and Wang, New York, 1957.
Phillips, Thomas R., editor, *Roots of Strategy*, The Military Service Publishing Company, Harrisburg, PA, 1941.
Tse-tung, Mao, *On Guerrilla Warfare*, translated by Samuel B. Griffith, Frederick A. Praeger, New York, 1967.
Tzu, Sun, *The Art of War*, edited by James Clavell, Delacorte Press, New York, 1983.
Westcott, Allan, editor, *Mahan on Naval Warfare: Selections from the Writings of Rear Admiral Alfred T. Mahan*, Little, Brown, Boston, 1943.

Other Secondary Sources

Alger, John I., Thomas E. Griess, series editor, *Definitions and Doctrine of the Military Art*, Avery Publishing Group, Wayne, NJ, 1985.
Bacon, Benjamin W., *Sinews of War: How Technology, Industry, and Transportation Won the Civil War*, Presidio Press, Novato, CA, 1997.
Barrett, John G., *The Civil War in North Carolina*, University of North Carolina Press, Chapel Hill, 1963.
Baugh, Daniel, *The Global Seven Years War 1754–1763*, Routledge Taylor & Francis Group, New York, 2011.
Benedict, G.G., *Vermont in the Civil War*, Volume II, The Free Press Association, Burlington, VT, 1888.
Brown, Kent, *Retreat from Gettysburg: Lee, Logistics, and the Pennsylvania Campaign*, University of North Carolina Press, Chapel Hill, 2005.
Calkins, Chris M., *The Appomattox Campaign: March 29-April 9, 1865*, Schroeder Publications, Lynchburg, VA, 2015.
Catton, Bruce, *Grant Takes Command*, Little, Brown, Boston, 1969.
Cohen, Stan, *The Civil War in West Virginia, A Pictorial History*, Pictorial Histories Publishing Company, Charleston, WV, 1976.
Colby, Gerard, *Du Pont Dynasty*, L. Stuart, Secaucus, 1984.
Cross, Gary, and Rick Szostak, *Technology and American Society: A History*, 2nd edition, Pearson Prentice Hall, Upper Saddle River, NJ, 2005.
Duncan, Richard R., *Lee's Endangered Left: The Civil War in Western Virginia Spring of 1864*, Louisiana State University Press, Baton Rouge, 1998.
Essin, Emmett M., *Shavetails & Bell Sharps: The History of the U.S. Army Mule*, University of Nebraska Press, Lincoln, 1997.
Gilbert, Martin, *The First World War: A Complete History*, Henry Holt, New York, 1994.
Glantz, David M., and Jonathan M. House, *When Titans Clashed, How the Red Army Stopped Hitler*, University Press of Kansas, Lawrence, 1995.
Goodwin, Doris Kearns, *Team of Rivals*, Simon & Schuster, New York, 2005.
Haselberger, Fritz, *Confederate Retaliation: McCausland's 1864 Raid*, Burd Street Press, Shippensburg, PA, 2000.
Helvestine, Frank, "The Development of a Great Railroad," *Norfolk and Western Magazine*, July 1923, 12–14, 73–76.
McPherson, James M., *Embattled Rebel: Jefferson Davis as Commander in Chief*, Penguin, New York, 2014.
Moore, Albert Burton, *Conscription and Conflict in the Confederacy*, Macmillan, New York, 1924.

Motter, T.H. Vail, *United States Army in World War II, The Middle East Theater, The Persian Corridor and Aid to Russia*, Center for Military History, United States Army, Washington, D.C., 1985.

Potter, E.B., and Chester W. Nimitz, editors, *Sea Power: A Naval History*, Prentice Hall, Englewood Cliffs, NJ, 1960.

Quarles, Garland R., *The Streets of Winchester, Virginia*, Prepared for The Farmers and Merchants National Bank, undated.

Raines, Rebecca R., *Getting the Message Through: A Branch History of the U.S. Army Signal Corps*, Center of Military History, United States Army, Washington, D.C., 1996.

Robertson, James I., Jr., *Stonewall Jackson: The Man, The Soldier, The Legend*, Macmillan, New York, 1997.

Ross, Charles D., *Trial by Fire: Science, Technology and the Civil War*, White Mane, Shippensburg, PA, 2000.

Ruppenthal, Roland G., *United States Army in World War II, The European Theater of Operations, Logistical Support of the Armies*, Volume I, Center of Military History, United States Army, Washington, D.C., 1989.

Sears, Stephen W., *George B. McClellan: The Young Napoleon*, Ticknor & Fields, New York, 1988.

Strickler, Theodore D., *When and Where We Met Each Other*, The National Tribune, Washington, D.C., 1899.

Summers, Festus P., *The Baltimore and Ohio in the Civil War*, G.P. Putnam's Sons, New York, 1939.

Trudeau, Noah Andre, *Southern Storm*, HarperCollins, New York, 2008.

Van Creveld, Martin, *Supplying War*, Cambridge University Press, New York, 1997.

Van Creveld, Martin, *Technology and War*, The Free Press, New York, 1991.

Vandiver, Frank E., *Ploughshares into Swords, Josiah Gorgas and Confederate Ordnance*, University of Texas Press, Austin, 1952.

Wayland, John W., *Stonewall Jackson's Way*, The McClure Printing Company, Verona, VA, 1969.

Wheeler, Tom, *Mr. Lincoln's T-Mails*, HarperCollins, New York, 2006.

Wills, Mary Alice, *The Confederate Blockade of Washington, D.C., 1861–1862*, Burd Street Press, Shippensburg, PA, 1998.

Periodicals

Battles of Winchester

Holsworth, Jerry W., "Winchester, Va., in the Civil War," *Blue & Gray*, Volume XV, No. 2, 6–26, 47–61, 1997.

Osborn, Patrick R., "Operation Unthinkable," *MHQ: The Quarterly Journal of Military History*, Volume 12, No. 2, Winter 2000, 26–31.

Patchan, Scott C., "Opequon Creek, The Third Battle of Winchester," *Blue & Gray*, Volume XXVII, No. 2, 2010, 6–26, 41–60.

Smith, David G., "Clear the Valley: The Shenandoah Valley and the Genesis of the Gettysburg Campaign," *The Journal of Military History*, Volume 74, No. 4, October 2010, 1069–1096.

White, Lorraine, "Strategic Geography and the Spanish Habsburg Monarchy's Failure to Recover Portugal, 1640–1668," *The Journal of Military History*, Volume 71, No. 2, April 2007, 373–409.

Effects of Geography

Brown, William Le Roy, "Confederate Ordnance during the War," *Journal of the United States Artillery*, Volume IX, No. 1, January-February 1898, 1–13.

Camprubi, Lino, "Resource Geopolitics: Cold War Technologies, Global Fertilizers, and the Fate of Western Sahara," *Technology and Culture*, Volume 56, No. 3, July 2015, 676–703.

Crimmin, P.K., "Searching for British Naval Stores: Sources and Strategy, 1802–1860," *The Great Circle*, Volume 18, No. 2, 1996, 113–124.

Kemmerly, Philip R., "Environment and the Course of Battle: Flooding at Shiloh," *The Journal of Military History*, Volume 79, No. 4, October 2015, 1079–1108.

Prados, John, "How Many Roads to Richmond?" *MHQ, The Quarterly Journal of Military History*, Volume 12, No. 2, Winter 2000, 54–59.

Rains, George W., "History of the Confederate Powder Works," An Address Delivered by Invitation before the Confederate Survivors' Association, at its Fourth Annual Meeting, on Memorial Day, April 26th, 1882, *The Newburgh Daily News Print*, Newburgh, NY.

Ramsdell, Charles W., "General Robert E. Lee's Horse Supply, 1862–1865," *The American Historical Review*, Volume 35, No. 4, July 1930, 756–777.

Ross, Charles D., "Outdoor Sound Propagation in the U.S. Civil War," *ECHOES*, Volume 9, No. 1, Winter 1999.

Smith, David G., "Clear the Valley: The Shenandoah Valley and the Genesis of the Gettysburg Campaign," *The Journal of Military History*, Volume 74, No. 4, October 2010, 1069–1096.

White, Lorraine, "Strategic Geography and the Spanish Habsburg Monarchy's Failure to Recover Portugal, 1640–1668," *The Journal of Military History*, Volume 71, No. 2, April 2007, 373–409.

Other Periodicals

Canfield, Daniel T., "Opportunity Lost: Combined Operations and the Development of Union Military Strategy, April 1861–April 1862," *The Journal of Military History*, Volume 79, No. 3, July 2015, 657–690.

Weekly Philadelphia Times, June 2, 1877.

Collections

Handley Library, Stewart Bell, Jr., Archives, Winchester, VA. This source has an excellent collection of books on the history of Winchester before, during, and after the Civil War. Some of the books in the archives are relatively recently publications but cannot be checked out. Any none book source I used at the library has its own entry in the bibliography with a note that it was found in the Handley Library.

Library of Congress: Any item I used that I found in the Library of Congress has its own entry in the bibliography with a note that it was found in the Library of Congress.

The Ohio State University Library Map Room.

Web Sites

Shenandoah at War, http://www.shenandoahatwar.org/ ,accessed 24 October 2014.

United States' State Department Website, http://www.state.gov/, accessed 14 September 2015.

Unpublished Sources

Fritsche, Carl H., interview of Carl H. on 27 December 2000 by Edward B. McCaul, Jr.—information on the impact weather had on flying a B-24 across the Middle East and the Himalayas.

Hanson, Luther D., United States Army Quartermaster Museum, E-mail message 21 January 2015—information on the weight of an Army supply wagon.

Macadamized Roads

C.T., *Road-Making on Mr. McAdam's System*, Bristol, 1819 (probably Thomas Codrington).

Codrington, Thomas, *The Maintenance of MacAdamized Roads*, E. & F.N. Spon, London, 1879.

Fletcher, Austin B., *Macadam Roads*, U.S. Department of Agriculture, Farmers' Bulletin Series, no. 338, Washington D.C., 1908.

Hofstra, Warren R., and Karl Raitz, editors, *The Great Valley Road of Virginia*, University of Virginia Press, Charlottesville, 2010.

McAdam, John L., *Remarks on the Present System of Road Making*, J.M. Gutch, Bristol, England, 1816.

McAdam, John L., *Memorial on the Subject of Turnpike Roads* (1817?).

McAdam, John L., *Notes on Practical Road Making and Repairing*, London, 1863.

McAdam, John L., *Remarks on the Present System of Road Making*, Longman, Hurst, Rees, Orme, Brown, and Green, Paternoster Row, London, 1824.

Parnell, Henry, *A Treatise on Roads*, 2nd edition, London: A. Spottiswoode, 1838.

Parton, James, "John MacAdam-Inventor of the Macadamized Road," *Scientific American*, January 16, 1869, 38–39.

Rolt, L.T.C., *Thomas Telford*, Longmans, Green, New York, 1958.

Salisbury, Marquis of, *Circular No. 21, United States Department of Agriculture, Office of Road Inquiry*, Washington, D.C., 1896.

The Valley Turnpike Museum, Harrisonburg, VA, visited September 2015.

Wayland, John W., *The Valley Turnpike Winchester to Staunton*, Volume IV, Winchester-Frederick County Historical Society, Winchester, VA, 1967.

Williams, John S., *Improved McAdamized Roads*, R.P. Brooks, Cincinnati, 1838.

Drawings and Photographs

Taylor, James E., "Sheridan with Wilson dashing through the Berryville Canyon at daylight to select the ground on which to form the infantry," The Western Reserve Historical Society, Cleveland, Ohio.

Ingram, David Lee, Photographs of the Valley Turnpike, Mt. Crawford, VA.

Index

Abbott, Capt. Lemuel 107
Abraham's Creek 104, 105
Academy Hill 12
Adams, Maj. Alonzo W. 76
Allegheny Mountains 17, 18, 20
Anderson, Gen. Richard 90, 101, 102, 200
Army of Northern Virginia 15, 23, 25, 27, 66, 77, 94, 97, 119, 131, 133, 134, 171, 172, 176, 177
Army of the Potomac 53, 70, 72, 97, 131–134, 156, 170, 172, 173, 177, 179
Army of the Shenandoah 21, 90, 135
Ashby, Col. Turner 30, 32, 33, 44
Ashby's Gap 18, 20
Athens 138
Atlanta 82, 90, 94, 119, 170, 180
Averell, Gen. William W. 84, 110

Baltimore and Ohio Railroad 14, 48, 69, 95, 96, 101, 132, 203, 205
Banks, Gen. Nathaniel 3, 31, 32, 47, 49, 53, 54, 56, 59, 60, 130, 156, 184, 199, 206
battles Adrianople 151; Antietam 27, 61, 66, 131, 203; Champion Hill, 174; Chancellorsville 66, 132, 133, 167, 189; Chattanooga 182; Chickamauga 82, 157, 170; Cold Harbor 12; Coral Sea 149; Drewry's Bluff 50; Fisher's Hill 24, 112, 119, 120; Fort Macon 51; Fort Pulaski 52, 181; Glorieta Pass 50, 203; Hupp's Hill 121; Island No. 10 51; McDowell 20, 21, 50; Pea Ridge 31; Perryville 66, 167; Port Hudson 66, 81; Shiloh 51; Stones River 66; Trafalgar 148; Vicksburg 166, 170, 174, 205
Beaufort 51

Beauregard, Gen. Pierre 159, 161, 166
Berryville 68, 73, 76, 95, 101, 108
Berryville Canyon 102–105, 107–109, 112
Berryville Pike 16, 75, 103, 104, 106, 107
Blackford, Capt. Charles M. 25
Blenker, Gen. Louis 130
Blotcher, Sgt. George 14
Blue Ridge Mountains 11, 17, 18, 32, 97, 99, 114, 121, 130, 133
Bowers Hill 55–58
Bradford, Gov. Augusta 92
Bradwell, I. Gordon 127
Bragg, Gen. Braxton 82, 158, 167
Braxton, Maj. Carter 108
Breckinridge, Gen. John 24, 84–86, 108, 110
Brown's Gap 18
Buell, Gen. Carlos 158, 167
Burnside, Gen. Ambrose 131, 132, 157, 189

Camp Hill 56–58, 69
Campbell, Col. Edward J. 106
Carlin, Capt. John 71
Catton, Bruce 11
Chambersburg 27, 79, 81, 87, 90, 134, 200, 204, 205
Chesapeake and Ohio Canal 15, 27, 66, 95, 96, 101, 106
Chester's Gap 18
Church Hill 12
Cincinnati 137, 193
Clausewitz, Carl von 6, 144, 145
cod 137, 138
Cooper, Gen. Samuel 173
Cravens, Maj. John O. 71
Crook, Gen. George 21, 79, 84, 85, 87, 104, 107–109, 122, 124, 125, 134, 200
Cumberland Valley 17, 72, 172
Curtin, Gov. Andrew 92

Dallas 136
Dana, Charles A. 113, 114, 184
Davis, Pres. Jefferson 4, 31, 53,
66, 81, 82, 96, 97, 119, 154, 156, 158, 166, 177, 178, 183
Denver 136
Diamond, Jared 138
Douglas, Henry Kyd 79, 112
Duffie, Gen. Alred N. 84
Duffield, Col. William 190
DuPont, Capt. Henry A. 19, 121, 122, 125

Early, Gen. Jubal 15, 24, 27, 72–129, 133–135, 184, 190, 200, 201, 206
Elliott, Gen. Washington L. 68, 70
Emancipation Proclamation 66, 153, 157, 203
Emory, Gen. William 14, 107, 108
Evans, Gen. Clement 122, 123
Ewell, Gen. Richard 54–57, 66, 70–77, 133, 200

Fairfield 16
Farragut, Adm. David 163, 166
Fisher's Gap 18
Fisher's Hill 24, 47, 112, 117, 120
Forbes, Edwin 14, 46
Forrest, Gen. Nathan Bedford 89, 190
Fort Clark 160, 161
Fort Collier 110, 111
Fort Donelson 175
Fort Hatteras 161
Fort Henry 174
Fort Hill 12
Fort Jackson 14, 75
Fort McAllister 174
Fort Milroy 14, 73, 74
Fort Pulaski 51, 181
Fort Star 73–75, 102
Fort West 70, 73–75
Frederick County 9, 11, 12, 64, 79, 89, 199–200
Freeman, Douglas Southhall 61
Fremantle, Lt. Col. Arthur 171
Fremont, Gen. John 130, 156, 157
Fritsche, Carl H. 148

225

Index

Front Royal 18, 22, 47, 54, 56, 57, 73, 64, 114, 121
Front Royal Pike 16
Fulkerson, Col. Samuel V. 45, 46
Fuller, Gen. J.F.C. 148

Garnett, Gen. Richard B. 45, 46
Geary, Gen. John 132
Gettysburg 27, 63, 78, 81, 133, 165, 170, 172, 173, 177, 205
Gordon, Col. George H. 59
Gordon, Gen. John 79, 86, 104, 108, 112, 122–127, 156
Grant, Lt. John T. 106, 107
Grant, Gen. Ulysses S 4, 12, 79, 91–84, 87, 88, 95–102, 112–114, 110–121, 128, 134, 154, 156, 157, 162–164, 169, 170, 174, 178, 179, 181, 184, 205
Great Britain 7, 138–142, 150–153, 161, 186, 191, 192
Greeley, Horace 155
Green, Col. Colton 173

Halleck, Gen. Henry 13, 67, 69, 84, 95, 101, 114, 133, 157, 166
Halltown 15, 90, 97–100, 114, 135
Harding, Capt. French 107
Harrisonburg 16, 17, 113, 120, 195
Harrow, Lt. Col. William 46
Hartley, Lt. James 14
Hatch, Gen. John 55
Hays, Gen. Harry T. 74, 75
Holly Springs 174
Hood, Gen. John 82, 164, 171
Hooker, Gen. Joseph 48, 70, 72, 133
Hotchkiss, Jed 61, 79, 122, 123
Howard, McHenry 58
Hunter, Gen. David 20, 25, 82, 83, 96, 122, 123, 134, 166

Imboden, Gen. John D. 70, 205

Jackson, Gen. "Stonewall" 2, 3, 16, 30, 32, 33, 41–50, 53–61, 66, 84, 129–133, 136, 159, 177, 184, 189, 190, 199, 200
James River 17, 31, 131, 167
Jerusalem 136
Johnson, Gen. Bradley 27, 81, 91, 205
Johnson, Gen. Edward 75, 76
Johnston, Gen. Albert Sidney 51
Johnston, Lt. Col. J. Stoddard 24, 25
Johnston, Gen. Joseph E. 24, 31, 32, 51, 53, 54, 82, 94, 129, 131, 159, 167

Jomini, Antoine-Henri 145
Jones, Maj. Frank 46
Jones, Lt. Col. Hilary P. 74
Jones, Gen. William "Grumble" E. 70, 79, 205

Kanawha Valley 21, 83, 203
Keifer, Col. J. Warren 77
Kelley, Gen. Benjamin 132
Kimball, Col. Nathan 9, 10, 32, 33, 41–47, 199

levels of command 4, 5, 54, 60, 61, 63, 71, 115, 151, 154, 157, 169, 179, 181, 186, 187
Lexington 16, 61
Lincoln, Pres. Abraham 3, 4, 31, 48, 50–53, 61, 66, 67, 81, 82, 88, 90–94, 114, 119, 128, 134, 135, 154–159, 161, 163, 173, 178, 179, 198, 203
Little Rock 82, 165
Locke's Ford 107, 110
Long, Gen. Armistead 79
Longstreet, Gen. James 25, 121, 131, 132, 164, 170
Luray Valley 17, 32
Lynchburg 22, 25, 26, 82, 83

Macadamized 6, 16, 32, 61, 71, 72, 86, 125, 147, 172, 189–197
Machiavelli, Niccolo 144
Mahan, Alfred Thayer 146
malaria 141, 146, 165
Manassas Gap 18–22
Manassas Gap Railroad 18, 21, 22
Martinsburg 16, 17, 70, 71, 87, 100, 102, 114
Martinsburg Pike 16, 70, 71, 74–76, 110
Mason, Capt. Eddy D. 44
Mason, James 155, 156
Massanutten 16–21, 26, 32, 54, 122, 123
McAdam, John 191, 192
McCallum, Daniel C. 170
McCausland, Gen. John 27, 81, 91, 134, 205
McClellan, Gen. George 16, 31, 32, 48–53, 60, 90, 130, 131, 156, 158, 159, 167–169, 199
McClernand, Gen. John A. 157
McDowell, Gen. Irwin 48, 49, 53, 60, 130, 156
Meade, Gen. George 133, 173
Memphis 89, 166
Merritt, Gen. Wesley 107, 110, 121, 127
Mexico City 136
Middle Road 40, 46, 85, 86
Middletown 16, 47, 54, 55, 72, 83, 124

Millwood Road/Senseny Road 16, 104
Milroy, Gen. Robert 14, 15, 66–77, 132, 200
Mobile 89
Moltke, Field Marshall Helmuth Graf von 144
Morgan, Gen. John 81, 204
Murphy, Audie 4, 46

Napoleon 8, 147, 148, 175
Nashville 31, 171
Neil, Alexander 21, 87
Nelson, Adm. Horatio 148
New Market 16, 82, 101, 134
New Market Gap 18, 31
New Orleans 51, 157, 181
New York 82
Newtown 83
Norfolk 51
North Fork 17, 18, 122

Opequon Creek 12, 15, 84, 95, 99, 100, 103–107, 110, 112, 114
Orange and Alexandria Railroad 22

Paul, E.A. 124
Pendleton, Gen. William N. 177, 178
Petersburg 82–84, 89, 90, 98, 101, 102, 114, 119–121, 128, 135, 169, 170, 178, 200, 205
phosphate 140
Piatt, Lt. Col. Donn 67, 70
Pittsburgh 137
Potato Hill 12
Potomac River 8, 11, 16, 17, 28, 55, 56, 72, 95–97, 99, 100, 129, 131, 172, 173, 184
Price, Gen. Sterling 90, 119, 165, 170, 173, 174, 206
principles of war 7
Pritchard's Hill 33, 37, 40–45, 81, 84–86
Pughtown Road 16, 72

Ramseur, Gen. Stephen 86, 87, 107, 108, 123
Randolph, George 61
Rawlins, Gen. John A. 113
Red Bud Run 104, 105, 107, 109
Richmond 22, 24–27, 31, 32, 49, 51, 53, 66, 72, 94, 97, 98, 101, 102, 113, 114, 130, 131, 167, 168, 182, 184
Roberts, Maj. Joseph 22
Rockfish Gap 18
Rodes, Gen. Robert 108
Rome 136
Romney Road 16
Rosecrans, Gen. William S. 22, 157, 189
Rowley, Lt. William 43

Index

Saint Louis 137
saltpeter 140, 161, 162, 181, 183
Saltville 25, 114, 119, 162–164, 185
Sandy Ridge 39–45, 81, 84, 85
Savannah 51, 165
Sawyer, Lt. Col. Frank 46
Schenck, Gen. Robert C. 67, 68, 70, 77
Schlieffen, Gen. Alfred von 4
Schwartz, Dr. Christian 46
Scott, Gen. Winfield 159, 160, 166
Seddon, Sec. of War James A. 82, 171
Sevier's Ford 107
Seymour, Capt. William J. 75, 123
Shenandoah River 9, 11, 17–20, 31, 84, 97, 122, 123, 128
Shenandoah Valley 1, 2, 6, 9, 11, 14, 17, 18, 20–27, 31, 63, 69, 72, 81, 82, 94, 97, 98, 112–114, 128–134, 156, 157, 163, 172, 176, 201
Sheridan, Gen. Philip 14, 15, 17, 20, 24, 87–90, 94–116, 119–123, 126–128, 133–135, 184, 200, 201
Sherman, Gen. Willam T. 90, 155, 164, 165, 170, 174, 175, 179
Shields, Gen. James 32, 44, 47, 60
Sibley, Henry H. 170, 171, 203
Sigel, Gen. Franz 61, 82, 134
Signal Knob 17, 18, 20, 122–124
Snicker's Gap 18, 20
South Fork 18
Spooner, Lt. Edmund D. 71, 75
Stanton, Sec. of War Edwin 53, 60, 61, 113, 166
Staunton 16, 21–23, 78, 122, 172, 195, 196
Stevenson, Gen. John D. 113
Stoughton, Gen. Edwin 178
Strasburg 14, 16, 17, 22, 32–34, 61, 83, 84, 114, 121
Stringham, Flag Officer Silas 160, 161
Stuart, Gen. J.E.B. 27, 162, 204
Sun Tzu 144
Swift Run Gap 18

Taylor, James E. 102, 103
Taylor, Gen. Richard 59
Thoburn, Col. Joseph 85, 86
Thornton's Gap 18
Timbuktu 136
Tompkins, Col. Charles 106
Torbert, Gen. Alfred 98, 110, 121
Tyler, Gen. Daniel 67, 70
Tyler, Lt. Col. John W. 22, 23

Upton, Gen. Emory 107

Valley Turnpike 16, 17, 22, 24, 30, 32, 33, 39–44, 54–57, 61, 69, 72, 73, 84–86, 104, 105, 116, 121, 122, 125, 127, 128, 189, 194–201
Virginia and Tennessee Railroad 22, 25, 163
Virginia Central Railroad 18, 22, 25, 98

Washington 24, 27, 29, 31, 32, 48, 53, 54, 60, 61, 68, 70, 71, 79, 82–84, 91, 94–97, 106, 121, 129–131, 133, 134, 155, 156, 159, 166, 167, 172, 199, 205
Watkins, Sam 171
Williams, Gen. Alpheus S. 47
Williams, Gen. Thomas 166
Williams, John 193
Williamsport 16
Wilmington 89, 183
Wilson, Gen. James 104, 108
Winchester and Potomac Railroad 21, 74, 100
Winder, Gen. Charles 58, 59
Wool, Gen. John 61
Wright, Gen. Horatio G. 84, 108, 119, 121, 122, 126, 127, 139, 166, 201

yellow fever 146, 165
Yorktown 51
Young, William S. 46